JUDAS IN KILKENNY

THERESA LENNON BLUNT

Flanker Press Ltd.
St. John's, Newfoundland
2002

National Library of Canada Cataloguing in Publication

Blunt, Theresa Lennon, 1931-
Judas in Kilkenny / Theresa Lennon Blunt.

ISBN 1-894463-19-6

1. Blunt, Theresa Lennon, 1931- --Childhood and youth.
2. Kilkenny (Ireland)--Biography. I. Title.

DA995.K48B58 2002   941.8'350821'0924   C2002-901286-4

Printed in Canada by Robinson-Blackmore

Flanker Press Ltd.
P O Box 2522, Stn C,
St. John's, Newfoundland, Canada, A1C 6K1
Toll Free: 1-866-739-4420   Telephone: (709) 739-4477
Facsimile: (709) 739-4420   E-mail: info@flankerpress.com
www.flankerpress.com

www.judasinkilkenny.com

FOREIGN PUBLISHING RIGHTS AVAILABLE

- DEDICATION -

For Jane
whose companionship and nonjudgmental nature
helped me be a better person.

****

- ACKNOWLEDGEMENTS -

Thanks to my husband Keith for his infinite patience with my constant outbursts during the initial stages of editing, and to my son Allan who gave willingly of his time and constructive criticism.

A mere thank you seems inadequate in expressing my gratitude to my publisher Garry Granford, his wife Margo and son Jerry and to Vera McDonald, for their untold hours of work in the preparation and promotion of the book.

To my editor Anne Hart whose skill and dogged determination added a new and important dimension to the story, my heartfelt thanks.

And last, but not least, a special thanks to my therapist Leslie Larsen, without whose insistence the story be submitted for publication, the manuscript might still be lying dormant in its drawer.

****

Introduction

To begin at the beginning: Twenty years ago in Ottawa, a psychologist looked at me and said, "Write down every detail of your life in Ireland that you can think of, leave nothing out." His suggestion was prompted by a breakdown of my mental capability, the inability to express, without a flood of tears, what I wanted to convey. I wondered about the logic of his thinking as reluctantly I set about the task. But set about it I did, and as the weeks progressed the entries in my notebook grew considerably.

With time the therapy succeeded, my sanity returned, and the diary was no longer needed. Yet, somehow I couldn't bring myself to part with it, for somewhere in that compilation of memories and emotions I felt sure there was a story. I set my mind to finding it. Lacking the necessary qualifications, and never having written anything worthy of mention before, I naturally had some ambivalence about my ability to organise and complete the task. Nevertheless, I persevered.

Sadly, some months later, my sister Jane was diagnosed with terminal cancer, ironically providing me with a stronger incentive to continue with my quest. Two years later a manuscript was born. Unfortunately, Jane died before it reached completion, and with her death and the fact that I had given no thought to publication the manuscript lay dormant until 1999 when I myself was diagnosed with cancer. Though surviving radical surgery and removal of a breast, I was once again in need of mental counselling. Then, and only then, was the manuscript revived and with the encouragement of my therapist submitted for publication.

The story itself is set in a small town in the south of Ireland, Kilkenny (The Marble City), a pretentious though historically significant little town. It is a true account of "the best of times and the worst of times" as experienced by myself while growing up as a young girl there. The tale has many facets, sad in some respects, humorous in others and interspersed throughout with fragments of history and hearsay. It must be added here, in case of any doubt, that the people and events described are factual, but the names of certain individuals have been changed to protect them and their families from pain.

As for myself: I was born Theresa Agnes Lennon in August of 1931 into a large working-class family, most of whom had left home before my tale commences. Life was anything but easy, our childhood blighted by an alcoholic mother and a proud but stern father. Like many an Irish lass before me, I left school early, worked in Ireland until I was twenty-one, then crossed the Irish Channel into England, where I met and married my husband five years later. The year was 1956, and precisely one year after that we set sail for Canada. Our son, and only child, Allan was born in Montreal in October of 1961.

If the purpose of writing is to inform or entertain, then, I hope dear reader you will find my story worthy.

Prologue

Years and years ago when I was still a child in the marble city of my mind, I sailed the sky in a silver ship with an old man and his goat. He was a fool they said, a crazy intractable old fool filling our heads with silly notions and shouting his insanities to an indignant world. Well, maybe he was crazy. Crazy like an old fox at a farmyard feast. He had no home that I knew of when we first met, living out his days in some secret place and appearing at night like a phantom sheik to fill our world with his magic. Ah! but it was a long time ago, a time of innocence and trust when old men revelled in deeds long done and the days went on forever.

How well I remember it all the same. Sitting naked like on an old log with only the sky for shelter, listening to a bedraggled old man telling tall tales and pouring his vinegary voice across the wind in an arrow of derision.

"Sure ye can knock forever on a dead man's door," he would say to us in exaggerated tones whenever Matty Cavanaugh the rent collector passed close enough to hear, or, "'Tis huntin' with th' hounds an' runnin' with th' fox that a man meets his folly," to Barney Callaghan the chief constable.

Little we cared about the motives in his mind, the hidden meanings in his metaphors, as around him we would gather like moths around a flame, blinded by the grandeur of his rhetoric and driven by the lure of his legends.

All that has changed now. The Old Man is long dead, as are most of the others. Their voices stilled forever in the stony silence of their graves, their faces broken unclear images floating in and out of my consciousness like gnats on a summer breeze. Only the words remain constant, filling my mind with memories best forgotten.

Kilkenny City,
Ireland

1

I was twelve years old when I met the Old Man. It was Saturday, the day little Marty Connolly died, almost sixty years ago. My mother, gone as usual to do the weekend shopping, had left me to mind the house. Through the open window in the scullery I heard footsteps approaching the back door. I paid little heed, sure that it was only my sister Peg who had been playing in the garden a short while before, and whose passion for companionship sent her racing to the door on every conceivable pretext.

I stayed by the kitchen door, scraping the crusted wax from around the brass doorknob, and attempting to make some sense of my distorted image in the orb. The room, heavy with the scent of red Cardinal polish, was spotless and shining like a new pin. A light warm breeze rustled the clean crisp curtains, carrying with it the scent of lilac from the tree outside. The fire, though low, was bright in the grate. Beyond the rustling curtains the world had long been up and about its day, though you never would have known it from the deserted street. Except for the occasional clip-clop of horses' hooves on the road out front, everything was quiet.

I looked around the room with girlish pride, trying to imagine my mother's face. I hoped she'd be pleased with

everything I had done, though one could never be sure with
Mother. For one thing, no matter how well you managed to get
a thing done, Mother could always have done it better. For
another, anything done without her prior consent was usually
subject to discredit. Of course there were times when she
didn't even notice, or at least showed no sign of having
noticed. But when she did, and bestowed her praise, it was
worth all the times that she had not.

Picking up my duster and my polish, I started away from
the kitchen door when I heard a small voice calling. I listened,
but everything had gone quiet. Then I heard it again, this time
with a light tapping sound against the back door. I walked
into the scullery and pushed open the door. A small timid boy
was standing in the yard, looking up at me with eyes as large
and green as pools of emerald. I was struck by the delicate
beauty of his face, and though I could not put a name to him,
I knew that I had seen him someplace before. How he had
managed to get into our yard I had no idea until he told me he
had climbed over the garden wall and showed me the scrapes
and scratches he had gotten while doing it. I guessed his age
to be about four, and learned that he was looking for my
brother Jimmy, who was nearing six, the youngest member of
our family.

Our house was situated on Stephen Street, and behind it
was a wide, enclosed space where children of the neighbourhood came to play. We knew it as the Fair Green because
once a month all the farmers in the county used to gather
there with their livestock and wares, to trade with other
farmers. Like other houses in the street, our back garden,
surrounded by a high wall, overlooked the Green. The
ground on the inside of our garden had been raised so that
we could look out over, but access from the Green was possible only by scaling the wall. Somehow this little boy had
managed to climb over.

"Is Jimmy not here then?" he asked again, with obvious pleasure at being out alone, and stretched his neck to see past me into the scullery.

Again I told him that Jimmy wasn't home. "If he isn't in the Green, I don't know where he is," was all I could think to say, for I recalled Peg telling me earlier that Jimmy had gone to the Cloch with his older brother Jack.

But what would be the sense in telling him that? The Cloch, a more primitive green next to the ancient burial ground of St. Rioc's, was a favourite gathering place for boys, but it was one street over and too far for him to go alone.

I was about to suggest that he go back home and get permission from his mother, when he voiced a sudden thought. "I know! He's gone to the Cloch, I'll betcha," and away he darted before I had time to stop him.

"Wait, wait," I called after him. "You haven't told me your name." He looked around excitedly but didn't stop.

"Connolly," he shouted across his shoulder.

I watched him race along the garden path, his tiny feet beating their freedom on the trodden earth, and as I stepped back into the house I heard his small voice calling "Willie! Willie!"

Looking through the scullery window, I saw him sitting upright on the garden wall, his pale face staring out across the Green, one leg dangling inside the wall, his golden curls blowing in the breeze. Then, swinging his leg upward with a sudden jerk, he heaved his tiny body and disappeared behind the wall. I stayed by the window for a moment looking out, not happy that I had let him go.

I turned and walked back to the kitchen, resuming my work on the brasses and soon forgetting about the little boy. When I had finished polishing, I mopped up the spills from around the floor and put the dirty flannels to soak. I returned the Brasso to its place behind the door and checked that the pots were simmering by the hobs, adding more turf and coal to the fire for good measure. There was only the small front room that I had not touched.

I crossed into the hall and stood hesitant outside the door. Nobody was allowed in there without express permission from my mother, for behind the confines of the locked door lay not only the family's one claim to fame, but all that was left of my father's link with his more privileged past. For a moment I stood looking at the long-stemmed key lying in the lock. All it would take was one quick turn. There might never be a better opportunity, for usually the key was never in the lock.

I went to the front door and looked up and down. The street was empty. No sign of Mother. I checked the clock. There was still plenty of time, so I reached out and touched the key. The metal felt cold and stubborn, but when I closed my fingers more firmly around the end it yielded. There was a click and the door swung slowly inward. The room was in semi-darkness, the curtains half-drawn. I looked around quickly. Everything seemed perfectly normal, yet there were changes. Changes so minor they were barely perceptible until you looked harder. Here and there was an empty space, or an out-line on the surface of the wood that told of something removed. I tried to remember what the object might have been, but could not. For several minutes I went over everything.

Above the mantelpiece were the two crossed swords that Uncle Jack had brought back from the war, and directly below was his medal. The Flying Duck, they used to call him, though I never knew why. A dead duck now he was at any rate, the result of shrapnel in his head; and the sum total of his life, devoted to an English king, displayed here upon an Irish wall. The medal, I suppose, was something for the family to be proud of, presented, as they said, by King George himself. Underneath on the mantel stood a little silver blacksmith, his powerful arms raised above his head ready to strike the waiting anvil.

There, near the china vase, was the papier mâché elephant. Long floppy ears it had, and a trunk that swayed from side to side, a gift to my mother from my older brother Joe. Poor lost Joe. Where was he now? Forever play-acting and getting into trouble, what harm had he done to anyone? God only knew what had become of him. The secret of his hasty departure in the middle of the night was still secure in a web of family secrets.

I could scarcely remember his departure: a moment of awareness in the dead of night, angry, muffled voices from some remote corner of the house, a door opening and closing, a voice calling in the dark. An extension of a waking dream, perhaps? I had no idea. But in the morning Joe had gone, and all my mother had left of him was the little elephant and his picture in the family album. On rare occasions that, too, was taken down from its shelf and we allowed to look at it. Women sitting stiff-backed on wooden chairs, their children mute against their sides, or squatting by their feet. Men standing rigid by a table or a chair, one arm lost behind their backs, or resting stiffly on a woman's shoulder.

"Well now, let me see," from Mother. "You wouldn't know him, or you wouldn't know her, but there's Uncle Willie with your father's sister Kate, the one that went to Canada, remember? Aye, and look now, there's Nelly Madigan, God rest her soul. She was before your time, but a great friend to the family."

And so it went, with Mother laughing or sighing as the case might be, but always snapping back the clasp with a sudden jerk and locking in the ghosts. Grandmother, they said, had had the greed of filthy lucre, and pinched and pared her pennies with the zest of a thrifty Scot, and though I suspect that criticism to be the hobgoblin of little minds, I remember well my mother's words, "as mean as ditch water, as soon part with a molar as with a penny." Whatever the truth of it, our family did well enough by her. Almost everything in the room had come to us from my grandmother's house, albeit through my father's brother Jim who lived with us—even the cabinet, with its sparkling glass and fine delicate china that never got used. There was something sacred about this little room with its clutter of ornaments, old furniture, and its haunting, mellow atmosphere. Nowhere else in the house was there such a feeling of stability. Yet even that feeling I knew now to be false, for I was learning to interpret the subtle influences at work in the destruction of our home.

My first real awareness that something was wrong had come about by accident. One day, suffering from an upset stomach, I had come home early from school. The front door was open, and there was a strange man standing in the hall. My mother, catching sight of me coming through the gate, had quickly shuffled me inside. Her obvious annoyance at my appearance and the man's immediate move to conceal the object in his hand made a strange impression on my mind. I had given little thought to it at the time, absorbed as I was with my own struggle for survival. Yet several days later, huddled in the corner by the backyard door, listening to the argument going on inside, I had reason to remember.

I heard my father, his voice raised in anger questioning my mother about some missing object, and my mother, her voice sharp and resentful, denying knowledge of it. Then somewhere through the mirrors of my mind came a reflection, and coupled with my father's words the forgotten scene took on meaning: Mother's hands steering me through the kitchen door, the stranger waiting in the shadows, a sudden, silent movement and, there in the corner of my eye, a furtive hand—something concealed beneath the fingers. The shocking truth broke upon me then, though it was all I could do to accept it. Many times I had heard about the skeletons in other people's closets, but I had never suspected we had one in ours. Everyone but myself must have known of it. The picture was as clear as day, with all those innuendoes from various corners of the street, but I had turned a deaf ear to it.

Even that day in the gaolhouse yard, with Nuala Brannigan saying what she had, the truth had not registered. Yet I had knocked her down on account of it. What else could I have done? Speaking that way about my mother! I hated the mean way she had said it, eyebrows raised, and speaking so loudly that everyone could hear.

"Your mother, I believe, is extremely fond of the bottle!"

So typical that was of Nuala, who had run home crying to her mother. In the evening I would have to pay the penalty.

"I'll not have one of mine brawling on the street," Mother raged as soon as she laid eyes on me, her knuckles heavy on my ear.

So stung was I by the unfairness of her action that without really meaning to I blurted out the reason for the assault. Only a slight change of expression in Mother's eyes betrayed her alarm, but a few minutes later, when she put on her coat and hastily left the house, I knew she had gone to the Brannigans'. You'd think I would have realised then that there was something wrong, but I hadn't—not consciously at any rate. It was easier to believe that Nuala had been lying.

The stranger in the hall turned out to be the rag-and-bone man from Parnell Street, who called to visit people too ashamed to visit him. I had not recognised him at the time, but I knew about his practise. Many times I had passed by his open gate and seen all the rags and feathers in squalid little heaps waiting to be weighed, and the solemn-faced women, the look of the Famine in their eyes, waiting mute beside the limestone wall hoping for a handful of pennies. That was how it was for many people then, but it had never been a part of our world, and I resented Mother forcing us into it. The implications of my father's questions had alerted me, and I remember well the feeling of despair that had come over me. My own mother, one whom I had imagined to be above reproach— better than all the others—a common drunk, selling anything she could get her hands on to support her habit!

The following months found me a regular attendant at evening prayer, filling up the coffers of the church and depleting its seemingly endless supply of candles. Self-denial and prayer became my constant companions, for I had no doubt that I could save my mother. Yet here I was, one year and a million novenas later, finding out for myself the futility of my efforts. Not one of my prayers had been answered. My petitions? Who knew? Lost in a letterbox without a bottom.

2

Mother was standing by the kitchen table, examining the bits and pieces from her shopping. The empty basket was lying on the floor. She didn't look up when I came in, unconcerned it seemed with my presence. Making a slight coughing sound, I moved across the floor and sat beside the fire, waiting for her to say something about the shining kitchen. She said nothing. I watched her take off her coat and brown felt hat, pushing the sharp pearl-tipped pin back through the felt like she always did. After she had put them both on the peg behind the door, she put on her apron and began to shell the peas.

The sun, coming in at a slant through the window, lit up her hair. A golden bronze it was with deep furrowed waves pressed firmly to the sides and forehead. At forty-five she was still pretty, with a tiny frame and slender shapely body. Today her skin seemed pale against the blackness of her dress. Her face still, the mouth closed tight. The worn lines about her face and her blue eyes, so warm at times, filled my heart with love for her.

It troubled me when she was sad and lately it seemed she was always sad. In many ways, too, she had begun to change, arguing all the time with my father and turning her anger so easily on us. "I reared a bad lot," she had started saying to any-body who would listen, and sadly for us there was always somebody who would. I can never forget that feeling the first time I heard her say to someone that none of us were any good. How could she have been so heartless with me standing listening, and she knowing that it was not true? To hear her speak one would think we were all her enemies. There was only one reason I could think of for her saying such a thing—she had no love for us. That was how it seemed to me, at any rate, and it hurt me deeply.

Never in her conscious mind could Mother admit to any weakness. Her drinking she considered to be her own affair. Why should she give it up for anyone? She drank so little in any case, and it helped her get through the miserable days. Trouble was, every day was miserable for Mother. The world itself was a miserable place, where nothing in her life was ever going to change. No, there would never be an end to the drudgery, not at least until we were all grown up, and then most likely it would be too late. So sick, she said, she had become of it, with Father always telling her to wait. "Wait! Wait! for what?" when he knew as well as she that nothing would ever change.

Of her life before coming to Kilkenny she seldom spoke. But I had learned from my sister Jane what little bits she knew. Mother, she had told me once, had had it hard. Seventeen was all she was when she left home. The second eldest in a family of five, she resembled her mother in her tiny frame but she had her father's eyes and temper. Him she had held in more favour than her mother, who she quarrelled with all the time—a pat-tern that would repeat itself with me in the years to come. Mother's father had died when she was fourteen. The Great War had broken out and she remembered well his leaving: standing on the shore with her mother, her heart aching. Six months later they received the news that he was dead. She had kept him alive in the locket on her neck, as she had the memory of Jimmy Cleare, the boy she was supposed to marry.

Of Jimmy she tried not to think at all, though the years had compelled her to endure the pain. The Cleares, by all accounts, had been a cut above them. Martin Cleare was a politician and a man of sterling character. Jimmy was an only child, doted on by his mother, a fact responsible for people's belief that he would turn out no good. But he had grown up fine and had shown good faith to Mother, even after she had had to take that job at the foundry and the neighbours had started to look down on her. Every evening he waited patiently by the foundry gate so that people would know they were walking out. She had risen in their esteem on account of it, and soon the whole town had expected them to marry.

Mrs. Cleare had made no objection. A quiet, genteel woman with a vacant face, she kept herself immaculate, her opinions to herself. Mother thought she was nice enough and often walked the distance to their house outside the village, and though Mrs. Cleare seldom asked her in, she always had a ready smile for her. There was no reason to feel that she disapproved until that Sunday by the river when Jimmy told her he was going to England. He had no good reason to be going, and a quarrel had flared up between them. Mother, too proud to plead with him, had let him go. He would be back when he got things sorted out, he told her, in August or September, and it had given her hope. But August came and September too, with no sign of Jimmy. He had sent one card renewing their pledge, but nothing more. In the end she had gone to see his mother who had received her well enough, but would tell her nothing. There was something odd in the way she had looked at her, Mother thought, something almost dishonest, her voice with an accent of forced concern. Had she had a hand in it after all? Mother recalled her own mother saying that she thought Mrs. Cleare to be a deceptive one.

Something must have happened that she knew nothing of. Why else would Mr. Cleare go shaking his fist in his wife's face, almost bringing on a row in front of her? A sudden feeling of panic had prevented her from asking more, and she had left without finding out the truth. The walk home had been miserable, her heart near to breaking. The shame of it.

What would they say about her now in the village, now that he had jilted her? They'd say she was a fool to have trusted him. Or that it served her right for not knowing her place. Or maybe they would say she was better off—a spoiled lad like that, *musha!* would cheat a donkey out of its own hind leg. They would laugh at her, in any case. Treat her the way they had Finoula Brien, whispering and going on behind her back. She didn't think she could face it, so she had run away. Had worked for a while at the convent in Clonmel, and later had come to Kilkenny.

She met my father at the county fair and thought all her troubles were over when they married. "He was different altogether when we were keeping company," she would say to us, "but he changed soon enough after we were wed. And look at him now! Just working in a shop, with no pension or anything."

I wondered if she was thinking those things now as I watched her intently, willing her to look up. Finally she did, allowing me only a fleeting glance before turning away again. Somewhere out back I could hear the chop-chop of Paddy Brennan's axe and the whooping and yelling of children in the Green. I longed to be outside with them, yet I wanted also to be with her. Any minute now, I thought, she might look up and say the house looked lovely, that she could see her face in the polishing, but she didn't. Not until a smouldering log fell apart in the grate, shooting sparks and flames up the chimney did she look at me.

"Don't sit too close to the fire, move back a bit," she said, eyeing the red-hot cinders just fallen on the hearth.

I drew my stool back noisily, hoping to keep her attention, but she had already returned to her shelling. Swallowing my disappointment, I watched the smoke go up the chimney. I could feel the hurt gathering in the hollow of my throat, and wondered why it was that my mother, who had so many kind words for other people's children, seldom had any for her own. How easy it was for her to stand there and pretend she hadn't noticed.

Inwardly I cursed the stubbornness that prevented me from encouraging her favour. Were it Jane or even Peg in my place they would have managed fine, for both had a way of drawing praise from her. But I could never bring myself to say the necessary words or overlook the fact that she might have drink in her. Even when I knew my attitude would bring on a row I could not yield. That aspect of my nature did not exactly comfort me and I knew it irritated Mother, driving her at times to say hurtful things and comparing me unfavourably with Father.

"Too cold and proud to bend," she'd say, and her voice would have so much hurt in it that I would feel overwhelmed with guilt, hating myself for being that way and angry with my father for giving me his traits.

I wanted to tell her about the little boy. How he had climbed over the wall all by himself, and the sense of foreboding he had left me with. But now with all this silence I could not bring myself to speak. She would only scoff, at any rate, say that I had imagined it, that I was too smart for my own good, always puzzling my head about things that weren't my concern. So I kept quiet, mulling the words over in my mind and searching for hidden faces in the coals. There I fancied I saw the little boy, clinging to the tail of an enormous kite, sailing above the Green. Away up he went, floating silently beyond the roofs, his tiny body bent backward toward the earth. Up, up he went into the waiting clouds, leaving only a tiny speck in the air. The image frightened me.

The clock ticked and ticked. The only other sound in the house was the rustle of empty pea shells as my mother dropped them back into the bag. I watched her silently for a while, not moving my eyes from her face, then followed her gaze to the grandfather clock, getting ready to strike the Angelus.

Ding-dong! Ding-dong!

It sang in cheerful tones, striking the hours off one by one until it had counted all twelve. A treasured scene from the past came drifting back to me, of Mother kneeling beside the clock and Father stealing up behind her. How happy and excited she had looked as she turned to him, and he, pulling her close beside him as she rose. How had I forgotten? Forgotten how they used to laugh, seemed always to be laughing. Why did she suddenly have to change? And how could childhood be so beautiful, yet growing up so fearful? Looking at Mother now I could see no difference in her face. Yet there was something at times in her manner, something cold and angry that caused me to shrink away from her. And even if I were too critical, as Jane said, it didn't change the way things were. I kept my feelings to myself, as Jane advised, but it hadn't stopped me thinking.

Finally my mother spoke.

"Here," she said, handing me a brown paper bag that smelled of sulphur. "Take this in to Mrs. Bourke, and then run down to Shaun Byrne's and get me a packet of Woodbine." She opened her small red purse and brought out a shilling. I stood up slowly but could not speak, my throat tight. I could feel the minted newness of the shilling as I pressed it into my palm.

"Is there anything else?" I asked, in a controlled voice.

No, there was nothing. But would I remind Jimmy Murray to send up the coal before five, and bring back the change from the shilling?

Making my way across the garden to the Bourkes' house I thought again about my mother and her philosophy of divine right. Because she had given us life she believed she owed us nothing, while we on the other hand owed her everything, including the right to direct and rule every aspect of the lives she had given us. At no time did our rights enter into it. Why should we have what she never had? was her favourite reply. How weary I had become of hearing it. Seldom did she ever show gratitude, in spite of everything we did. Yet all of us went on loving her. Had she not done her share for us when we were little? First up in the morning and last down at night. The household chores she tackled by herself, perspiration at times in beads upon her forehead. It wasn't easy bringing up a family.

The years had gone by too quickly and she felt old and trapped. Besides, she had not had the advantages my father had enjoyed, and didn't know how to be happy. The years she had spent in servitude had hardened her. Marriage, she had believed, would put an end to the struggle. But she had been wrong, for added to the drudgery of everyday life was the burden of bearing many children. That more than anything had finished her, robbed her of the will to carry on. And yet, as low as she may have felt at times, she never stooped to beating us. The odd swipe with the kitchen towel from time to time, but nothing more, unlike some children I could mention who took their share of punishment be it rain or shine.

Little Billy Corrigan for instance, tripping *moryah* up his own front steps and ending up in hospital, or Lizzie Ryan with the droopy eye, falling off an invisible bike and giving herself a broken arm. Oh! there were many I could mention, but Mother had never been like that. The most she ever did was complain. Father she considered puritanical and proud, unwilling to acknowledge her predicament. The house, after all, belonged to him. None of her friends were welcome in it and his, she felt, barely tolerated her. After Mikey left she had nobody. Mikey, her first-born, her passion. He had been her confidant in times of stress. Seldom did she argue with my father in those earlier days, but if an argument did break out Mikey would always side with her. Someone to confide in was all she had ever wanted. She had not meant for anything bad to happen, for him to turn against his father. But that was precisely what happened.

One Saturday afternoon she had come home to find them quarrelling, my father seated in his chair beside the fire, grim-faced and ashen, and Mikey, his breath fouled with the smell of drink, standing over him. She had tried to intervene, to find out what had happened, but the argument had ended, and when she looked to Mikey for some clue he had turned on her in anger. A few days later he had left for England. My father never spoke to him again, because Mikey died in England of pneumonia before they had a chance to make things up. For that, Mother could not forgive my father, and the wedge between them widened.

Then, after Joe left, it was open war. She began to despise my father, to blame him for everything. Yet to this day I believe he cherished her, and in my memory lives the little bunch of roses he had plucked one day from the garden vine and left upon the table for her to find. I remember, too, the dark winter evenings when everything was quiet and there was heard only the crackling of the fire in the grate and the sound of their whispers in the red glow of the embers. All that had died. Died as the fire dies in the grate, one dull spark amid the greying ash. Nothing, it seemed, could be done to rekindle it.

3

It was past one o'clock by the time I got back from the store, and too late to go to the river. Some of the neighbourhood children were already drifting home, their jam jars swarming with their morning's catch. Joey Fahey had caught himself an eel and all the boys had gathered excitedly to look at it. I, too, had a look, and watched it squirm about in the bottom of the jar. Every time he shook the jar, it arched its back in a menacing way and rose to the top.

Y ou should have come," called Nuala Brannigan, catching sight of me outside our gate and racing over to enlighten me with her particular version of events. I pretended I didn't care, but inside I was seething.

"Was Jane there?" I asked casually, wondering about my sister, who was two years older than myself and who, through artful engineering, managed to disappear on Saturdays to avoid the morning chores. Nuala didn't answer, her mind already occupied with something else, so I left her and went inside.

No sooner was I indoors again than I heard Jimmy Murray on the garden path. "One hundredweight of coal for the Lennons!"

I hurried to the yard and watched him empty the bulging sack, his back bent beneath its weight. Mother appeared in the open door and he moved off to speak with her. I lingered in the garden listening, but I couldn't hear a thing for Jimmy had his back to me. I saw Mother hand him the money. Then there was a pause and a quick glance around by Jimmy to check my whereabouts, followed by a sideways movement of his head to indicate to Mother he had something to confide. She moved closer and Jimmy's voice fell to a whisper. I heard the intake of Mother's breath and saw her grave expression as she backed farther into the hall. A few minutes later Jimmy came out, picked up the empty sack and hurried off along the path. I followed Mother inside.

"I have to go out again," she said in a curt tone as soon as she saw me, and then with a subtle change of expression, "there's been an accident."

"Oh!" I responded eagerly, pushing aside my resentment in a rush of newfound enthusiasm at her unexpected confidence.

"One of the Connolly children," she said, and my heart stopped.

"Do you know which one?" I asked, fearing what she might answer.

But she shook her head. She hardly knew the family, she said, and instructed me to mind the house until she got back. Mind the house! After I being stuck in here all morning, and without a word of gratitude. It was too much! Why did it always have to be me? Anyone would think I was the only capable member of the family. And where did she get off using me like that? Always calling on me to do everything, even for people in the street. "Send her," she'd say, when a neighbour needed an errand done. "No one can cheat her out of anything," and both of them would look at me as though I possessed some sinister trait that other children did not.

"The house can look after itself. I'm going outside," I said. It was the first time I had ever spoken back to Mother and I expected the worst, but to my surprise she said nothing, just gave me one of her warning looks. Then all at once the tightened lines around her mouth sort of fell away and her face softened.

"I won't be long," she said, and off she went.

I sat in the kitchen fuming, the ever watchful eyes of William Ewart Gladstone staring down at me from his picture beside the door. Sad eyes I thought they were. Eyes of another time that seemed to speak to you as they followed you about. On that wall behind that door he had been hanging for as long as I could remember, his great melancholy face a stark reminder of the troubled times when he had tried in vain to win justice for Ireland.

Mother came back while I was thinking this, but she had nothing to say, her face straight and solemn.

"Was it one of the children then?" I asked, aware that she wasn't going to tell me. Her reply was noncommittal, but I detected an anxious glimmer in her eye that told me of something serious, something that she didn't want me to know.

4

By five o'clock the family had arrived home to supper, and the story of the little boy's accident told and retold. With a sinking heart, I listened.

I s he dead?" Peg asked the unpardonable question, and we all held our breath.

"That will be enough," my father answered, forbidding us to speak further on the matter.

I sat in my chair until I could bear it no more. Then, draining the last dregs of tea from my cup I excused myself from the table. Outside in the freedom of the cool air I tried to extract some meaning from the isolated words and images floating around inside my head. He couldn't be dead, I told myself, for if he were there would be a black crepe on the Connellys' door and we would have heard about it.

News travelled faster than light in our neighbourhood. Mr. Murphy on his way home from work, it seemed, had heard the screams and had run to the house to investigate. He couldn't say exactly how it had happened, but saw that the boy was badly burned. Later we heard that the little boy, finding himself alone in the kitchen and curious about the simmering cauldron above the fire, had somehow tipped it over on himself. I felt numb with anguish that I had let him go away that morning and knew of only one way to find out the truth. I would go myself to the Connolly house, and if Mrs. Connolly thought it odd that I had come alone I would say that my mother had sent me to inquire about the boy. I waited until the coast was clear and nobody in our house watching, then I left.

The Connolly house was clearly visible from our front gate, and I could see some people on the street outside. One old woman, a black shawl covering her head and shoulders, was standing in the garden muttering to herself and crying out repeatedly. Her behaviour frightened me, and I turned to go home when I noticed Mrs. Connolly standing by the door. She had obviously been watching, and seemed curious about my hesitation. So, with some uncertainty, I passed through the gate.

Mrs. Connolly was a stoutish woman whose youthful appearance on that day startled me, because I had imagined her to be much older behind the confines of the shawl she usually wore. On this day, however, she wore no shawl, her long black hair falling loosely around her shoulders. I approached her nervously, going over in my mind what I would say. But I had no need for words. Her eyes told me everything.

I looked past her into the narrow hall that was now clearly in my vision, and a cold mantle of terror descended upon me as I gazed in panic on the lifeless form of the little boy already in his coffin, or a small white box resembling one. To a mind like mine, cultivated more by imagination than by common sense, death was an inconceivable thing that happened to old people only, or to animals. Children never died. They were simply borne away by angels to become angels themselves or to replace a burned-out star in the heavens. An inexpressible sensation of terror swept over me and I felt the urge to turn and run. Mrs. Connolly glanced at me without saying anything, then nodded toward the coffin.

"I'm sorry for your trouble," I heard myself say, as though I had known about it all along, and had come expressly to offer my condolences.

Somebody came up behind me then and pressed me farther into the hall. I had not wanted to go inside, but I took the few steps nearer and stood beside the coffin. A black-edged card lying on the body told me the name. Martin J. Connolly.

I rested my eyes on the little face. How still and silent now the little body that only hours earlier had raced along our garden path. Where had the sparkle in his green eyes gone, and the spring of his little curls, now limp upon his forehead? How could he have died at all? There was no evidence of burns on him, at least not on his face or hands. What lay concealed beneath his gown I didn't want to imagine. On impulse I placed my hand on the little head. So cold it felt to my fingers. The grim reality of death came home to me. Was I to blame? Could I have prevented it from happening? Confusion swept over me and I felt my head begin to swim.

The candles flickered and spat, spilling hot wax down upon the white lace cloth and throwing eerie shadows over the walls and ceiling. I heard a muffled sound from behind a creaking door, and glancing into the shadows saw the figure of a man standing back against the wall, a dim ghostlike figure, stiff and silent. I guessed it to be the dead boy's father. Then a small girl, sobbing, pulled open the bedroom door and hurried to her mother's side. Evidence of poverty showed itself in the damp sagging wall and sparsely furnished room beyond, and in the girl's undernourished body, barely discernible beneath her torn dress.

The father came forward into the light and I saw he was a man of about thirty-five, of medium height, with hair already greying and a large bald spot around his forehead. His suit was worn and wrinkled, with a washed but rumpled shirt protruding from his buttoned vest. His large eyes, red-rimmed from crying, fell for a moment on the little boy. He bent to console the little girl, stroking her head with loving hands, then looked at me with searching eyes. In them I saw the misery of his tortured soul and a wish, perhaps, that he himself might die or never to have begun living.

I seized upon the moment to extricate myself, and muttering some final words of sympathy I slipped outside. I stood a moment at the gate looking down the street, but with no desire to go home I walked the other way.

5

The evening had suddenly turned into night as I rounded the corner to Friary Street. Avoiding the people from the Confraternity at the gates of the Friary Chapel, I hurried along the narrow path, stopping only to look at the large goose egg in the window of Slater's shop. When I reached the bottom of the street, I turned left onto High Street, the main shop-lit centre of the town.

No children played in this street, for here was the heart of the city where only business was transacted. Most of the shops were closed and shuttered, the street almost deserted. Signs above the doors displayed the owners' names, the largest and most prosperous in quality gold lettering: Elliott, The Home & Colonial, Monster House, Murphy the jeweller on one side, O'Connell on the other, and farther down the Ulster Bank, followed by Delahunty, and Smithwick where my father worked. Across the road from that was the main post office.

Here and there a couple stood whispering in a doorway, or huddled together under the shelter of the Tholsel roof. A few passed quietly on their way to the Regent Cinema. I saw by the town clock that it was past seven. My mother would already be at her friend Julia Nevin's house, my father at the Workman's Club, so I could be away from home for some time without them knowing I was out.

Outside Coogan's restaurant a derelict man rooted in a metal dustbin. The sight disgusted me. Maybe in the slums of Dublin one expected that, but not here in the Marble City, this articulate town of Anglo-Norman fame and sublime respectability. I stood in the shadows watching as he rummaged through the bin. Finding nothing in the first one he moved silently to the second. Here he found something which he picked out and examined with both hands before slipping it into his pocket. Then, placing the lid back on the bin he made off along the path, keeping close to the wall. Something about the way he walked, bumping his elbow against each passing door, puzzled me. I slowed my pace and followed quietly behind. The curious way he cocked his head from side to side as if listening for something reminded me of a story I had heard once about a drunken man who had had his eyes plucked out by crows while he was sleeping. This man wasn't drunk, though, I was sure of that, and for some reason that gladdened me. I walked behind him for a little while until I felt an urge to pass him. Then I quickened my step, and keeping to the outside of the path overtook him at the Market Slip. I looked back once and saw him grope his way around the corner. The tilt of his head and the blank expression on his face told me he was blind, and I wondered if he knew of the flight of downward steps in front of him. I listened for a moment, but heard no sound of stumbling and so I hurried on.

It was on the stroke of seven as I passed Dore's clock and found myself outside the old marketplace. The farmers had long since taken down their stalls and cleared away their wares. Most of them, like their customers, had gone home to supper, but a few stragglers had as usual found their way into the pubs, leaving their unsold rabbits hanging unguarded by the market gate. A tired old horse stood alone by a lamppost, a piece of dirty cord hanging loosely around his neck. I looked at him for a moment but did not go close, for I remembered what had happened to Billy Meany when a horse had tried to pick him up by his head.

There was a softness in the air now that smelled of hot bread from Crotty's bakery, mingled with the more pungent odour of malt from Smithwick's brewery. From somewhere I could hear the sound of a violin playing and somebody singing, the voice rising and falling on the still air. I listened vaguely to the melancholy tune. It reminded me of my brother Mikey and the stories he used to tell about the Black and Tans, how they used to come to our house in Abbey Street for him, and in spite of my father's protests carry him down the hill to Conway's pub. Everybody in the town hated them, he said, the very mention of their name sending fear into their hearts. They had brought pain and misery, and too many doors still showed the marks of their hobnailed boots.

Mikey was only eight when they first came to our town, and some of them took a liking to him when they learned that he could sing. Sit him up on the counter of Conway's bar they would, and people passing outside would listen in disbelief to the words of the outlawed "Kevin Barry" in his fine soprano voice. It was the only song he could sing all the way through, and when he finished they would fill him with lemonade and biscuits and send him home, his pockets jingling with coppers.

I had never been inside a pub during business hours, but I knew that men went there to drink the beer that sullied their breath and dulled their senses. I wondered about the lure of it, the attraction of those smoke-filled sanctums that turned timid men into bullies, cursing and fighting with each other, some spending their whole week's wages before going home drunk and empty-handed to a family of hungry children. It was all so stupid and it made no sense. Better, I thought, not to think about it.

Ahead I could see the narrow span of road that forged the River Breagagh. A line of small shops and houses snuggled on either side. I had reached the boundaries of Irishtown, the breeding ground of my ancestors. Residents here were proud of this little street with its ancient heritage and culture. Not only was it one of the oldest in the city, but also the gateway to St. Canice with its medieval history and famous ninth century tower. Some days the paths here streamed with people; tourists come to see the old church and tower, rubbing shoulders with ragged barefoot boys and their coal-filled barrows.

I began to move faster when I had passed the first shop, every step now taking me back again to home. When I reached Lenehans' I turned the corner into Dean Street. Here everything suddenly turned dark, the only light coming from the row of houses on the other side. Somewhere a child began to cry, the sound cutting through the stillness like a ship in distress, reminding me again of the little boy. Where was he now? I wondered. Had he gone to heaven? The chimes from St. Canice cut through my thoughts.

I had reached the Water Barrack. Just ahead I could see the banks of the Breagagh, its waters gliding silently, one minute glimmering in the moon, the next plunged into darkness before passing from view beneath Fryers Bridge on its way to the River Nore.

But it was not the river itself that interested me at this point. It was a voice. The voice of a man unknown to my ears.

6

Could be the tinkers, I thought with sudden alarm, reducing my gallant stride to a canine crawl. But it was not the tinkers. It was an old man, as old as Methuselah himself. I could see him clearly from my place in the shadows. He was on the other side of the road, sitting on a wooden bench, his great feet almost touching the red cinders of a glowing brazier. His long arms were flailing in the air like old straw in the wind. A few lads older than myself and from various corners of the town were sitting or standing about him on the grass. I strained my ears to hear what he was saying, but the words, caught in a sudden breeze, were lost to my hearing.

I moved around the corner and crossed from the curb upon which I was standing to the low wall overlooking the river. I stood flat against the wall listening. The air was still and tranquil, the night starry. His voice was strong and filled with feeling, at times sinking almost to a whisper, then becoming gradually louder. Though I cannot now recall exactly what it was saying I remember well the sound of it. In it you could hear all the accents of Ireland, from the Gaelic brogue of Donegal to the mild Elizabethan of the Pale, and all the rich variations in between, from Tipperary to County Kerry. At first glance I took him to be very old, ninety years or thereabouts, but this I soon discovered was due to his white beard and the way his hair hung limp about his head.

He stood up just as I reached the wall and I saw that he was wearing a gabardine coat tied around the middle with a leather belt. A tall man, I thought, powerful around the shoulders once but never fat. On his head was an old tweed cap which he shifted back and forth every now and then. I decided to leave my place beside the wall and join the gathering.

All the faces were known to me. Closest and to my left was Eddy Byrne, and beside him sprad-legged on a rotting log was Paddy Farrell. In front I saw Milo Mac with Billy Bood McGuire and Tommy Connor, and over by the big oak tree, slumped against its massive trunk, his hands deep in his trouser pockets, was Billy Meagher. Paddy, always the bloodhound, detected my arrival and alerted the others, who immediately began with withering looks and muttered oaths to show their disapproval. The Old Man, in the act of placing something on the fire, looked up inquiringly. His look was not encouraging so I threw a quick glance at Eddy whom I hoped might come to my defence. But Eddy regarded me with blank disdain, his mouth firm, as though holding back the things he would like to say to me for my insult of the day before. I turned again to the Old Man, who was still watching me.

"I heard your voice from across the road," I said by way of apology for my intrusion. His eyes narrowed.

"Did ye now, an' I suppose yer curious t' know what i'tis we're doin'."

He kept his eyes fastened on my face, but I could see in them a glimmer of curiosity. The others saw it too.

"Be off with yourself," somebody called out rudely, and instinctively I turned to go, but with one last look at Eddy.

"Ah! leave her alone, what harm is she doing?" Eddy beckoned me across.

No sooner had I started over when the Old Man offered me a place beside him at the fire. Not so much, he explained, to avoid the damp, but so that he might have the pleasure of my company. He asked me no questions about myself and I offered no information, just sat where he had bundled me and listened while he picked up the threads of his conversation exactly where he had left them.

So began my long association with the Old Man, that night the first of many visits to his side. With it began my awareness of myself, my country, and a whole wide world beyond the boundaries of Kilkenny. I cannot attempt to relate all that was said that evening, for I have forgotten most of it. Nor can I pretend to have understood it all, for they were dealing to great extent with experiences common to themselves or to people older. The one thing I do remember is the way the Old Man's thoughts kept mingling with my own, half-realised thoughts that had been stewing in my mind, but never quite spilled over into articulate form. Occasionally he would look down at me with an encouraging smile, wanting me to say something, but I was still shy of him and wanted only to sit and listen and to study his face when I thought he wasn't looking. A kind gentle face I thought it was, reddened by the frost of countless nights.

Who was he? Where had he come from? And how was it I had never seen him before? To all these questions I would find answers, but not that night. That night I had to be content to wait, to listen and take in everything. And so I did, and learned, for example, of his love of birds. Of Meggie his bunty one-horned goat, grazing nearby in the bushes. I learned, too, about his feud with Barney Callaghan and how he loved to be one up on Mickey Mulligan. A republican, he told me later, was what he was, but listening to him argue on the subject then one might be inclined to think that he had become one simply to irritate those whom he disliked the most. Spideogs he called the politicians; hotgospellers the clergy. Newspapers he said were the devil's tools, though he read them all. His solutions to everything fascinated me, as did the things he said and the peculiar way he had of saying them.

He was not what you might call a religious man, not in the way we understood our faith, for he had his own ideas on how it should be practised, ideas which did not conform to all that was laid down by the Catholic Church. On the contrary, he said, people should learn to do their own thinking, and they might be amazed at what they would discover. He would give a funny sort of laugh after some remark like this, as though he knew some wicked secret the rest of us did not. He talked about things we were not supposed to hear, ideas disapproved of by our churches and our schools. Young minds, he felt, should be free to choose, not fettered by tradition or coerced into accepting an established order. Many people felt the way he did, he told us, but were afraid to speak out. But given half a chance they would show you they could have minds of their own. Rosaries and scapulars would vanish from their homes and be replaced with nourishing bread and butter.

Of course there was truth in everything he said, but I didn't know that then and his words frightened me, for I was only twelve, and to my mind religion was a serious thing. One did not mock nor make fun of it. I saw Tommy Connor watching me and then whispering something to the Old Man, who stopped talking and looked at me. He threw his head back and laughed.

"Ah! 'tis all right alana, no need t'fret. No harm is goin' t'come t'ye. Sure God an' meself are th'best iv friends. Isn't that so lads?" The boys laughed in confirmation.

Men worship God in many ways I was to learn later, and despite my uneasiness that night it was clear to me even then that He had a special place in the deep, deep things of this Old Man's heart.

It was a night like any other, a few souls come together to exchange ideas. But to me then it was something more. Something wild and wonderful, like a page from David Copperfield, with the moon peeping out behind the old church spire, and casting the Old Man's shadow on the wall behind. Even now I can smell the crispness of the cool night air and the pungent odour of the Old Man's tobacco. And I can feel the hair stiffen at the edges of my neck when I think of the spooky tales and thoughts that followed.

His words opened up a whole new world to me and sparked the beginning of a friendship that would prove a blessed distraction and comfort to me in the turbulent years to come. Listening to him that night, I learned more in the space of one short hour than in all my days at school. I wanted to stay and listen more, but the time was passing and I knew my chances of slipping through our front door undetected were getting slimmer. Thanking the Old Man for having me and asking if I might come again, I said goodbye and left.

7

On Monday they buried the little boy. There were only a few people at the church to mourn him. The small procession, made up mainly of women and what few men as could take time off from work, moved away from the cathedral and wound its way slowly through the city streets. A few straggling children filed in behind the coffin, which was born aloft on two men's shoulders. The grieving parents followed. There was no hearse, no car, only the steady plod of feet along the concrete roads.

I followed along behind until I merged with the others, trying with little success to blot out the memory of events of two days before. People stopped along the streets or huddled in open doors, whispering with curious respect about the little coffin. Shopkeepers pulled down their shades as the procession passed in the middle of the road. Ahead one could see the Grand Parade, its cobbled slope leading up to the castle.

A few holidaymakers moving slowly up the steps or walking in the shaded terrace lined with tall trees lingered to watch the procession as it rounded the corner into Rose Inn Street. Here the quiet air was shattered by loud strains of music pouring through the open windows of the Imperial Hotel.

"Can I forget you, or will this heart remind me?" the singer's voice resounded in the air. People raised their heads in disbelief as it continued, and someone raced ahead along the path to the hotel. Nobody had expected it. It had not been planned, it had just happened. But the singer's voice plagued my mind long after it was silent.

We reached the top of John Street and started out along the Comer Road to the cemetery. Small grey clouds were gathering in the sky when we reached the gates, and the quiet procession, somewhat larger now, passed inside. Coming to an open grave set apart from a cluster of old headstones, the bearers set the coffin down. The mother, scarcely able to walk, was assisted by her only surviving son on one side and her husband on the other. Leaning heavily on their stout arms, her long hair concealed once more beneath her shawl, she moved closer to the grave. The priest began to read the service and we all bowed our heads.

I stood there listening, thoughts drifting through my mind. A ghoul is at home in a cemetery. I had laughed when I heard that, but I wasn't laughing now. Looking along the rows of tombs spread out along the daisied grass with splashes of sun from between the rain clouds, one felt no fear. But what about at night, when the moon had dominion over all things dead and the spirits walked the land?

A sudden splash of cold against my face returned me to reality. A light rain had begun to fall.

I heard the damp earth thump-thumping on the coffin as the last solemn words were spoken. The world had scarcely known nor would it long remember that he had been here, but I knew that I would not forget. Something strange and terrible was creeping into my sheltered world and the realisation made me feel keenly the extent of my naïveté. I felt suddenly older and alone as I looked around the bleak enclosure, knowing full well now that age had no relevance here. People earn and must carry their own crosses, we had been told all our lives, but what terrible thing could a mother do to deserve such a heavy cross? And what of the suffering of an innocent child, now nailed down in a wooden box beneath the earth?

I waited until the small gathering began to disperse, and when the last few people prepared to leave, I followed.

8

In the days following the tragedy, my mood of apprehension began to lift and I was less despondent. I began to feel as though it had all been a dream, and that the events of the past few days would vanish, as always, in the warmth of the sun. For a few days the weather was cold and wet, and we were obliged to play indoors, but then the sun came out again and we ran outside.

Inside a hole in our garden wall lived a host of grimy earwigs. Their presence had always been a source of worry to me, fearing their migration to my unsuspecting ears. I never had the courage to tackle them before, but now, for some reason, I knew I could. Grabbing the stout end of a broken stick I marched along the garden path and plunged it deep into their lair.

A morbid satisfaction mixed with a kind of fear went coursing through my veins as I watched their frenzied flight. Out of the hole the earwigs poured like a mass of living lava, stampeding over each other's bodies as they spread in a brown carpet across the wall, some dropping to the soft earth below with a silent thud and scurrying to the safety of the nearest rock. Then I plugged up the space with small stones and clay, making sure that nothing could get in or out. I threw away the stick and was about to leave when I heard someone approaching. It was Madge Bourke who lived next door and who, by dint of her lanky legs, had cleared the wire fence between our gardens.

"What were you doing with that stick?" she asked, crouching down beside me, her eyes travelling to the plugged-up hole.

She was my dearest and closest friend and usually I told her everything, but for some reason I didn't want to tell her about the earwigs.

"Let's go to the Water Barrack!" I suggested suddenly, by way of cutting short her interrogation. To my relief she readily agreed.

We went inside to tell my mother. Then off we went to the river. It was nice having Madge's company and I wished I could tell her about the little boy and why I had scattered the earwigs, but I couldn't. Madge had always attributed to me more cerebral horsepower than I actually possessed, imagining me the wisest most far-seeing person in the world, and bombarding me with questions to which she was sure I had the answers. Needless to say I seldom had, though I had felt it wise to keep that fact to myself. So I knew I would have some explaining to do if I told her anything. I stayed quiet and so did Madge. In fact today she was very quiet, with no questions or enigmas to be solved.

We crouched together in the clear shallow water of the river, all our attention focused on our two empty jars lying on the sandy bottom. It was only a matter of time, we knew, before something found its way into the open ends. Today we were fishing not only for brinkeens, but the coveted little red-breasts that swam close to the bank, hiding themselves in the long slender grass. They couldn't fool us no matter how they tried. We were well acquainted with their wily ways. So we waited patiently for one more daring than the rest to leave the safety of the weeds and venture forth with courage.

The Breagagh was a trouting river, usually teeming with all kinds of life ranging from tiny inch minnows to fat black eels over two feet long. It ran through the heart of the area we called the Water Barrack and was at times high in flood, with deep muddy water plunging down from the mountains and creeping up over the old mill and bridge. At other times it was narrow and confined, barely covering the large rocks and weeds. I suppose it was never really a wide river, not in comparison with those I have known since, but to us then it was great and gushing. So clear you could snatch a trout from it, no rod required.

On certain days it had a scent all of its own, of wild flowers and sweet grasses that crept down from the hills and settled on the banks like a morning mist. The spot did not belong to us, but we thought it did because we lived so close to it. Sometimes children from other corners of the town would come to play, but their visits were usually short and at times unpleasant, for we had many rivalries. But never did we shoo anybody away, unless they posed a threat to our authority.

We had no special games that we played around there, just walking barefoot in the river or rambling in and out of the derelict mill. It was a place where the younger lads sought to impress us girls with their knowledge or their manly deeds. The older boys and girls, supposedly keeping vigil over us, would lie upon the bank or lean or sit on the bridge ogling each other. Today there was nobody there but us; the whole place seemed deserted.

Sometimes the whole city was like that: so quiet you would think that nobody lived in it. Kilkenny in those days was a well-kept town. The Marble City it was called, a city mainly by virtue of its earlier parliament, and later its cathedral, but a prosperous place in comparison with some. Most of the streets were respectable. We had no slums or tenements to embarrass us, except for one area on the outskirts of town where people lived in houses the size of cardboard boxes and emptied their slops into the street. But the last of these had vanished by the time I left home. Unemployment was everywhere, however, in spite of our mills and our bakeries. The people were mostly poor, the majority belonging to that proportion of the population that had to be kept in hardship in order that the road to heaven might be made easier for the others.

Two faces the city had, my mother used to say. One that looked out over the poor and one that looked the other way. But it was for the most part a respectable town. Respectable that was until the military returned to the empty barracks, and soldiers walked the streets. Young girls began to part with their virginity. The population of the city began to climb, and fear hung like fog over every mother's heart until every respectable father locked up his respectable daughter. Still, the population continued to increase. My Auntie Mary was right about the soldiers on that account: they brought much pain and suffering. Families who up until then had no skeletons to hide now strove to conceal their shame.

My own father was a fine example. He locked up my sister Mary Brigid every chance he got and forbade any soldier to even look at her. Yet in the end she defeated him. Got herself pregnant and had to marry one.

The town was not large by any means, its boundaries, roughly speaking, running in a line north and south of John's Bridge which spanned the River Nore. The ancient part of the city lay to the north, its origins in the settlement of St. Canice from which it took its name. Later, it became known as Irishtown, and the newer, more selective half as Englishtown. At that time the English influence was everywhere, and the differences—the grace and elegance of the English half, the poverty and degradation of the Irish half—were conspicuous. I remember my father telling me once that even when he was

51

growing up it was not always possible to walk along High Street to the Grand Parade without feeling conscious of one's origins. Those were the great days of Smithwick and the Railway, their massive drays clattering through the cobbled streets to unload crates and wooden barrels into open gratings in the ground.

Eventually the two parts came together, and in the Kilkenny of my day things were different. It was difficult to say with accuracy what English influence remained, for more and more the Gaelic heart had begun to throb and people less inclined to deny their heritage. In general they were well informed, the men honest and hard-working, the boys with a manliness that could never be bred into their bones at school, a manliness that came only from tradition, either from the father's side or the mother's side.

Yet the people had one black mark against them, I always thought. They were too much in league with the men in black, who kept their minds focused on our mortal sins instead of on our virtues. Everything ran by the law of God, not by the County Council. Most of us believed what we were told and had no particular opinions of our own. At age twelve, however, none of that was of consequence to me. Kilkenny was a fine town and I loved it well. It was a grand place to grow up in, so many lanes and corners to explore. We had our round tower and our castle, our quarries and our canal. And outside the city were the country roads, the bosheens and the meadows, every inch of which we travelled, leaving home early in the morning and returning home only when the sun went down. No river escaped the imprint of our feet along its bottom, and often we would walk the length of one from the heart of the country to the heart of town.

The Breagagh was that kind of river. You could spend all day in it fishing, paddling or doing very much as we were doing now. We seldom lifted our eyes from our carefully concealed jars, for we had to be quick and ready for any eventuality. Once

Madge caught sight of something moving in the swaying grass and pointed to the flurry of mud spreading out around the bottom. We kept our eyes on that spot for a while, and when the film of mud had cleared we saw the long sleek body of a bloodsucker winding its way through the weeds. Wisely we kept our distance, remembering what had happened to my toe the previous summer. The bloodsucker wound its way along the muddy bottom for a while, and then with a furious wriggle it moved out into the fast-flowing water and glided away in the current. Relieved at its departure, we resumed our slow survey of the bottom.

Sometime later Madge began to fidget. I asked her what was bothering her and she said "nothing." But I knew by the way her eyes fell down that something was. I waited, and a few minutes later she sighed a heavy sigh and said it was a secret known only to her mother. Then for some reason she changed her mind.

"Oh well! I don't suppose it will do any harm to tell you, but you won't tell anyone, sure you won't?"

Wild horses couldn't drag it out of me, I assured her, and crossed my heart and hoped to die if I ever told.

She told me then that her father was sick and was being sent to the sanatorium. The heart went out of me, for Mr. Bourke, as far as I knew, only had bronchitis and people sent to the sanatorium had tuberculosis. Furthermore, if and when people were admitted, we children were the last, if ever, to be informed. So I couldn't help but wonder where Madge had gotten her information.

"And how do you know that?" I asked, sure that something in her answer would contradict her statement. It didn't. Dr. Purcell had been up to their house, she said, and told her mother. She'd been skulking in the scullery at the time and had heard everything. She looked at me imploringly, her eyes begging a solution, and I racked my brain for something plausible to say, but for the life of me I couldn't think. Managing to inject a note of confidence into my voice, I suggested that we not worry until we heard something more.

"Lots of people go in there and come out fine," I told her. Doubtfully she shook her head.

"They do, Madge—honest—only we never hear; we only hear about the ones that die."

The words sounded shallow in my ears and I wished I could believe them for Madge's sake. Though we were not aware of statistics then, tuberculosis was the country's number one killer. Not many people recovered from it, and Madge knew that fact as well as I did. We had good reason to fear it with people dying every day.

Why! only that year two lads we knew had succumbed to it, and nobody at the time could believe it had happened. For some time we had suspected it of one of them because he had taken to sleeping in a wooden hut behind their house. At first we gave it little thought, but as time passed and he never came out we began to get suspicious.

The sad thing was that families stricken with that disease felt instant shame and went to extremes at times to conceal the fact. A few months later when we heard the lad had died we were not surprised. But I will never forget the shock on people's faces in the street when his brother died. He had never been sick that we knew of and had planned to marry that same year. The next thing we heard he was being buried. What was I to say to Madge in light of that? There was no sense in trying to deceive her. So I suggested we go to the Abbey Chapel and offer up a prayer. Her face brightened at the prospect of a miracle, then clouded over.

"Do you think it will do any good?" she asked.

"Of course it will," I lied brazenly, remembering all the months I had spent there myself with nothing to show for it but sore knees and empty pockets.

We pulled our still empty jars out by their strings and climbed onto the bank. After drying our feet on the long grass and pulling on our shoes and socks we walked in silence to the Abbey Chapel. All I kept thinking about was Madge, so dear to me and so much a part of my fretful life. I had no memory of our first encounter. It seemed to me we just grew out of the ground together. She lived in the house next to ours, her parents having moved there the same time as mine.

Madge was an only child, though Mrs. Bourke made mention once or twice of a dead son whose framed picture she kept above the window in the kitchen. I used to look at it wondering whether the little boy in it was simply sleeping in his bed or whether the picture had been taken after he had died. Madge either didn't know or didn't want to talk about it so I never pressed her, and I didn't like to ask her mother.

They were like a second family to me in any case, though at times Mrs. Bourke was apt to fuss when I was present. Ignorance, you see, had bequeathed to us a higher place on the social scale, simply by virtue of my father's reputation. People thought of him as a man of standing, though I don't know why, for men of standing usually had lots of money, and all my father had were friends with lots of money. Apart from his connection with his sister Mary, who might have been classified as "well to do," he had no material riches. Unlike many, though, he had a decent job, secure with average wages. I suppose as the butler is a man of consequence in the servants' hall, so it was with my father.

Mr. Bourke on the other hand was less fortunate. He was compelled to accept whatever jobs were offered, and these were usually poorly paid and physically unsuited to him. But he was a decent man, my father said, and he did not discourage our mingling.

Despite the supposed advantages of my own home, I envied Madge the tranquility of hers, the comfort of her own bed, and never having to share as I did with others. I envied her straight blond hair and porcelain skin, as compared to my red kinks and freckles. She did not have to endure the misery of names like Carrot Head, or Titch, for she was tall and thin, not stunted like myself. When people called us Mutt and Jeff it never seemed to bother her. Most of her spare time was spent in our house, taking my mother's praise and punishment in like manner.

She was truly my closest friend, and the bouts of anger and resentment I sometimes felt when shouldering the blame for some forbidden act in which we were both complicit were usually short-lived. I couldn't bear to think of any misfortune falling on Madge or her father, for I was very fond of both of them. Many were the long wintry nights I had spent in their house beside the fire listening to her father's stories. At times, after telling one story scarier than the rest he would disappear and then reappear a short while later with a sheet around his head. It was meant, of course, to frighten us, and so it did. For even though we suspected it was him all along, we would scream in terror and scramble for a safer place beside Madge's mother. Then he would pull the sheet off and we would all laugh, with Mrs. Bourke saying he was a silly man.

Off she would go to the scullery then to prepare something nice to make up for it. And when we had eaten all the brown bread and jam and drank all the tea I would go home.

9

Hiding our jars in a corner of the Abbey's hall, Madge and I pushed open the heavy inside door and stepped into the chapel. The familiar scent of burning wax and centuries of mould wafted over us. Tiptoeing across the red and green tiles, so as not to disturb people already at prayer, we slipped into the wooden pew nearest the altar and bowed our heads. Then we took turns kneeling at the shrines; first before one saint and then before another, with extra devotion to the little Christ child.

The church was silent and softly lit. A few candles burned brightly at each shrine, their flickering flames throwing fingers of light against the stained glass windows and making blobs of colour on the whitewashed walls. Kilkenny, like most Irish towns, took a lively interest in its saints, erecting shrines and statues in their honour. The churches were filled with them and the Abbey had its own fine selection.

This little Dominican church, over seven hundred years in age and one of the country's oldest, was known to us as the Black Abbey because of its association with the Blackfriars. It was a favourite place of worship for many, especially those of the old settlement of Irishtown outside whose boundaries the church had been founded. Plundered again and again by Norman and English alike, one could almost feel the shadow of their presence and catch the whiff of sweat from Cromwell's mares. Yet despite my years of attendance there I knew little about its founders. The friars, shy and retiring, preferred to seclude themselves behind the stone walls of their monastery. Only the brothers, usually engaged in the janitorial services in the church, were known to us. Not one of them was evident today, the pitter-patter of their sandalled feet lost behind the privacy of the sacristy door.

Except for one or two parishioners in another section of the church, we knelt alone in silence and lost ourselves in prayer. After we had been kneeling for some time we noticed a woman walking along the aisle. There was something odd about her manner, some little quirk. We watched her as she ambled toward us, stopping every now and then to fiddle with her bag or gaze about distractedly. She was neatly dressed, but we couldn't tell if she was young or old because the veil of her hat hung down around her face. I kept my eyes downcast as she came closer, but watched her from the corner of my eye. Her flat brown shoes went past me on the tiles and I ached to raise my head. A jab from Madge's elbow gave me the excuse.

Looking up, I saw her standing at a nearby shrine examining the opening that channelled the coppers dropped in for candles. She had bent her body and was peering into it. What happened next has become a jumble in my mind, though I remember distinctly a flat metal object in her hand and the coppers sliding through the slot. She must have drawn out a dozen or more before she finally gave up and dropped the metal object back into her bag. Then she promptly added a handful of candles.

Madge looked at me agog, and I knew what she was thinking—a compound mortal sin, right before our eyes.

"Would you believe that?" she exclaimed, when we heard the thud of the closing door and knew the woman had departed.

Without ceremony we took off after her, but when we reached the outside gate she had already gone. We looked up and down the street, but there was no sign of her. Disappointed and still curious we crossed the square to home. Then, just as we turned the corner into Blackmill Street we heard the clip-clop of shoes behind. Darting back, we saw her cross the road from the chapel gate and head off along the street.

"Do you think she is from the asylum, Tess?" Madge asked excitedly, and I said I did, for I knew well enough it was possible. In those days it was not uncommon for mental patients to slip out of confinement on the Dublin Road and make their way into the town.

We decided we should keep an eye on her. Ducking in and out of doorways we followed behind until she reached a point in the street where the road branched off. Here she stopped and turned in our direction. A wild scurry of excitement followed as we tripped over each other's toes trying to create the impression that we had been walking the other way. Sure that the woman had detected us, my heart thumped. Any minute I was sure she would come bounding after us, but when I didn't hear her feet in mad pursuit my heart settled and we remained with our decision to follow her.

"Looks like she's going to cross Fryers Bridge," Madge said, taking a quick glance around, and I looked to see the woman heading in that direction.

Rather than face the stench of the slaughterhouse in that street, we gave up the chase and wandered off to the Brewery Lane. By the time we had reached the sluice opposite the brewery and saw the apples floating on the water, we had forgotten about the woman.

We raced into the old lough yard looking for a stick with which to trap the apples. The sluice gates were open, but no water was flowing, only a little leakage trickling through the wooden beams at the bottom. We fished as many apples as we could from the dammed-up section of the river and then searched the vacant fire grates of two derelict buildings to see if the old stray hen we knew so well had left us anything. Both fire grates were empty and no sign of the old hen anywhere, so we sat down outside the door to eat our apples. Within a very short while we heard the voice of Jack Mulcahey in the lane outside.

"Whoa Nellie, whoa."

We ran into the lane and saw the long wooden cart with SMITHWICK printed on the side, coming around the corner. Nellie's hooves clattered on the cobbled stones. The cart stopped outside the brewery gate and Jack climbed down and disappeared through the little door in the centre of the gate. We hurried over to Nellie. She was standing with her head bent, shaking the reins noisily and stamping impatiently on the hot stones. We told her what a good horse she was and reached up to stroke her nose and forehead. She looked at us lazily from behind her long lashes. Then Jack came out.

"Stand back, girls," he said, and began backing the heavy load toward the open gate. Leaning his body against the mare's side he talked to her in whispers.

"Easy girl, easy," he said, when she pranced too jittery on the slippery stones.

The lane was very narrow and left little room for manoeuvring. Caught up by the urgency of the moment we ran to the back of the cart and busily called warnings any time the wheels came too close to either side. In due course the cart passed safely through and we were rewarded with a handful of sweets. With spirits high and egos fat we headed home discussing the pros and cons of equine companionship.

"Do horses have souls?" Madge wanted to know, and I decided that they did, for why else would they be so gentle?

Then Madge said that her father knew a fellow once who got wedged between a gatepost and a lorry. The driver didn't even know he was pinned against the wall until he saw every-body waving. The man almost lost his leg on account of it. No such thing would happen with a horse, we decided. They were safer and friendlier and nobody ever heard of anybody getting squashed by one. Some months later I would remember those words while watching Mrs. Marshall's stallion stomp poor Matty Morrison almost to death.

We came to the end of the brewery lane, crossed over the road, and tired but happy trudged up James Street to home. That evening when the sun had gone down and night had begun to fall, the ambulance came for Mr. Bourke.

10

There was seldom a quiet moment in our house anymore. Nothing my father did or said seemed to satisfy my mother. Today, she was complaining about everything. She had no friends, she claimed, and blamed my father. The people in the street were good enough for her, she said, if not for his high and mighty. My father, a quiet, retiring man who hated the sound of raised voices, concealed his hurt and said nothing. It was not true, of course, that she had no friends, for she had many.

The problem lay with her preference for the few whose manners offended my father's sensitivity, the ones he considered an affront to his efforts to exclude from our lives all that was coarse and common. I don't believe he ever really was a snob—intensely shy would be more accurate—though he seldom passed another in the street without taking off his hat or giving them the time of day.

A tall handsome man, he was, greying at the sides, with large sunken eyes that were round and hazel. "Sheep's eyes," my mother used to say when she was mad at him, but I thought they were beautiful. A gentle man, he liked to sing and tell us stories, and I can hear him now sitting by the fire polishing our shoes after we had gone to bed.

We knew of course that mother's anger was not entirely directed at my father, the arrow of her discontent going further back, way back to his mother. My grandparents, whom I never knew, had lived in a modest house in Abbey Street. They were not wealthy by any means, but neither were they considered poor. Both were self-employed, my grandfather a master tailor and she a tailoress. Fashion and fine tapestry had afforded them a decent living and gave them admittance to a social circle they could not otherwise have reached.

"Beggars on horseback," Mother said, and maybe she was right. But they could see no harm in fraternising with people of influential means, with an eye to furthering their own. Besides, Grandfather was a respected member of the community, well known for his tenor voice. The whole family were singers and their regular appearance in amateur operatic performances had brought them a small measure of recognition. In a country where jobs were as scarce as diamonds and at a time when education was considered the prerogative of the rich, it was to my grandmother's credit that she managed her family so well. There were no labourers in her house. All her sons were respectably in business and both her daughters had become teachers. None of the children, she thanked the Lord, had allowed their fancy to become entangled below the circle which she felt was best for them.

My father at eighteen was her youngest and already apprenticed to the largest retail marketer in the city. Grandmother's hopes for a favourable marriage within the boundaries of her prescribed zone were on the way to becoming reality until Father announced that he was going to marry my mother. It came as a great shock to Gran, who opposed the marriage with every fibre of her being. A domestic, after all! Not even a native of Kilkenny, but just a blow-in from another town. What prospects would poor Tommy have? This bias to outsiders was not confined to

Granny. For Kilkenny at that time had its own form of nepotism apt to discourage an ambitious newcomer, a fact that had not changed appreciably fifty years later. All new arrivals of later than a hundred years were resented, especially if they were associated with the economic weakness of the country.

It was mother's belief, however, that big fish swimming in a shallow pond deserved to be caught. Not that she considered my father such a big fish, mind, but he had, after all, a steady job, a decent reputation and a glimmer of hope for their prospective future. It was he who persuaded her to remain in Kilkenny. So here she was and here she would stay, and woe betide the one who tried to budge her. The wedding date was posted and Grandmother, faced with a situation she could not change, acknowledged her defeat and eked out her blessing. The resentment nonetheless lingered, according to my mother, and revealed itself later when my grandparents died. My father, the last born of their children, received not a penny piece of anything they left.

After they were married, my father, hoping to reconcile his mother's hurt feelings, set up house in the very same street. One year later Mikey was born. Named after my grandfather, he became a buffer between the families, healing the wounds to some extent. By the time my sister Mary Brigid came along my grandmother had relented somewhat, and a state of relative neighbourliness existed between them until her death. Unfortunately, however, the stored-up resentment Mother felt too often found an outlet in her anger against my father.

She often spoke of their home in Abbey Street, though, and I knew she had been happy there. It was there that I was born. But of those early years I have little memory; my mother was but a starched white apron with soft-scented hair and loving hands. I wasn't even three when we left Abbey Street. By that time the family had increased to seven.

Those were the happy carefree years; my father still in a decent job and Mother fair content. But changes were abroad in the world the breadth of which they could not foresee nor indeed prevent. Two years and one brother later, Father came home from work with the gloom of death upon him. He had lost his job. The company, it seems, having survived the first onslaught of depression, had floundered and was now going under.

To my father, who had had years of service there, the shock was great. Gone were his hopes of rising to the top. Gone, too, his salary. Too proud to go to the Labour Exchange to file for income he was entitled to, he was forced in a short time to use up what little money he had saved. Unlike my mother, he had not learned to tackle life like an angry bull and soon began to give way to despair. With savings all but depleted and no prospects in sight, Mother took the reins.

"When I married you it was for better or for worse, and I see no reason why it should be for the worse."

She was not timid or embarrassed about sharing her troubles with her friends as my father was, and in no time at all she had found herself a job. Lucky for us that she did too, for we had never known or would again the unexpected luxuries that flowed from her decision. Her reputation for cleanliness preceding her, she was soon installed in the home of Mary Duggan, one of the wealthiest families in the city and proprietors of the Monster House, the largest department store in the county.

To Mrs. Duggan we owed the comfort of the following years, for it was through her generosity and her honest affection for my mother that we were able to enjoy one of the nicest homes in the neighbourhood and the pleasure of clothing we could not otherwise have afforded. Life had blossomed and grown bright again. A few years passed and Father, after months of temporary work around the city, found himself a job with Smithwick, the leading apothecary and distiller. It was not the job he had hoped for nor the wages he expected, but it would save him from the horror of the Labour Exchange. Soon after that, however, Mother found herself pregnant again, and the pendulum of fate took another swing when a year or so after Jimmy was born the Duggans left Kilkenny.

A strict policy of thrift was more necessary than ever. Save more and spend less became my father's motto, and life for us became dreary again.

More and more my mother began to look for comfort in Smithwick's Ale, the local panacea for everybody's ailments be they real or imagined, yet my father refused to acknowledge it. He knew of course that she took the odd drop, as Mother put it, but he refused to admit it was anything more. Mother on the other hand was beginning not to care, and when Father was out of the house she started to drink openly, relying on us to cover up for her. She might go for weeks without her fits and nasty temper—sweeping, dusting and chatting with us all. Then the tide would turn and she would be unbearable.

While this must have disturbed my father inwardly, outwardly he behaved as if nothing untoward was happening. His protectiveness, conversely, was doing him no good, for gradually without meaning to he began to isolate himself. His every remark became a weapon for my mother to use against him. Moreover she had gained a sort of ascendancy over him during her term as the breadwinner, leaving her mistress of her own actions. Now it was too late for reversal.

Most of these incidents had taken place when I was little, stories told and retold leaving flimsy impressions of a sly whisper here, a cold glance there, but with no real impression on my carefree life. All that had changed, however. I had seen the glint of the Devil's steel and felt the crack of his whip around my ankles. At last I was beginning to recognise my mother, or one who I perceived to be my mother, standing now on the kitchen floor glowering at my father. All morning she had been looking for a fight, picking on the family like a bird of prey. I had hoped the fire would burn itself out before my father came home, but it had not. She started in on him as soon as she saw his face in the kitchen door.

The insults, the oaths and the horrid accusations. I could understand then why it was that Father went to such lengths to avoid her tongue. I closed my mind to the things being said, especially the unkind things about his mother. Could any of them be true, I wondered? Was my father in some remote way responsible? It seemed unfair to be blaming him. Yet how could I be sure of anything?

Around the room there flowed an emotion that I could hardly bear. Jane was crying quietly in the corner, her sobs muffled by her fist, and I could feel splinters tearing at my stomach.

11

Some days the arguments were more violent than others, leaving us terrified and drained. This morning's argument had been like that. Such a heavy feeling had come over me when our parents left the house and we were finally alone. I helped Jane clear away the dishes, and when we had dried and stacked them in the cupboard, I told her I was going out.

Where?" she asked dejectedly, not wanting to be left alone. I didn't really want to tell her, for I was hoping to see the Old Man, though I wasn't sure of his whereabouts. I had never seen him in the light of day, but Tommy Connor had told me once that he spent his weekends at the Mulligan farm. I had told Jane something about him, but I had not mentioned his name to anyone else, even though I had seen him a few times since. I didn't want my parents to find out about our friendship and was reluctant to share it with anybody else. What few boys joined him in the evenings were older than myself, so they didn't count. I knew Jane would never betray me, so I told her what I was thinking. She livened up and wiped her face with the kitchen towel eager to come along.

"Don't worry about Dad," she said, as we walked along. "He knows her better than we do. Besides, she doesn't mean all the things she says."

I said nothing. Poor Jane, I thought, always sticking up for Mother. If only I could have felt the same; but at some point I had stopped believing in my mother, had begun to lose respect for her. It wasn't even so much the drinking as it was her treatment of my father. Her behaviour was slowly managing to turn the rest of us against him, with her not wanting him to know what she was doing and we not wanting him to find out. Conspiring and concealing facts we were, partly to spare him pain, but partly from allegiance to our mother.

Then there was that other thing, the hypocrisy, the need to pretend that we didn't notice when she had drink in her. The others I suppose had learned to conceal their feelings, but I could never hide what was in my heart nor the contempt all too clear on my face. So Mother and I had begun to quarrel. And as the years passed and I began to gain some measure of independence, we would quarrel more. For the time being, however, I tried to behave as Jane said I should and smother my resentment.

We continued walking, our walk one of many of the past few months, precipitated by the turbulence at home. Along the College Road we went, all the way to the Sceilp Inn (a pub believed to have been a refuge for Fenians on the run) and then right toward Kenny's Well. On these occasions Jane was usually quiet and thoughtful, but today she was lively and full of chatter. Two years older than myself but with a milder disposition, she had begun of late to act older than her age, partly because of responsibilities that had fallen onto her by our sister Sheilagh finding a full-time job and partly because of adolescence.

Jane had taken to putting on makeup, too, when there was nobody home to see it, and lately I had noticed the looks of admiration she was getting from the boys. Her hair she usually kept long and rolled outward at the bottom in a sausage roll, but today it was combed loosely on her head, with little curls and frizzy pieces hanging by her ears. It looked nicer and less severe, especially with the yellow ribbon. Her eyes were large and blue like Mother's, her skin pale. I glanced at her as we walked along, noting the contrast of her skin against her dress and wondering if there was any truth to the story that she and Maizie Dooley smoked cigarettes at the matinee on Sundays.

. As we strolled along she seemed to have forgotten the unpleasantness at home and began talking about her future. She had big plans, she told me, and would soon be a stranger to us all. I didn't find that statement odd because it was the dream of all of us, but then she said something that astonished me. I knew she would be fourteen at the end of the year and old enough to leave school, but now here she was telling me that she had already left school and would be leaving home right after the summer holidays.

I looked at her in disbelief. She laughed nervously, adding that it had all been settled. The look on her excited face and the smugness in her voice provoked in me a spasm of jealous anger. My immediate thought was one of dread, for if it were true, and I had my doubts that it really was, it meant that I would be left at home, the eldest, with the task of keeping an eye on the younger ones. Having given me this news she became quiet and refused to say more, except to add that she was going to Youghal to work as a chambermaid at a large hotel.

"You must be codding me," I said, adding that Father would never agree.

She pulled her lips into a grimace.

"I'm not a complete gomme now, am I?" she replied, meaning of course that she had not told him.

"Well, I wouldn't get your hopes up then," I said, "because he will have to know."

"Oh! no he won't," was her reply, so nonchalant and flagrant. I saw with clarity then that she had been working on my mother, and I recalled how every day of late she had started hanging around the house, making herself useful at every turn. I also knew that she had manoeuvred Mother into letting her stay home from school on more than one occasion. Resentment rose like bile in me as I pictured their collusion, but I fought the urge to say what I was thinking, for I didn't have the heart to destroy her hopes. Besides, one worm out of the can, I knew, and all the rest could follow.

We walked in silence for a while, gazing at the empty peaceful fields that made the world seem calm and normal, while inside my mind was churning.

"Will she ever give it up do you think—the drink I mean?" I finally asked, as casually as possible. Her face went wistful and she said she doubted it, because Mother had been like that too long. Did she know when it had started? I asked, and she said she didn't, only that it was a good while back according to Mary Brigid. Mother, she said, had gotten sick once and almost drowned herself in the river. The drinking had started soon after that. Before I was even born most likely.

"I hate it every time she does it," I told Jane. "I can't bring myself to look at her, and she knows it too."

Jane nodded and said she felt the same way at times, but that my attitude didn't help. "You could try letting on a little more," she said.

"I can't, it doesn't work for me. Besides, she can see it in my face; I can't hide it anymore."

"Well it doesn't make her feel any better. She doesn't do it to hurt anyone, and it's not fair to keep blaming her."

How I hated it when Jane said that, making it seem as though Mother was not accountable. I didn't know what I wanted her to say, but I did know that implicit in that remark was the belief that somehow Father was to blame. My stomach knotted.

"You can't blame Daddy either," I responded angrily, and Jane sighed.

"I didn't say you could, now did I?"

"No, but that's what you're implying," I said. She stood still and looked at me.

"You just can't let it go, can you? You must keep on and on until you hurt someone. Why can't you accept that no one is responsible, that it is just something that happens?"

She was right, of course, but I didn't care, because all I could see was my father's face so white and shaken.

"Who can you blame if you don't blame her? Nobody forces her to do it."

Jane replied in that sombre tone of an adult giving counsel. "Lots of people drink, Tess. I don't know why, but the problem only starts when they can't give it up. I don't think that Mam can give it up, and that's why she won't admit to even doing it. You'll understand it better as you get older."

She had started walking faster and I knew it was time for me to quit or risk having her go a separate way. Not wanting to spoil our day completely, I let it go.

"Why don't we take a shortcut to Mulligans'?" I suggested, when it became clear that the Old Man was nowhere on the road. And so a short while later we were standing on the steep slope overlooking the glen. From there we could see the river winding its way through the meadows. We looked along the length and breadth of it but saw no one we recognised. Across the fields we could see the Mulligan farm, its windows golden in the sun. Knowing that the Old Man often went there, I wondered if he might be there now.

The yard and fields around looked empty as did the boreen leading to the house. Tall elm trees lined both sides and stout stone walls separated the farmhouse from the fields around.

Everything seemed tranquil.

"What do you think?" Jane asked, and started down the hill.

I followed and we jumped across the narrow brook, climbed the broken wall at the bottom and raced across the fields to the nearest barn. Everyone was welcome at the Mulligan farm so we had no fears of trespassing. Except for an old sheepdog that barked loudly at our approach, there was little evidence of life, the children of the family long grown up and moved away. In the centre of the yard was an ancient chestnut tree from whose widespread branches there hung a swing. It was arranged with tiny pillows, and beside the swing was a wooden bench with a cast-iron pump at the side of it. The house itself was very small but comfortable, with a thatched roof and rambling roses twined about the walls.

The back door opened and Mrs. Mulligan appeared. She nodded pleasantly and said a few kind words to us. There was no special introduction necessary, but we told her our names and why we had come by way of the fields. She smiled, saying that there would be fresh milk in the barn any minute now and went back inside. A few minutes later Mickey Mulligan came out rolling back his sleeves and collar. He acknowledged our presence as he hurried to the pump, gasping as he splashed the cold water up his arms and over his face.

We had known Mickey for many years. People still referred to him as "the rent man" though he no longer worked in that capacity. A small man he was with merry eyes, a quick laugh and a kind word for everyone. Wispy locks of hair strayed at random around his otherwise bald head. His mind was a storehouse of information, especially on farming and economic matters. He was an authority on everything, from the interesting to the ridiculous that had happened in our city in the previous twenty years. His house was a kind of neighbourhood club where on any given night a person might drop in. Mickey, usually in his stocking feet before the fire, made everybody welcome. Like the Old Man he loved to talk, but he also loved to listen.

A few years before he had suffered a stroke which not only left one arm disabled but deafened him a little in both ears. His mind remained clear and lucid however. After the stroke he had given up his job in the city and retired to the farm. He seldom left it now, except to go to Mass on Sunday or stroll with the Old Man along the river. I wanted to ask him if he had seen any sign of the Old Man, but didn't have the courage.

In the cowshed we watched the cows give up their milk and listened to Mickey praising them. Shorthorns, we learned, were his favourites and Dolly his favourite cow, the one that he admired most.

Admired? I threw a glance at Jane. Who but Mickey Mulligan could admire a cow or think of them as beautiful? Great ugly heaps I thought they were. Pancake makers of the world, not to mention their aroma! I looked along the row of chewing heads, the large vacant eyes just staring, and noted the telltale splatter on their behinds.

"I'm going outside," I said, and Jane followed, giggling.

"Evening in Paris with a moo-moo twist," she teased, equating the terrible aroma with my favourite perfume.

We moved away to a nearby pond and wandered idly around the edge keeping a lookout for the Old Man. A few ducks and drakes waddled by the pond and there, in the centre by a floating log, a mother goose and her goslings. Jane picked up a stone and lobbed it in the water, scattering the goose and her little brood.

"What did you do that for?" I yelled at her, annoyed.

She shrugged, and picking up a flatter stone skimmed it along the surface.

"I don't see any sign of this Old Man," she said sulkily, kicking up some loose stones with her toe. Angry with her I made no reply, but moved away to another spot, to a log that was damp and smelled of mould, with little white grubs crawling over one end of it. I sat down in any case, pretending not to notice Jane. At that very moment I heard her scream, and with a few leaps she was at my side. I leaped up in panic.

"What is it?" I cried, and she pointed to a spot just beyond the water where the ground dipped to a hollow. I strained my eyes but could only see tall grass waving in the breeze.

"There's nothing there," I said.

Jane held my arm.

"There is so," she insisted.

I suggested we creep over to get a better look. At this she took fright and was about to run when suddenly the long grass parted and the thing appeared. It looked to me like an enormous pig, but not like any pig I had ever seen. For one thing it didn't have the usual mud caked onto it, and its skin was black with pink patches. At first whiff of us it raised its head, grunted noisily and sprinted toward us. Jane screamed, her one thought now for immediate flight. Then we heard a voice I recognised.

"Ye don't mean t'tell me yer afraid iv Boc?"

And the Old Man sauntered toward us.

12

He was without his coat, and his grey hair looked even greyer. A long red scarf dangled from his neck, and on his feet he had Wellingtons. I turned to the touch of Jane's fingers on my arm and saw that she was pale, her eyes telling me that she wanted to go home.

It's him," I whispered. "It's the Old Man," but she seemed past caring, her eyes glued to the strange black animal.

"C'mere alana, come t'me," the Old Man called to Jane, but she wouldn't budge.

Then he offered something from his pocket to the animal, and we saw it disappear into a frightening mouth.

"That's all that fella wants," he said, as the light dawned on Jane.

"A pig! Is that all it is?" she laughed, adding that she had never seen such a huge pig and thought all pigs were supposed to be pink. The Old Man laughed.

"I used t'think th'same meself 'til I met this lad. Ye've heard iv th'horse iv a different colour, haven't ye?"

We said we had.

"Well, this is a pig iv a different colour, a male pig, a boar. Sure, th'head on him is bigger than me own."

He told us then that Boc was no ordinary pig but a paragon of pigs in the porcine world and had already distinguished himself as a champion.

"Every day he gets more pictures took iv him, an gettin' a great swelled head on account iv it," and indeed Boc did strut about the field with an elegant air. He had long black hair all over and large drooping ears.

"Pigs bite you know," Jane said, telling about our Mikey who had had his thumb snapped off by one.

"Did he indeed?" The Old Man looked amazed, then added, "Well, this fella's not keen on fingers. All he cares about is apples."

He pointed to a spot a little distance off where another pig, more common to our eyes was penned up with her banivs. That was Sadie, the saddleback sow. Unlike Boc, she had no black on her and her ears were short and standing up. As soon as she observed us coming she flung herself into a merry rage, leaping up from her place in the straw and plunging in wild spurts about her pen. Indigestion was what the Old Man said was bothering her.

I could have told him a different tale had I not seen the threat in Jane's eyes, as surely as I had seen the fear in Sadie's. For only I knew of the perverse pleasure Jane derived from sticking pigs with hatpins. Judging from the look in Sadie's eyes, I was sure she had had a premonition. I reached over and patted her gently on the head, telling her everything would be all right, and after I had whispered in her ear that Jane had no hatpin she settled down.

"A great many people hate th'sight iv pigs," the Old Man said. "I usen't t'like them much meself until I met these two. Now I like them better than any iv th'rest."

"Not better than horses, surely?" Jane exclaimed, and the Old Man laughed.

"No, not better than horses."

"And not better than Meggie!" I put in, for I knew that he loved his little goat.

No, but better than all the others, he told us chuckling. We walked around the back of the sty past the fairy's wreath, and a few minutes later we reached the meadows. All the time I noticed Jane hovering close beside the Old Man chatting. We stood on top of a nearby hill and looked across the land. The sun was sinking low in the sky, the afternoon passing, and long deep shadows had begun to creep across the valley. Below in the meadow by an old oak tree two horses lingered in the shade, and close by, a family of rabbits.

"Yo-ho. Yo-ho-o," the Old Man suddenly yelled through his hands, and I thought for sure he had outgrown his wits. Then I saw the reason for his call: Meggie was still standing at the bottom of the hill. She started toward us. The Old Man stretched out his arms to her and with all the tenderness of a little girl fondled her head with loving strokes. Some words of endearment followed as he fed her a length of straw and from his pocket bits of food which she gobbled greedily while following him about the hill in little halting rambles.

How the Old Man could find in her a companion was a mystery to me, yet it was clear that he did, keeping her close beside him all the time. Jane cooed and coddled her for a little while, but this scene of tender mothering soon ended when the goat in a moment of greed snatched up the bottom of her dress and began chewing. Jane tried to shunt her away but to no avail. Finally, tired of persuasion she landed her a hefty wallop. The Old Man looked at her in astonishment but said nothing, and Jane meekly apologised.

Suddenly, without warning, the whole sky went black and a slashing rain began. We dashed for cover to the nearest barn and called to Meggie to follow. We sat ourselves down on some old boxes inside the door where the Old Man and Jane continued chatting. They seemed to be ignoring me, and I felt hurt.

"Oh, no I won't. I wouldn't go to one even if I could," Jane was saying, and I knew she was talking about leaving school and why she wouldn't go to the Technical School. "I'd hate it there. I'll never make a scholar."

It was a simple statement of fact, because Jane had never been much good at school and hated going there. But the Old Man tried to convince her otherwise, saying that she was still young and clever and could succeed if she wanted to. His reasoning only angered Jane.

"Oh! grown-ups always say that, and it makes me mad. Maybe they believe it, but it isn't true." She looked at me.

"Ask Tess," she said, "she'll tell you. She's better in school than I am."

It was a chance for me to include myself in the conversation, as I had been trying to do all afternoon, but now that the opportunity was here I hesitated. Jane either didn't care or didn't notice.

"Anyway, I'm going to be an actress, just like Bette Davis," she told him.

"An actress! Is that a fact?"

His grey eyes were kind, but it seemed to me he was holding back his laughter.

"Faith an' ye'll be on th'pig's back so," he said, and Jane giggled, grateful that he hadn't trampled on her dream as the rest of us often did.

It wasn't that we did so intentionally or that we didn't understand her longing, it was simply the inevitability of our situation. Our lives and environment were hardly geared to any grand ambitions. Fashioned in the same way as our parents and our grandparents, we tended to accept meekly what was ordained. Why should Jane's life be any different?

Maybe in America she would have a chance. Things were different there, where an ordinary person could make it to the top, but not here in Ireland. Here in the land of the rainbow, where myths grew like mushrooms, only the privileged could afford to separate the glue from the glitter. But Jane loved to talk about the movies, where she spent the greater part of her spare time unbeknownst to my mother. The resemblance to Bette Davis was real enough, made even more noticeable by her efforts to emulate the star by copying her hairstyle and daubing scarlet lipstick on her lips.

13

The excitement in Jane's voice and her big blue eyes suddenly seemed to turn the Old Man sad. "Ye know, alana, ye remind me iv my poor wife Ellie. 'Twas in this very field I caught first glimpse iv her. Right there, beyond that shed." He pointed to a spot nearby.

I was helpin with th'hayin at th'time, an she came across the field bringin tea an sandwiches. Th' loveliest sight I'd ever seen. Mickey's fathur, Matthew, was beside me at th'time an told me who she was. His brother Sammy's girl, down for th' summer t' visit her aunt, an help around th' farm."

Her father, he told us, owned a grain store in the city and lived in a fine house on the Dublin Road. He rubbed his gnarled knuckles across his eyes and said no more.

"And where is she now?" Jane prodded.

"Dead," was all he answered, and abruptly rose.

The rain had stopped and we followed him out of the barn.

We heard no more about Ellie that day, but later I was to learn something of his own life. That he was born in Clonakilty and had lost his mother when he was only five. Then four years later his father had died. That left only his two older brothers, Peadar and Paulie, who brought him up the best way they could. Then one day Peadar went off to America and after one or two letters from him they heard no more. A few years went by before one cold night in January Paulie died, his patriotic blood washing over the cobbled streets of Dublin. Overcome with grief he had tried to drink himself to death, and when that failed he had left home forever.

"The travelling man. The man from Clonakilty," people would say when they saw him coming. And indeed that's what he had become, but never a tramp, for he worked hard for his living at each place he stayed.

Ellie had come into his life like a burst of sun, he told me, and he had waited all that week for another glimpse of her. That Saturday evening at the village dance he had seen her again. Danced all night with her. He loved her as he had loved the mountain air, he said, and one evening had asked her to marry him.

"Iv coorse I was young an' handsome then," he had added jokingly.

"And what did she say?" I asked.

"Ah! she laughed at first, said we weren't suited. She was a young teacher ye see, an' I was nothin'."

But after he had told her of his plans for a better future and how he planned to follow his father's trade of creating stained-glass windows, she accepted. He hadn't given much thought to her parents' opposition, their glum faces at the wedding. He had taken up his father's trade as he said he would, and was making a decent living.

Ellie seemed to be satisfied, but as time went on he noticed a change in her. His pride had been in his workmanship and in building their own little home. Hers, it seemed, was in putting on a show and accepting favours from her mother. Exactly when she stopped loving him he wasn't sure, but he knew the hating had begun.

One evening when he came home from work eager to tell her of the day's events, she had prevented him. Had looked at him with pure contempt, his mud-stained footprints on the floor flaming her temper. He didn't want to recall the ugly things she said, the names she had called him. A tramp! A clod from Clonakilty! Of course, he knew that he was not good enough for her and would never be respected by her family, but a tramp he had never imagined her as seeing him. In that moment he realised he would never be anything different in her mind.

When the next train left for Dublin he was on it.

For years he avoided the Marble City, though he sent money home to keep the mortgage going. One day he came back. He had no intention of calling in on Ellie, just catch a glimpse of her perhaps. Stay a little while around the town, maybe, and find out how she was doing. It never occurred to him that she might be dead, and couldn't believe it when he was told she had died only months earlier. In shock he had made his way to the Mulligans'. Old Matthew was long dead, but Mickey and his wife made him welcome.

From them he learned everything to be told about Ellie. How she had chosen to remain in the house despite her family's objections. Of her going back to teaching, and finally, her death. For a long time he had mourned her, visiting her grave whenever he could. Then he took up his travelling life again, read many books and became something of a scholar.

When he learned of Mickey's stroke he came back to help, settled down to a quieter life, listening to the young lads talk about their lives and driving Mickey mad with his philosophies.

We followed the Old Man up to the farmhouse, leaping over great rivulets of mud from the rain. A few minutes later we were seated by the fire, logs hissing in the grate, and the room filled with the smell of resin. There was no sign of Mrs. Mulligan, but Mickey, in his stocking feet, was already by the fire, his head resting on the back of the chair and the daily paper spread across his chest. Opposite stood an empty chair

which the Old Man settled into, and Jane and I seated ourselves on a low bench in between. There was a peaceful silence
in the room. Except for the dog's tail thumping on the mat and
the logs crackling, everything was quiet.

"D'ye know these girls Mickey?" the Old Man asked, emp-
tying his pipe into the grate. Mickey gave an irritated cough.

"And why wouldn't I? Haven't I known Tommy Lennon
the best part of my life?"

Then with a jab of his finger at me, "This one is the image
of her mother."

The Old Man smiled but made no comment. If he had
known who I was before Mickey mentioned it, he had not let
on and I had never told him, for fear he might find out about
my mother's drinking. Mickey shuffled back from the fire and
began to talk as usual about the trials of farming.

"It's hard work when you're not used to it," he said,
though he had been doing it on and off for fifteen years. If he
weren't used to it by now, when would he be? The truth of it
was that Mickey was inclined to be indolent, the whole farm
was in disrepair and everything needed mending. Pieces falling
off buildings in the wintertime were never nailed back, left to
rot until the spring and then forgotten.

A good man otherwise, though, the neighbours said, trying
to turn a blind eye, because for warmth of heart and public
affability Mickey had no equal. People had come to regard him
as an authority and would run to him with their problems. He
could tell them how to fix an axle or a broken wheel, how to
handle an unruly horse or how to stack hay at threshing. The
Old Man, who had heard all of Mickey's complaints before,
looked slyly at us.

"A nod is as good as a wink to a blind horse," he whispered, and aimed his spittle at the grate.

If Mickey heard him he didn't show it. They talked for a
little while of history, politics and the Garda, subjects of little

interest to us. Bored, Jane rose and walked across to the window. I followed, and we both stood there looking out.

"I want to go home," she whispered, urging me to interrupt the conversation. But I was spared the task of doing so when Mrs. Mulligan bustled in.

"Are you going to keep these children here forever?" she demanded jokingly of Mickey. "The gards will be out searching," she said to Jane, taking hold of her by one arm and me by the other.

"But you two must be starving!"

We shook our heads politely and mumbled that we weren't, but the very thought of food heightened our longing.

The Old Man rose and offered to see us home, but Mickey objected, pulling on his boots.

"The fresh air will do me good," he said.

Mrs. Mulligan interrupted.

"None of you are going anywhere until these children have some tea."

She ushered us through the kitchen door and made extra places at the table. Jane and I were nervous as we sat down, never having eaten in someone else's house before. But there was neither fuss nor bother, the meal was just a simple ordinary meal. But to us, accustomed to wartime measures in the city, the huge piles of homemade bread and salted country butter and the meat with a flavour all its own—and the apple pie with cinnamon made a banquet by itself.

We ate and ate until we nearly burst. There was little talk during the meal, because Mrs. Mulligan was worried about us getting home. After we had eaten all we could and Mickey had readied the pony and trap, she hurried us out.

"Take that home to your mother," she said, handing Jane a burlap bag filled with berries. We both thanked her and left.

Waiting in the trap were the Old Man and Meggie. Jane and I sat where Mickey directed and he drove off briskly along the road. Evening had come to the country, the air filled with the scent of hay and of turf smoke from the nearby farms. Finally we came to the very last hill and reached the bend in the road, where years ago the Ghost Hound of Lady Bell had appeared for the very first time. Pretending to be frightened, Mickey whipped up the horse and sped away.

And so we reached the city. The church bells were silent. The shadows long vanished and night already fallen. Scattered lights throughout the streets were beginning to come on. But a deeper shadow than night had fallen on our house, as we were soon to learn, for that evening, and for the very first time, my mother had come home with a step a mite unsteady.

14

Jane, her hand through the letterbox, found the key, pulled it out on its string and unlocked the door. She went inside, leaving me to follow. I pulled the key back inside and eased the door shut, not wanting to alert everyone to our late arrival. Before me the hall was in darkness and I could have told then, even before I heard Sheilagh's voice beckoning us into a bedroom beyond, that something terrible had happened. The whole neighbourhood, I gathered from her whispers, was privy to some awful secret about our family.

K eep your voices down," she warned, her face as grim as a mortician's. She peered about the shadows making sure the younger ones were asleep and not just lying in the dark listening. In the big brass bed by the window Peg was lying, her knees drawn up beneath her chin. Protruding from her ear was a wad of cotton wool, Mother's attempt of the day before to remove the abscess inside. Never would Peg's hearing be the same again. I could still hear her scream as the hot oil landed on her aching ear. Yet according to her testimony, the pain had vanished. In the little bed opposite, his legs bare above the covers, was my brother Jack, tossing and turning in one of his perpetual nightmares. And close by in his cot was little Jim.

Tom, the eldest of those three boys, was at that time in another room.

The story Sheilagh told us was disheartening. It had happened earlier, when she was coming home alone up James Street. The evening had grown dark, the streets still shiny from the heavy rain and a stiff wind blowing. A little distance ahead she noticed a figure moving slowly along the path, the shoulders hunched against the wind. It was Mother, and Sheilagh hurried to catch up with her. They both wanted to pay their last respects to poor Danny Dunlop, whose body had been brought to the church that day. Mother, Sheliagh learned, had been to the store to pick up the meat for the Sunday dinner. She had no drink in her. She thrust the paper bundle she was carrying into Sheilagh's hand, the juices soaking through the print like warm milk.

It was coming out of the church that it had happened. They had closed the door behind them and started toward the gate, the wind tugging at the bottom of their coats. Just as they were passing through the gate, the burly shape of Father Chapman in his usual hurry to go nowhere collided with them both. Sheilagh escaped undamaged but the impact sent my mother staggering. It was all she could do to keep her balance. The priest, unperturbed, grappled with his hat, which toppled from his head and whirled off along the path. Sheilagh raced after it. My mother, feeling foolish, stood beside the priest and waited. He did not speak, not even to apologise, or to ask how she was feeling.

On her return with the hat, Sheilagh, aware of Mother leaning heavily on one foot, asked if she was all right. The priest answered for her, saying that there was nothing the matter with Mother that a drop less of the other would not cure. His sardonic voice carried clear across the street. It was like a slap to my mother's face, Sheilagh said, as much as accusing her of drunkenness and she that evening as sober as a judge. She couldn't believe the nerve of him. But that wasn't all, she told us, for this was followed with a lecture, no less, on the disgrace and indecency he encountered on his weekly pilgrimage through the town.

"Drunken men and begging women," he thundered, for all to hear.

And sure enough, just as Sheilagh had feared, across the road was Lyla Fogarty stopped dead in her tracks with curiosity.

"Oh! my God, we're finished so," Jane lamented, for Lyla, we knew, was a terrible gossip.

"But that's not all," Sheilagh whispered, and continued. There had followed an ominous silence, she said, and she thought for sure that Mother was going to lose her temper. The hurt and humiliation on her face filled Sheilagh with rage. She glared at the priest in his fine cut clothes and arrogant air. What did he know about anything with his foreign ways and education? He had begun to speak again, his voice still critical, when, as though on queue from heaven the door to the rectory opened and there in the floodlit hall they beheld the welcome frame of Father Joyce. It was the chance they had been hoping for, and they both made off along the path.

They had not gone far, however, when they heard behind them the rising voice of Lyla Fogarty, hurrying like a demon to catch up.

"Wouldn't you know it?" Mother growled, and Sheilagh wondered furiously why it was that Lyla always happened to be around when she was not wanted.

There was nothing for it now but to suffer her intrusion. How much she had heard they could only guess, but it mattered little in any case for whatever she had missed she would surely invent. Panting and puffing she arrived at my mother's side, her face red from hurrying. Her eyes, green in colour, peered out from under umbrella lids. Her lips, thin and lost beneath a parrot nose, were drawn back in greeting. The rest of her wiry body was hidden behind a bearskin coat which Lyla swore was genuine mink and wore the whole year round. With sympathetic hands she reached for Mother's arm.

"Isn't that a nice how-do-ya-do when a priest can talk like that to a parishioner?"

"Oh! you heard then?" Mother answered.

"What gives him the right is what I'd like to know, a skit of a man like that. It's a pity he doesn't find something better to do with his time."

"I don't know I'm sure," Mother sighed, smiling wanly at Sheilagh.

"He did the same the other day to my poor Paddy, and he without a drop in him at the time."

"Oh, don't tell me!" Mother gasped, putting as much sympathy on her face as she was able. For God forbid that anybody should say a word against Lyla's Paddy.

But Paddy without one drop in him? That would be a thing worth witnessing.

Mother managed to conceal her laughter, wishing at the same time she had not run into Lyla. It wasn't that she didn't like her or anything like that. In fact Mother was one of the few people willing to tolerate Lyla's nature, for she had a terrible bent for gossip and a habit of staring after people that continually got her and whoever happened to be with her at the time into all kinds of trouble.

The daughter of a journalist once removed, she had inherited her father's knack for sniffing things out and had a taste for cream sherry that only my mother knew about. Paddy, we all knew, was her baby brother and lived with Lyla in their little house down Chapel Lane. Lyla didn't hold with marriage, or so she said, and never lost an opportunity to voice her opinion on the sordid struggle of the matrimonial state. Paddy, she made sure, was of a like mind. Yet she was not a bad sort, my mother said, if only she would show a little sense. We children were of a different mind, however, and would band together on the Fair Green wall waiting for Lyla to appear around the corner. At first glimpse of her hairy coat we would begin:

Down in the meadows, imagine if you can,
Lyla is awaiting with her frying pan,
Along comes Paddy with a girl on his arm,
Her young heart a-melting with his manly charm,
In behind the bushes old Lyla has sped,
And oops! poor Paddy has a bump on his head.

It used to drive Lyla crazy and she would chase us clear across the Green shouting threats of murder, but never catching one of us.

Her lips moved closer to Mother's ear.

"This town has gone to the dogs altogether, for wait until I tell ya what I heard about himself." She manoeuvred my mother out of hearing range of Sheilagh's ears.

Mother's exclamation carried back to her. "Oh! no, don't tell me...tennis shorts and what! Is he a priest at all I wonder?"

From Lyla. "I'm telling ya now, by God, I'm thinking seriously of complaining to the bishop."

To us this was hilarious. The idea of Lyla, unable to express herself with any degree of clarity, marching up to the bishop's door, her face prim and proper, was just too much.

I mimicked her. "Axcuse me yur holiness. Ya probly don't amember me, but I'm from a dacent fambly."

Jane laughed at my comic routine. Sheilagh, however, was not amused and had to be coaxed into continuing. She had dropped behind, she told us, but she could hear the voices ahead and see my mother nodding at everything being said.

They reached the corner of Black Mill Street where Mother stopped and looked around to see if Sheilagh was following. The wind was blowing fierce around the bend, she said, as the two women, hunched together, set off across the road to Shaun Byrne's pub where the light and sounds of laughter from the bar were reaching out to them.

"Come on," encouraged Lyla, laughing and looking fixedly at the oversized poster of draught beer advertised in the window. Mother had not wanted to go in, but caved in to Lyla's prompting.

"Ah! well, I suppose one drink won't do me any harm." She moved toward the hall and then turned around to Sheilagh.

"Will you not come in and have a lemonade with us?"

Sheilagh thanked her and shook her head.

"I'll wait here for you," she said, avoiding the argument of one drink leading to another.

"Right so," my mother called. "I'll not be long," and off she went behind the swinging door.

Reluctantly Sheilagh took her place outside the door, hoping that no one else had seen Mother enter. It was bad enough for men to be seen going inside a public house, but worse still for women. A man could drink whenever or wherever he pleased, and providing he did it liberally it would not reflect against him. A woman, on the other hand, could be known to drink, but God forbid she should ever be caught doing it, especially in a public place. If it happened once or only on rare occasions it might be forgiven, but if it happened frequently the whole family was shamed.

Where one drank was another consideration. Places like the Metropole and Imperial Hotel where the priests and Protestants frequented were a cut above the pubs, and anyone affluent enough to go in there was usually ignored.

Buttoning her coat up around her ears, Sheilagh waited. She could see the silhouette of Mother's head and shoulders behind the frosted glass of the snug marked PRIVATE.

Several times her hand went to the brass door handle, but each time she drew it back again, afraid of provoking an argument. Worried that Father might come around the corner any minute and find her there, she finally went home.

As it turned out, Father had been home all evening reading by the fire. An anxious glance from time to time in the direction of the door told Sheilagh he was watching out for Mother. After depositing the meat quietly in the scullery, she squatted down beside him at the fire and waited for her footsteps on the path. Sometime later she arrived, her face red and rosy, her hat not altogether straight upon her head, and her coat open at the collar.

She had probably been happy enough when she left the pub, but walking home alone, battling the wind and brooding in the back of her mind about the priest, she had become dour. She knew she had stayed too long in the pub and cursed Sheilagh for going home without her. When my father opened the door as he sometimes did, she immediately became cantankerous.

"Waiting for me are you?" The words were flat and accusing as she pushed past him through the hall into the kitchen where she saw Sheilagh snug beside the fire. A rage built up inside of her. As was her habit when she had drink in her, she looked around the room for a reason to complain. She found it in the baking pot still hanging on the hook.

"That bread not done yet?" she asked angrily, going to the pot without taking off her coat and lifting up the lid to inspect the crust.

"Indeed if it isn't, it should be," my father remarked, following her to the chimney. Sometime before he had cleared the smouldering embers from the lid and raised the pot to the finishing peg. But that did not satisfy my mother. Dropping the lid back angrily she began to remove the pot from its iron peg. My father moved to help her. The smell of stout was strong upon her breath and Sheilagh saw his bitter smile.

"Why is it," Mother demanded, "that nothing I ask to be done in this house ever gets done? And why isn't the meat ready for tomorrow's dinner?"

The complaints went on and on as did the banging and slamming of things about the house, with Sheilagh being ordered from the fire to do her bidding. Father tried to intervene and a terrible row had started, ending with Sheilagh sobbing and Mother marching in fury to her room, slamming the door against them.

"I wouldn't mind," Sheilagh finished, "but Dad probably thought she had been visiting friends, when all the time she was in a pub."

All the lights in the house had been turned down then, and Father retired to his bedroom.

WHEN I WOKE THE NEXT morning it was drizzling rain, and I heard my mother calling us to rise for Mass. The family gathered at the table, Sunday being the only day we sat down together as a family. All were present except Father. Somebody asked if he was up, and Mother grunted, obviously still in a dour mood. He usually appeared as the tea was being poured, but this morning there was no sign of him.

"A grand day for walking," Uncle Jim said, coming through the door, his cheeks rosier than apples. Mother glowered at his muddy boots, and only then it dawned on him what he had done. He threw his hands up in despair.

"Oh! sit down and eat for heaven's sake, before everything gets cold," Mother said.

If he had been aware of the scene of the night before he did not show it. It was his habit after a night of arguments to make himself scarce, rising even earlier than usual to be out of the house before anyone else got up. For days after, however, he would look uneasy. He was seldom home and never interfered in the family feuds. His business he kept strictly to himself, rising in the early morning and retiring at an early hour. He neither drank nor smoked cigarettes, for he thought them vile. His pipe was all the consolation he desired. And he loved to walk.

Every day, except Saturday, he went to early Mass. On Sunday he managed to get the late one as well. Then out to the country roads with him to walk for miles and miles, and on the way back to meet his friends by the old stone bridge and watch for trout in the river. In winter he sat at home by the fire, but only on the coldest days, muttering to himself and—when he thought nobody was watching—spitting at the fire. This habit used to irritate my mother, to say nothing of ourselves, because the spittle often missed the embers and sizzled down the outside of the polished grate.

Ah! but he was a rare one, my Uncle Jim, tall and straight as a ramrod. A Titan you might say, chiselled by Michelangelo. Not the Irish stereotype at all. His eyes, blue and brilliant, were lodged in hollow sockets and set wide apart. His nose, long and slender, was always red. His hair and his moustache were short, cut in the fashion of the day and slicked down with a little oil for tidiness. No one I knew had a mind more quick, more clear or more precise. He loved to be asked questions and could remember almost everything. Yet so unyielding he could be at times in matters he knew nothing of, always trying to make us see things as he thought we should.

If my father's pride was plentiful, Uncle Jim's was excessive, and this kept him from associating with people in the street. Very little was known to us about his past, except that he had lived alone for years in his mother's house and had never married. He hated women as he hated wasps. Any man who got himself married was automatically stupid to his mind, and for a while he despised my father for marrying my mother.

It must have been a great sacrifice he made when he came to live with us, giving up his home and his belongings, not to mention his freedom, and at a time when the family fortune, so to speak, was in full decline, and he trying desperately to hang on to his image. They must have thought it a good idea at the time, pooling their resources in an effort to keep Father's head above water. It might have worked, too, had it not been for Mother. By the time he found out about her drinking it was too late. His days of influence had gone forever and he reduced to a nobody.

Nevertheless he managed to retain an air of grand respectability. Never stooped to labour. Lived as much as possible on what little money he had yet accepting suitable employment whenever it was offered. Such a meticulous man he was about his dress, polishing and repolishing his boots until you could see your face in them.

"You are what you wear," he always said, and would never go out without something on his head.

Did everyone have uncles just like him? I wondered, bumping into him one Sunday while out walking, himself and Galtee Murphy. The sun was streaming from the heavens and the two of them buttoned to the eyebrows, too proper to undo their collars. Had he but known what was in store for him, that he would end his days in Thomastown in that dreaded home for the aged and the derelict. All his life he had been in fear of that happening, so great was the stigma attached to it, and Mother had promised she would never let it happen. Yet when the time came and his health gone, that was where she sent him. For that I would never forgive her. In spite of his pretensions and stuffy ways, he was a dear man and would never willingly hurt another. Yet, I remember once asking his opinion of the Old Man, for I was curious to know what he thought of him. I regretted having done so by the way he glared at me, coughing and spluttering and making a fuss, threatening to tell my father if he ever saw me with his likes. Needless to say, I never asked him again.

This morning he was extra quiet, stabbing at his sausage with his fork and sopping up the gravy with a piece of bread. When he finished he got up and went to smoke beside the window. That ritual completed, he left the house and we knew we would not see him until the sun went down.

"I see no reason for you lot to go on sitting there," my mother said to Jane and me, interrupting my thoughts. She was extra sour now because my father had not appeared. Even the younger ones felt it, and moved about the kitchen in silence before going out to play.

"You two get a move on," she said to us when we had finished washing up. I sensed that she wanted us out of the house and got ready quickly. As I waited in the kitchen for Jane, hoping she would not take all day looking in the mirror, I was conscious that behind his closed bedroom door my father was lying in misery. I was torn between my desire to call out to him and my reluctance to incite my mother. Before I could make up my mind, Jane appeared and we left the house.

15

The summer holidays were almost over, and a few of us had planned an outing for the last weekend. We had been saving our pennies, or at least our ha'pennies—pennies being hard to come by in those days—hoping to collect enough for a real picnic. We had agreed to meet by the Water Barrack a certain Sunday morning after early mass. Madge, myself and Jane were the first to arrive. As we reached the bridge, we paused to take a summary of the weather.

I t was a clear calm day and getting warmer. Overhead the sky was as blue as ice, streaked only here and there with feathery mare's tails, a sign, Jane said, that the good weather would keep up for the remainder of the day. Jane, the eldest of the female contingent, had appointed herself leader of the expedition and clearly looked forward to being in charge. Nothing in the blue sky gave any hint of the calamities to come.

We sat on the old bridge waiting for the others to arrive and looking down into the clear flowing water. Today the river was as clear as glass. The bridge itself, its flags worn to a glossy sheen, had long been a gathering place for old men tired of living in the present and clinging like vines to the glories of the past. Here from sun-up to sundown they held converse with each other, enriching the treasure houses of their minds with the mythical stories of Ireland. But this Sunday morning the bridge was ours.

After we had been sitting for some time we saw Nuala Brannigan running toward us down the hill, her grey skirt flapping out behind. She began to wave when she caught sight of us and we could hear her shouting "Hey lads! Hey lads!" as she neared the bottom. The expression on her freckled face told me we were about to be subjected to another episode of *A Day in the Life of Nuala*, dictated of course by her own flights of fancy. I saw that she was wearing her white straw hat with the blue satin ribbon. Her mousy hair, usually hanging like old straw around her head, was arranged in neat plump curls. Still wearing her made-to-measure smile she clambered up beside us on the bridge, her rabbit teeth protruding.

"I see you decided to come," she said to Madge and me, as though there had ever been any doubt about it. Her eyes registered disappointment. Madge and I exchanged looks but said nothing. Nuala's delusions of grandeur did terrible things to my nerves as did her belief that she was entitled to an elevated position in our group by virtue of her premature maturity, her budding sexuality. From the moment of this transition she had become unbearable, treating Madge and myself like her inferiors. Her only duty on earth now, she believed, was the perpetual exhibition of her body; life for her had but one focus—boys.

Then of course there was the little matter of her father. "A tonsorial specialist," she would always reply to the inevitable question from new children to the neighbourhood, delighting in the blank reaction on their faces as she had done with us the first time we met. For weeks she had enjoyed special status in our group while we laboured under the mistaken impression that we were fraternising with the daughter of a prominent physician. A soldier was what her father really was, before becoming a barber.

I sat on the bridge watching the water leap against the arch and fall back again into the crevices, making a lapping sound just barely audible above Nuala's voice. "If you ask my advice," she was saying to Jane, and I tried to visualise a situation in which any of us might need her advice. When the sky rained turnips maybe!

We waited for another fifteen minutes for Maizie Dooley to arrive, and when she didn't we left. At the corner of Deanery Hill we saw Paddy Farrell, who never went anywhere without our Jane, waiting by the lamppost, and we knew without being told that Billy Bood McGuire, who never went anywhere without Paddy, was there as well. Billy was leaning on the other side of the post, his head tilted toward the sky, a Goldflake hanging from his lips. As always he was dressed in his George Raft coat and white silk scarf, the tassels trailing below the hem. His thick black hair was brilliantined and plastered to his head.

Like Jane, Billy's current ambition was to be a movie star, and he honestly believed that if he cruised about the town with an air of mild indifference and an avant-garde expression he would eventually be discovered and whisked off to Hollywood to become a great star like Robert Mitchum or Dennis Day. The fact that he had a closer resemblance to Donald Duck didn't seem to matter.

In his efforts to rid himself of his Irish accent, Billy had acquired a sort of honky-tonk that no one but himself could understand. How well the two were suited, Billy with his honky-tonk and Paddy with his nasal twang, and a manner of speech more aptly suitable to the wholesale slaughter of the English language.

Unlike Billy Bood, however, Paddy had no delusions. To hear him speak, he already had the world by its proverbial tail and would with the help of nobody make his mark upon it. For the stories had not been invented nor the books written that could supply Paddy with more knowledge than he already had. Unable to bore a hole through a cardboard box or use a phrase correctly, Paddy would set about teaching a carpenter his trade or a lettered man his alphabet. Yet he was a likeable well-trusted lad, and all of us enjoyed his company.

"It's about time," he said, addressing Jane. "What kept yee?"

"We came as soon as we could, Paddy," I replied, seizing the moment to let him know that Jane was in charge.

Fifteen minutes later we were still standing there with Paddy in the throes of a figayre and threatening to go home. In the end it was Billy Bood who settled it, pleading that Paddy, being the eldest, be given the responsibility. Reluctantly we yielded.

Our plan was to stroll along the meadows to the weir and stop to picnic when we got there. Afterwards, anyone who wished could continue on to Talbot's Inch, the next village. We started up the hill in an eager mood. Even an encounter with the Headless Coachman, a ghost believed to inhabit the hill, could not have dispelled our good humour. Above us the Cathedral of St. Canice shone brightly in the sun, and close by, the ancient tower of O'Connell, built in the ninth century as a lookout against invaders, was ever watchful of its city.

We pushed open the heavy iron gates leading to the church grounds and crossing the gravel path came out in a lane beyond. Skipping and laughing along the lane we reached Vicar Street where we stopped to pick up fruit at Sweeneys', and then on to Mullhalls' for lemonade and biscuits. We stopped outside the wide glass window and looked in.

There was Peggy's Leg and scented sweets, liquorice watches with little red hands and real numbers, Rainbow and Mickey Mouse toffee, and Moneyballs as big as a boxer's fist. And way at the back out of the sun's glare were soft cream pies with chocolate topping. Luck was with us when we went inside, for there behind the counter was Mrs. Mulhall with her pink puckered face and silver hair. Unlike some merchants in our town who hated parting with their sweets, dropping them in one by one and never ever letting the scales hit the bottom, she filled our bags to the very brim. We each told her what we wanted and she smiled broadly, selecting all with a liberal hand.

"Mind yourselves now and don't get into trouble," she called after us as we departed.

The boys agreed to carry the heavy bags, and after opening up each one and taking out a biscuit we closed them up again and continued on our way. Leaving the street behind at last we made our way along the bosheen to the Meadows. It would be a six-mile walk to the weir, which was located at the last of a long string of fields stretching out along the banks of the River Nore. The stretch of grassy land between the first and last field we called the Meadows.

As Kilkenny is an inland town with no beach of its own, the Meadows became our Riviera in the summer. All through the warm sunny months people would flock there to bathe in the shallow waters or relax along the edges of the river. Each field along the river gave access to the next by means of a wooden stile. I had been to the Meadows many times but never past the third stile. Only the older, more courageous, ever ventured past the BEWARE OF BULL sign in Brannigan's field in their eagerness to reach the weir. Today would be a first for Madge and myself, though Jane and the others had been there before. A spirit of adventure was coursing through our veins as Paddy began to chant:

> *Miser Matty Gombeen*
> *Went down the Meadow's bosheen,*
> *Mickey Meaney came out*
> *And gave him a clout,*
> *Miser Matty Gombeen.*

We all joined in and had begun to quicken our pace along the narrow high-hedged lane when suddenly a large rock whizzed past our heads, crashing to the ground with a loud thud. Everybody ducked low against the wall. Somewhere ahead an assassin lay in waiting. We all looked at Paddy. The smile had faded from his face, replaced by a grim expression. With fingers pressed against his lips he beckoned us to follow, and we crept silently along the bottom of the wall to a low spot farther down from where he thought the missile had been launched. Here he stopped suddenly, reached behind the wall and dragged out a struggling red-faced boy. Holding him firmly by the ear he leaned over and dragged out a second, smaller boy, who was squirming and kicking at everything in sight.

"Don't hold him by the ear," I called to Paddy, remembering the pain inflicted on ourselves by the well-meaning but sadistic Canon Cavanagh whenever it was our misfortune to bump into him on the street or in the playground at school. To my relief Paddy released his hold on the boy's ear but kept a firm grip on his shoulder. The smaller one picked himself up from the ground, rubbing his knee and glaring at us as though we were the enemy, and he but an innocent bystander.

"Didn't yur fathur ever tell ya not to pelt stones?" Paddy asked. The little one shrugged.

"We don't got no fathur, and don't take no orders from no one. Do we, Slugger?"

His chest swelled as he looked with reverence at his brother. The older one said nothing, just stood gazing at the wall, his hands hidden in his pockets.

"Gimmie back my catapult or I'll tell the gards," said the younger one, and Paddy laughed.

"The gards! Well, that's a good wan for ya. An what d'ya think they'll do ta you?"

The boy didn't answer and Paddy, softening, handed him his sling, advising him to use it carefully in future. He turned away then and we were about to follow, when Nuala, bubbling with importance, stepped in front.

"You two should be ashamed," she said, "just look at the dirt of you. Go home this minute and change those dirty jumpers."

Clutching each one by the shoulder she turned them to face the street.

"Don't let me catch you in this lane again," she added, giving them both a shove. It would never occur to her, of course, that the boys might not have had any jumpers to put on. Her arrogance was lost on nobody and her emphasis on "this lane" as though it were her own private property surprised only the little boys. She was about to walk away when the older boy, having neither said nor done anything up to now, swung around suddenly and brought his heavy boot down solidly on her foot. If he had been wearing sandals it would not have been so bad, but his boots had metal studs around the heels and toes.

"Oow! Oow! Oow!" Nuala cried, hopping about on her good foot and scared to take a look at the injured one. The two boys made off along the lane like bullets from a gun, and I was relieved as I watched them disappear around the bend.

"They're only children after all," I reminded Nuala, and Madge agreed, saying that Nuala need not have been so bossy. That made Nuala angrier, and she bunched herself into a tight ball, shrieking that it was easy enough for us to say because we hadn't been the ones he'd kicked.

"So don't go making up excuses for them," she cried, "they're nothing but a pair of hooligans."

I caught the look in Jane's eye, for only a few days earlier we had been called the same for our part in the rifling of Mol Houghney's raspberries. We walked along in silence, the excitement gone forever. But forever, I am happy to say, was only a matter of minutes in our world, and soon our lively mood returned. Within minutes we were out of the lane and racing along the path to the river.

We reached the first stile and climbed up on the wooden plank. Behind us we could see the river spread out along the fields before passing under the Great Bridge on its way to Fennessy's Mill, and we could follow its course with our eyes all the way down the Quay to John's Bridge. We heard someone shouting from the bridge, saw arms waving frantically, and decided it was Maizie Dooley. Paddy climbed up on the highest point of the fence and waved for her to follow.

Ahead in the distance lay the Woollen Mills, where Madge's mother worked, its chimney stack just visible above the trees. On any day of the week but Sunday, black smoke from the mill could be seen rising into the sky and its waste spewing into the river. Today there was no smoke, only the metal rim of the chimney glinting in the sun. Nothing but fields and bushes lay on our left, but far away in the distance, over the brow of the hill and hidden by the tall trees and shrubbery, we could hear the dull throb of Brannigan's tractor.

We stood for a short while looking along the riverbank toward the weir. We had lots of time ahead of us and nobody to interfere.

16

The Nore was a temperamental sort of river, covering several counties on its journey to the sea. Every few years it would overflow its banks, washing away all in its path. The old suspension bridge was still there, however, a little more rickety than the last time I had seen it. The boys loved to play on this bridge. It had been built originally for easy access to the Meadows by the residents of Green's Hill, a small community high above the river.

The bridge spanned the Nore at a height of only a few yards and was supported by huge wooden posts and steel cable ropes. The structure itself was made of wood planks about six inches wide with large gaps in between.

It used to terrify me to walk on the planks, but today I managed to make it to the middle and join the others looking down into the water. No sooner had my fear subsided, however, than the boys commenced to set the bridge swaying, jumping up and down like monkeys and swinging from the railing. In minutes the whole bridge was heaving, causing the rest of us to scream. We were saved by the sounds of shouting.

"Hey look! Here comes Milo and Peggy Cullen." Everybody stopped to watch the two figures hurrying toward us along the bank.

A few minutes later they were through the stile and we all ran to meet them. Milo, who everybody liked, was one year younger than Paddy Farrell, but a serious illness had impaired his health and at times he looked much older. Only a few of us knew the truth of his condition. Tall and well built with a head full of curls, his appearance gave no indication of his illness. Yet, as it turned out, he had but a few years left to live.

Michael Machan was what he had been christened, but everybody called him Milo Mac. The son of a local businessman, he had come to his parents late in life and spent some years at the local college. But in his final year of study he had been stricken with paralysis. After months of agonising uncertainty he had been released from the County Hospital with his heart in a critical condition. He had accepted his fate with a calm reserve, and even when his mother died some months after that he never once complained.

His companion, Peggy, was a younger girl of fair complexion. Of her background I knew little, except that she lived on the Kenny's Well Road and was the youngest in a family of boys. She had a certain something that attracted people to her. Her blond straight hair covered her head like an old mat, and her blue eyes had a singular expression. When she became excited they would light up like lanterns. Nobody could heave a hurl like Peggy, and she could split the core of any competitor's conker with her black-gnarled champion with a single blow. Only the toughest boys would challenge her.

The river looked seductively cool on this hot humid day. At Peggy's urging we kicked off our shoes and socks and darted to the water, leaving our food upon the bank and the drink to cool in the shallows. Billy watched us from the bank, refusing to come in.

"Ah! go on wi'cha," teased Peggy. "'Tis swimming in your own pool you'll be one of these fine days."

This thought made Billy happy, but removing his heavy coat he spread it on the grass and lay on it. No amount of coaxing could get him to remove his shoes and join us in the river. Nuala said it was because he had holes in his socks and didn't want us to see them.

"Isn't that so, Billy?" she teased, but Billy didn't answer, and we could see by his expression that he had left us and gone to Hollywood. We left him with his fantasies and played for some time in the shallows. Then we scrambled out onto the warm grass and spread our feet in the sun.

Nuala examined her foot, still tender from being stomped on earlier, and exclaimed, "That brazen little brat!" To everyone's surprise it had turned a nasty black and blue.

Behind us in the field a yellow mist of cowslips swayed among the bracken, its fragrance floating down to us on the breeze. Farther back a small herd of cows had broken through the hedge and was grazing its way lazily toward the river.

"Look over there," Madge said, pointing way out behind the sun. Shading our eyes we all looked at a tiny black speck circling high above.

"It's a kestrel," Milo said, and we followed its course as it circled wider and wider over the trees. Then, hanging in mid-air for a second, it dropped like a stone, soaring low over the nearby fields and filling the air with its shrill cries. We watched as it swooped a second time, tumbling down from the sky, its outstretched talons ready to seize its unwary prey.

"Thurs a fella over in John's Well who can tell ya anything ya want ta know about hawks," said Paddy. And despite our protests he proceeded to instruct us on the characteristics of our feathered friend. His monologue was brought to a sudden halt by an ominous bellow. I knew without looking it was Brannigan's bull, and I felt the strength go out of me.

"Run for it lads," said Milo Mac, who started off across the field before we had time to collect our wits. We all leaped up, only to be assured by Paddy that there was no need to panic. A bull, he said, would never bother you when he was with the cows. And besides, you had to be wearing red for him to notice. None of us were wearing red, but Milo, I noticed, was halfway to the stile and still running. Black fear went coursing through my veins as I saw the bull move away from the cows. His head was lowered and he was digging up the earth with a front hoof.

"Don't listen to Paddy!" I yelled in terror.

Everybody reacted to the panic in my voice and the sudden realisation that the mythical beast of Paddy's mind was in reality twenty tons of snorting flesh, already astir in a hurried trot—and moving steadily in our direction. With minds paralysed and muscles moving by their own accord, we pulled on our socks and shoes. I looked around for Jane, whose fear of these animals was greater than my own, and to my relief she was already running. In a wild shuffle of feet everyone took off after her.

Nuala Brannigan began to cry, big wet tears spilling down her cheeks. "I can't run," she sobbed, holding on to me and hobbling on her swollen foot.

I yelled to her to remove her shoe, holding out my arm to steady her. Then we ran like the wind to keep up with the others. Only a few yards from the stile somebody raced past and I saw that it was Paddy, the ground moving beneath his feet. I saw his legs leap almost to the clouds before he disappeared behind the hedge to safety. I raced on, anger mingling with the fear. Somewhere I heard a dog barking and a man's voice shouting.

Thundering hooves told me the bull was close. Only a few more feet and we would be safe.

I was almost crying with relief when I heard Nuala scream as she tripped on the long grass and tumbled to the ground. I glanced back. She was struggling to her feet, and when she lifted her head I saw blood running down her face. She began to scream again in a voice that didn't sound like her at all. It terrified me, and I knew she couldn't make it, and neither could I go back for her.

God! I was so afraid.

As I scrambled through the narrow opening in the stile I heard low muffled sounds from behind. Peering through the hedge I saw Nuala crouching in the grass, her head buried in her knees, and above her the hulking figure of the bull. His great head was only inches from her back and swinging slowly from side to side. Beyond Nuala and the bull but too far away to help, a man was racing through the field, shouting excitedly and brandishing a pitchfork in his outstretched arm.

It was then I saw the terrier, leaping and bounding through the tall grass. With ears flattened against his head and jaws bared, he sank his teeth into the soft flesh around the bull's nose. Its great head reared, knocking the dog to the ground, but in a moment he was up again, growling angrily. The bull charged at him in fury, but the dog was too quick this time, throwing his body to one side as the massive hulk brushed past.

Out of the corner of my eye I saw Nuala creeping through the grass toward the stile, and I reached out and helped her over. She crawled to the nearest tree and heaved herself against it, her foot stretched out in front of her.

"Oh God! Oh God!" she kept repeating, the tears spilling down her face.

"It's all your fault, Paddy Farrell," I cried, beside myself with anger. Paddy glared.

"Now lookit here Miss Bossy Boots," he began, and broke off as the man with the pitchfork appeared at the stile. He looked around at each of us, then walked over to Nuala.

"Is it trying to kill yourself you were?" he asked, and stroked her face with the back of his hand. "You had a narrow escape, little girl, no doubt of that."

Nuala nodded and stopped crying. Then the stranger asked about her injured foot, bending down to look at it, and the presence of a sympathetic listener brought a fresh supply of tears. He dried them with his handkerchief, wiped the blood from around her mouth, and bound her foot tightly with a piece of rag.

He stood up then and looked at the boys who had banded together a little way off. How did it happen? he wanted to know. Had they not seen the bull? His question was met with silence as Billy Bood, wrapped in an air of noble gravity, pretended not to hear. Milo, who as we all knew could extricate himself—and everyone else for that matter—from any situation, cocked his head to one side and waited to hear what Paddy had to say. What plausible explanation might he dredge from the depths of his microscopic mind? To our surprise he had nothing to say.

Nuala, her confidence restored by the ecstasy of all this attention, sobbed out the story which included a detailed description of the boy responsible for her injury. The man listened patiently, nodding. Bulls, he told us, were dangerous and could not be depended upon even by their own. Why only recently a man in Freshford had been gored to death!

By now Paddy had regained his usual know-it-all composure and was eager to re-establish himself as leader.

"Thur valuable animals all the same," he offered, and the man agreed.

"They are that," Nuala's rescuer said, and paid for his agreement with a lecture from Paddy on the merits of livestock breeding, followed by an exhaustive analysis of the virtues of bully beef, no doubt gleaned from the back of a Bovril bottle. One couldn't help, all the same, but admire his nerve.

Finally, our kind rescuer headed back to his farm.

"What shall we do now?" someone asked, and everyone looked at Nuala, who wiped her eyes with the back of her hand

and gave a shrug. She could still walk, she told us sulkily, but she was not going any farther than the weir.

"A fine picnic this turned out to be," moaned Paddy. He didn't see any sense in continuing, he said, seeing as the day was spoiled already.

"Oh, shut up, Paddy!" Jane snapped. "Go home then if you want to, but we're going on and we'll drink your share of the lemonade."

The lemonade! We had forgotten all about it, still cooling in the river. We all rushed over to the stile and peered into the field. It was empty, except for some boys crossing the bridge to Green's Hill. The cows were nowhere to be seen, but from way back beyond the trees we could still hear the terrier, his excited bark muffled by the sound of the tractor. The bottles stood where we had left them, their metal caps glittering in the sun.

"I'll get them," Peggy offered, and raced back across the field before anyone could stop her. In a few minutes she was back, the bottles bumping noisily against her side.

We gathered up our belongings and started for the weir. When finally we reached the last field, passing the old Mill wheel as silent now as the Sabbath, I could see the wide expanse of water spilling like a glass sheet over the incline.

I knew then that I had done it. I had walked the six miles to the weir.

17

We found a comfortable spot on the bank and arranged ourselves on the grass. Jane handed around our drinks and food, and we each shared our favourite biscuits. I took my Kimberlies and went to sit beside Madge, who had already started eating her favourite Mikados. As usual, the food tasted much better outdoors, and, with the joy of eating and talking, we soon forgot about our misadventure with the bull.

The whole world seemed motionless. Even the water spilling over the weir seemed turned to glass and behind the weir itself the water was as smooth as velvet, flickering like sequins in a mirror. Far off across the fields a bell was ringing, the sound coming to our ears in a clear tone, and then fading again with the shifting breeze.

Billy had drained his bottle of lemonade and began looking around for more, offering to trade his apple for what Milo had left in his bottle. But when he failed to separate anybody from their drink he contented himself with preening, combing his hair with long elegant strokes. We had all been laughing and making jokes, thinking that we were alone in the field, when all at once to our surprise we saw a man crouched near the river only yards from where we were sitting. How long he had been there no one knew, for we had not seen him coming, and we began at once to think of moving. But the man appeared to be absorbed in the river and paying no attention to us. With his knees pulled up close to his chin he stared out over the water.

We thought he hadn't noticed us until he turned his head in our direction and began to speak about the river, saying that when he was a boy you could swim in any part of it. He wouldn't swim in it now though because it was too dangerous, all weeds and currents. The bottom, he told us, was forever changing and it was hard to tell where the danger lay.

"Never go beyond that point in any case."

He pointed with his stick to the sandbar in the middle where the wide waters crowded through a narrow space. Were any of us able to swim? he asked then, and we all said no, except for Peggy Cullen who could swim like a fish. The man talked for a little while and then left. Some minutes later Maizie Dooley arrived, hallooing loudly when she saw us and plonked herself down beside Jane, wanting to know if there was anything to eat.

Maizie was a girl of about Jane's age who lived a street down from Paddy. Her mother was well known to us as a kindly soul who took in orphans from the street and looked after them. A myopic girl with grey-green eyes and auburn hair, she was inclined to be mischievous and strange in her behaviour, finding pleasure always in other people's fear. Insanity in the family is what we were told, but we had only Paddy's word for that.

"Nutty" was how he referred to Maizie and her brother. And who better qualified to make that judgement, himself a pistachio of the highest order?

But there was something queer about Maizie, there was no mistaking that. Besides her annoying habit of following you about and gazing up into your face, she would often lag behind, and like a cat watching an unwary mouse mark with grim intent the rhythm of your moving hand. Then with the speed of a rattlesnake she would snatch your little finger and bend it back as far as all resistance would allow, her eyes lighting up like beacons at your shrieks. I made sure to keep a safe distance from her.

We lazed about the bank doing nothing in particular. Nobody wanted to go beyond the weir. Jane wouldn't go because she had been there before. Peggy did not want to, Madge was afraid, and Nuala couldn't because of her foot. Only the three boys were left, and Milo and Billy had already said no.

That left only Paddy who had not as yet said anything, and whom I had suspected might want to go. I looked at him without asking and he instantly responded.

"Are you axin' me?"

I shrugged but didn't answer.

"So," he said, looking smugly at the others, "when all fruit fails welcome haw."

That did it. The last thing I wanted was to be obliged to Paddy. "Never mind Paddy," I said, "I don't want to go," and meant it.

I don't know who suggested that we cross the river to the sandbar, but somebody did. At first Jane objected, said it was too dangerous, but, after some teasing from the boys, she gave in.

"We'll make a body chain," she exclaimed. "That way there won't be any danger." To my surprise, the others agreed and began immediately to plan their strategy. I couldn't believe what I was hearing, after what that man had told us! I looked at the excited determined faces.

"I'm not going out there," I said. "It's too dangerous."

"No it's not," Jane replied, insisting that the body chain would make a difference and that we wouldn't go past the sandbar, as the man had advised. Body chain or not, I had no desire to go and told her so. Billy Bood said he was staying on land and I decided to stay with him. Then Madge had second thoughts and began to dissuade Nuala. Before I knew it I was the culprit. Why did I always have to spoil things, the others moaned.

"I just don't think we should go out there," I told Jane worriedly.

She knew that I was genuinely scared and tried to convince me not to be.

"Nothing will happen, I promise you," she said. "The water isn't deep, and even if someone did fall, they could get up again."

I didn't want to go, but I could see that Madge was disappointed, and Nuala beginning to change her mind. In the end I agreed. Paddy said he would act as vanguard and Madge as rear, because they were the tallest. Milo would take the centre and the rest of us in between.

"Hold hands tightly now lads," Paddy warned as we started out, our skirts tucked in our bloomers. I was holding tight to Madge's hand on one side and Peggy Cullen's on the other, feeling reasonably secure. As Jane had said, it was not too deep, rising only to the level of our thighs in the deeper part.

How it happened I never did find out, but to this day I suspect foul play, for only minutes after we started out amid shouts and laughter, there was a sudden wrenching of arms and the body chain was broken. Pandemonium set in as everyone began to scream and stumble.

Madge and myself were closest to the bank and managed to remain upright, though I could feel the pull of the current. I clung to Madge's arm like a barnacle as it forced my body sideways.

My feet were sinking as though into sand, and I heard Peggy Cullen yelling from behind. Only seconds earlier I had been holding her hand, and I wondered how she had gotten behind me. Turning my head I saw her splashing violently, her body half submerged. I reached to grab her hand and she reached for mine, but just as I closed my hand on hers she was torn away by the current. Terror gripped me like a vice and I began to scream. Paddy, who had almost reached dry land, heard and leaped in after Peggy, but it was too late. The water had taken her too far ahead. There was nothing we could do but run along the bank to keep up with her as she was swept along.

Every now and then we saw her shoulders rise above the water as though she were making an effort to swim, but then she would sink down again with only her head above water. Her eyes tried to say what her lips could not. At last the water brought her closer to the bank and we saw a chance of saving her. We called out to her, pointing to every overhanging branch, pleading with her to cling to one. Finally she responded and grabbed onto one, struggling to keep her face above water. Then the branch bent beneath the strain and the river tore it from her grasp.

Panicking now, Milo began to race across the field to find help, for he knew that beyond a point just a little farther on the river curved, and we would no longer be able to reach her as the water carried her farther from the shore.

A great hammering thought had occupied my mind and seemed about to swallow me: Peggy was drowning before our eyes. I couldn't believe it, and she such a powerful swimmer.

Suddenly, above the tumult in my head I heard Milo's voice as he raced back to us, and behind him saw the long lanky legs of Johnny Dougherty. Not waiting to remove his shoes or clothing Johnny dashed ahead to an overhanging tree, the last one before the river curved. Hanging from its lowest stoutest branch, the water covering his legs and hips, he waited for sight of Peggy.

A few seconds later her head appeared above the spray. With one arm around the branch Johnny reached out with his other hand, grabbed Peggy's hair and pulled her to safety. The gravity of events was still upon us as we crouched around her on the grass and watched Johnny atttend to her. He set his hands below her shoulder and began hammering on her back, expelling water from her mouth. Then he turned her over, face upward in the sun, and spoke to her. She lay still and silent, her face deathly pale. After a few minutes, though, she opened her eyes and began to cry, her shoulders heaving beneath her sodden dress. It was at that point that Madge and myself did the unforgivable. Peggy had scarcely opened her eyes when we were both beside her asking.

"Did you hear any bells, Peggy, did you?" and we peered into her vacant face.

Johnny raised his arms in anger.

"Bells! Bells! I'll give the pair of you bells," he yelled, and shunted us away.

"Well, I never," said Madge, offended, as we waddled off along the bank. What had we done that was so terrible? All we had wanted was to confirm the fact that drowning people actually did hear bells. Anyone would think we had comitted a crime. And who did Johnny Dougherty think he was? Peggy was a friend of ours and not of his. We consoled ourselves with illusions of an intellectual depth that the others had failed to comprehend.

When we reached the stile to the other field we climbed over it and waited for the others to catch up. Sometime later they arrived. Peggy, her light dress almost dry, was back to normal. Her face, though, still had an ashen look to it and her hair was wet and straggling.

"It was terrible," she told us later. One minute she had been standing upright on the sandy bottom, and the next was sinking under. Her lungs, she said, had been near to bursting, and she thought she had really breathed her last every time her body hit the muddy bottom.

And, no, she had not heard any bells.

Nobody confessed to having broken the chain but we all knew it had been deliberate, and I had my own idea as to the culprit. But nothing more was said about it, so I never knew for sure. We had come back again to the first field of our adventure, and we trudged heavy-hearted back along the lane and through the streets. The Town Hall clock struck seven as we filed past Brannigan's coal yard toward St. Canice's.

Nuala was still limping and Paddy strangely quiet. Milo and Peggy left us at the corner of the street, with Peggy instructing everyone to say nothing to her mother. The rest of us, tired and filled with thoughts of school tomorrow, turned the final corner into Abbey Street and home.

18

School days are the happiest of your life, at least that's what we were told by our parents, but the memories I hold of school, outside of kindergarten days, are mainly unpleasant. Have you ever wondered why it is that the faces of little children before the age of seven are usually happy, while those of older children so often sad? It seems to me that most children are happy, carefree little souls until they have the misfortune to run up against certain teachers, and lose their innocence forever.

I stood alone for the very first time at the bottom of the steps looking up with innocence at the inscription above the door. ABANDON HOPE ALL YE WHO ENTER HERE, it might just as well have read, so great was the fear in some of our hearts.

Our school was much like any other, I suppose, though the nuns and ladies of the sodality would have had you believe otherwise. The Loreto Convent was the only boarding school in the city and as such received the patronage of the privileged class. For what poor man could afford to send his children to a private school? Only the daughters of the prosperous were awarded that distinction.

The rest of us were herded like cattle to the National side, apropos our station. Only the highest windows of the convent could be seen from our schoolyard. The grounds and buildings of the convent itself were surrounded by a high stone wall, and separated from us by means of a narrow lane outside, under which a tunnel had been gouged for access to the nunnery.

The school itself was new and modern for its day, with large sunny rooms strung along a corridor and brought together in the middle by means of an entry hall and a cloakroom equipped with ceramic tiles and bowls. At one end of the corridor was the nuns' private room, the door to which was always locked. Beyond that were the lavatories, usually blocked and so overflowing they were impossible to use. Outdoors on one side of the spacious yard stood a long open shed furnished with a wooden bench that ran the length of its three sides, and beneath which fat salacious spiders lurked in dusty webs. Several tall conifers sheltered the open side from the constant wind and rain.

It was here we huddled in our leisure time, talking over lessons or sipping watery cocoa from tin mugs, always under the watchful eye of the dreaded Bull Neck Berrigan, one of the two lay teachers in our school. She was the most formidable, a woman of enormous size and strength with shoulders broader than a blacksmith and legs as stout as wireless poles. Her face more fearsome than Attila's boasted tusklike teeth, making it impossible for her to pronounce her V's.

We were educated in the manner and custom of our time and class, taught the proprieties and treated to a smattering of the genteel arts, music, poetry and needlework. There was no special method of teaching, just a senseless coercion of mind and body in a repetitious mumbling of words and phrases. The pursuit of knowledge for reasons other than the glorification of the convent was not encouraged. Aspirations beyond the realm of parlour maid, shop assistant or seamstress were considered ludicrous. Nor was discrimination unheard of, for even our school with its deflated status had its own subtle hierarchy

121

of values whereby a girl's clothing might be her badge of class or her social skills a medal of distinction.

The assembly bell began to ring and from every corner of the yard the girls came running to take their places in the line at the bottom of the steps. For a while the air was filled with their murmuring. Then the silence came, that all-consuming silence as the school door was flung open and Mother Superior appeared. The shock of her appearance ran through the lines like an electric current, for seldom did the mother superior grace our assembly with her presence. Forever in a delicate state of health, it seemed, it was important that her person not be contaminated too often by contact with our germ-ridden bodies.

She stood on the top step looking down, her face soft but not smiling, her head high. Tall dark and imperious she descended the steps, nodding at our upturned faces. A bundle of heavy keys dangled from an iron ring about her waist and clanked against her wooden beads. She was happy to see our smiling faces, she said, and told us the reason for her presence. The annual festival of Gregorian chant was to be held that year, and she hoped we could be counted on to bring home the Shield. The Bull Neck came and stood beside her, and they began to chat.

Something brought my eyes to Jane. She was looking over at me, her face pale and her eyes red from crying. Mother had reneged on her promise to let her leave school early and had insisted that she finish out the year. Jane had cried the whole way from home. Unlike myself, she had an unnatural fear of school and devoted a great deal of her time to devising ways of avoiding it. To make matters worse, Jane was about to be at the receiving end of Berrigan's wrath for no other reason than her failure to recite without error passages from our current subject of study.

The *Tain Bo Cuailgne*, a mythological saga from an ancient epic of Irish grandeur written in the vernacular of the time, and considered by many to be the greatest piece of literature in the western world. It had become in our day an object of passion by certain schools seeking to revive the Gaelic culture.

The story tells of the struggles of the warrior queen Maeve, and her battle to win back the prized bull of Ulster. The epic itself consists of many intriguing tales that many an Irish child has learned and loved at its father's knee, but to memorise the Gaelic form was a task most children dreaded. However, Jane had more in common with the Saxon tongue than she had with the Gaelic soul. Conchobor, Deirdre, and Oisin, or who begat who in the halls of Macha had little place in her troubled world.

A whisper of fear ran through the class as she stammered and stuttered in a failing voice, trying to give expression to words that held no meaning for her. She mumbled along for a few agonising minutes, doing her best to keep the words flowing long enough to find escape by the inevitable "Next," but a few seconds later her tongue cramped, her brain thickened and the words died upon her lips. There was an instant of deathly silence as Jane's head fell forward.

"I don't know anymore," she mumbled.

Berrigan spent a moment glaring, and then accused Jane of not studying it. I knew that Jane had in fact spent considerable time on it, despite a nagging toothache. She attempted to tell Berrigan this but the Bull Neck wouldn't listen, insisting that she had not spent enough time on it.

"Take it home and study it again," she said, "and spend all day on it if necessary."

"Yes miss, thanks miss," Jane replied, and slumped into her seat, forgetting the first rule of conduct in the school's list of proprieties: REMAIN STANDING UNTIL GIVEN PERMISSION TO SIT. Too late Jane saw her peril in the little white constriction at the side of Berrigan's nose, a symptom we had all come to recognise as the calm before the storm.

"How dare you?" Berrigan thundered, and Jane stiffened. She rose from her desk and walked to the front of the class where stood Berrigan, her cane poised. I watched Jane's quivering fingers and saw the shame in her eyes each time she drew her hand back in terror. Finally the cane found its mark, and Jane gasped.

The caning itself was brief, one slap to each hand, but the thing that happened next was unforgivable and set in motion a train of events that we would long remember. The Bull Neck, not content with the suffering she had already caused, resorted to a form of punishment that no other teacher in the school practised. First she looked around the room, her face conspiratorial, as though the rest of us were in league with her. It was her way of gaining our support and reducing the risk of one of us reporting her. The eyes of the class were on her as she drew from her desk the one thing we all feared more than the cane itself, and pushed it roughly against Jane's chest.

The enormity of Jane's shame permeated the room and a sort of numbing silence passed through my mind as Jane, the dunce cap hanging from her fingers, took her place in the corner. Unable to bring herself to wear it, she held it in her hand, hoping, I suppose, that she would not be forced to put it on. But Berrigan was determined, and Jane's hand rose slowly to her head, the tears streaming down her wretched face.

Then it happened. Something queer took hold of me. The Beast of Hades had possession of my soul as a surge of hatred swept across my mind. I gave no thought to the consequences of my action as I left my seat and marched with a purpose to my sister's side. She looked at me astonished, her eyes grateful but afraid as I snatched the paper symbol from her hand and trampled it beneath my feet.

The Bull Neck was beside herself with anger, her eyes smouldering, the muscles of her jaw tensing. But I was not afraid, for technically she had no authority over me. I did not belong officially in her class but was one of a few selected to compete in the County Council scholarship exam and only temporarily in her class for advanced tuition. She can't do anything to me, I remember thinking. But as I walked back to my desk with a feigned composure, she sprang up from her chair, came around her desk and pulled me to the centre of the room.

"In this school, we show respect to teachers," she said, her voice low but menacing, her expression so mean I couldn't bear to look at her. I kept my eyes downcast.

"Look at me when I speak to you," she ordered, but try as I might I could not bring myself to do so.

"Very well, then." Her hand settled on my shoulder with a pressure so strong it forced me to my knees. She raised her cane, and I held my hand out as bravely as I could. I felt the sting of the cane's descent but I did not flinch. Something mean but merciful had taken hold of me, clenching the anguish behind my teeth and gluing the tears to my eyes. Six times the cane found its mark on one hand and six times on the other. My body shook beneath the pain, and just when I imagined I could bear it no more, it ended. When the final blow was landed and the silent cheers of comfort from the class began, I knew that I had won.

Without Bull Neck's permission I walked back to my desk. Unendurable pain was pumping through my hands as I lowered myself into my seat. Yet even as my bottom touched the wood, I felt the elements of my nature change, as with a benumbed calmness I rose, crossed the room and turned the handle of the door. A screeching pain shot through my fingers as they closed about the knob, but I managed to get outside.

In the empty corridor I saw Mother Dolorosa arranging flowers at the Virgin's altar. A strange little nun with a gammy leg and an uncanny ability to see around corners, she had but to raise her head and my escape would have been halted. But her back was to me, and tiptoeing through the cloakroom I slipped through to the outside door.

I raced along the path to the iron gate, my heart beating wildly for fear it would be locked, but it was on the latch and I managed to get it open. Without looking back I hurried off along the street. Then ran and ran until I could run no more.

When finally I reached the summit of Clooney's Hill and saw the welcome river down below, I stopped to examine my aching hands. What I saw revolted me. The palms of my hands seemed to be no longer there, but were replaced with grapelike flesh that had swallowed up my fingers, leaving only my nails and the backs of my hands visible. All the pent-up feelings I had managed to control now escaped in a sea of scalding tears. I stopped running the second time only when I reached our house, and stood in the scullery looking at my mother's back bent over the weekly washing.

"Holy Mother of God!" was all I heard, before a tide of dizziness swept over me.

When I opened my eyes again I found my mother kneeling by my chair. I told her everything. Mother's face was livid. In that rasping voice I was happy enough to hear now that it was directed at someone else, she asked if I felt strong enough to walk and I told her that I did.

"Right so," she said, getting to her feet and pulling down her sleeves. "I'm taking you to the Gard's Barracks."

19

GARDA SÍOCHÁNA, *the writing above the door proclaimed, inscribed there sometime after I was born. The words meant nothing special to people thereabouts. It was just the local police station down the road, handy for information, complaints, and the handling of minor injuries. Police constables were known as gards when I was growing up, and I had never heard them called anything else. One did not say Constable Sinnot or Constable O'Brien, but Gard Sinnot and Gard O'Brien. The station was known as the Barracks.*

Though I knew most of the gards by name and all of them by sight, it was the first time I had been inside the building. We passed through the front doors into a long narrow hall lighted here and there by an occasional bulb. I wondered vaguely where they kept the prisoners, for I could see no iron bars or heavy bolts. From somewhere behind a closed door I heard the click-click of a typewriter. I thought about walking down the hall to investigate, but before I had time I was whisked behind a counter by the officer in charge, Chief Contable Callaghan, who had been talking to Jimmy Patterson at the inquiry desk.

Mother, still in her white apron and her hair scraggy on her head, spared me the ritual of interrogation with her own account of what had happened. She insisted that a warrant be written out against the school, because nobody was going to do to one of her children what she wouldn't do herself.

"For the child's sake I'll keep a civil tongue," she said, "but I'm giving you fair warning, that if something isn't done, I'll take the law into my own hands."

I remained in my chair listening, the pain in my hands momentarily forgotten as I watched the expression on Barney Callaghan's face. He was clearly not impressed with Mother's boldness and was doing his best to hide the fact. Walking over to where I was sitting he inspected both my hands. Then he walked back to his desk and sat down. Gard Sullivan, who had been conferring privately with somebody in the corner, looked up and asked if there was anything he could do.

For a moment Barney did not answer. Then he said, "You might see to her hands," and indicated me with a nod of his head.

Gard Sullivan said he would surely and stepped outside the counter to the room across the hall, returning a few minutes later with a bowl of water and some gauze. He picked up my hands and looked at them, shaking his head in disgust at what he saw. From behind him he produced a scalpel and I closed my eyes, waiting. But there was no pain, not even a needle prick, as with a few deft strokes of his blade and the practise of a skilled surgeon he freed my hands of blisters.

Barney in the meantime was sucking on his pen, pretending not to notice Mother still standing by his desk. She had ignored his direction to "just take a seat." Finally, with a weary sigh he looked up.

"I don't know," he said, shaking his head and mumbling something which I did not catch. I saw Mother stiffen.

"I don't care what the teacher has to say. Nothing a child that size might do could justify such a beating. And, since I know what you are going to say next, let me tell you now I won't stand for it."

If Barney didn't feel inclined to deal with her complaint in a forthright way because of whom it might offend, she demanded, then would he kindly pass the matter over to somebody who would? Barney's jaw set against his collar and he looked sternly at my mother.

"May I remind you, madam, that this building is a barracks, where business is conducted with decorum!"

Mother looked at him amused, then turned to Jimmy Patterson.

"This is all your fault," she said, knowing full well that it was Jimmy's presence more than anything that had prompted Barney's call for respect. Jimmy, whom Mother had known for twenty years, and soon to be mayor of the city, laughed.

He knew as well as Mother exactly what was going through Barney's mind, for Barney was a class-conscious man in his early fifties and considered himself a person of importance in the Royal Irish Constabulary. When officiating in the line of duty he spoke with a formal accent and regarded anybody with a little money or an iota of education above the normal, deserving of special consideration. Needless to say Mother did not qualify.

Jimmy, though reluctant to become involved, agreed with Mother. No school, he said, should be allowed to use such harsh punishment on its pupils. With a few sympathetic words to Mother and some advice to Barney, he excused himself and left. No sooner had he stepped outside the door than Barney began to plead with Mother, who despite her harsh words earlier eventually gave in and agreed to withdraw her demand for a warrant. She remained perverse, however, to his suggestion that she run along home and let him handle everything. On the contrary, she replied, she intended to handle a great part of it herself.

"The worst is over," she said to me, when we got outside, but I didn't believe a word of it, nor would anybody else who saw the resolve in her swinging arms, the battle warning in her eyes as she headed down the hill in the direction of the school.

A breeze was blowing steadily, and the sight of Mother's hair every which way on her head caused me some embarrassment. At the school door we were intercepted by Mother Dolorosa, an indication that Mother's visit was expected. She took Mother's hand and began to apologise for the Reverend's absence. Mother made a great effort to be polite, but the scowl never left her face.

"Pardon me," she interrupted finally, "but I have not come here to discuss the Reverend Mother. I have come about my daughter." She grabbed my hands and held them out for the nun to see. A faint sound escaped her withered lips and she begged of Mother some moments to explain.

"Explain what?" asked Mother, and insisted that she speak with Berrigan.

Reluctantly the little nun led her to the classroom door, then clasping her hands in momentary grief hurried off along the hall.

"Go get your sisters," Mother said to me, walking up to Berrigan's door and pounding on the glass.

"Where is she, the bull-necked butcher? Where is she 'til I murder her!'"

I could hear her voice clear along the hall as I went from door to door calling out the others. I had to help Peg find her coat in the cloakroom, and when we came out Berrigan was standing by the open door staring at my mother. Mother, five-foot-nothing in her stocking feet, seemed awed by Berrigan's great size and height. Evidently she had not expected so large a woman.

"Look at you, you great lump," she said. "How dare you beat a little girl like that?"

Berrigan barely answered, her face flushed. Except for a plea for understanding ventured in some muffled words of apology, she simply stood and listened. Mother said she could judge her only according to her actions and refused her apology, for anyone that size to beat so badly a defenceless little girl had no right to expect forgiveness. It was painful to watch the Bull Neck's face. Several times she swallowed hard and gave me a sheepish look, her eyes searching my face as though she might find some sympathy there.

All at once the Reverend Mother, who had evidently been hovering close by, hurried to take charge. Clearly offended by Mother's apron and the sight of her unkempt hair, she hardly noticed the rest of us. Grand words began falling from her lips like berries from a bush as she launched forth with a confidence drawn from her years of learning. Pausing only to take in air and to exhibit the strength of her position by backward glances at Mother Dolorosa, she proceeded to inform my mother that teachers under her supervision were both educated and civilised individuals and any punishment meted out to pupils in their charge was usually well deserved.

Perspiration beaded on Mother's forehead and she dabbed it away with the corner of her apron. I thought for sure she had met defeat in the wake of the Reverend's erudition, but when she fixed those pale blue eyes on the Reverend's face I knew otherwise.

"You can stop right there, if you don't mind," she interrupted boldly. "What civilised person would beat a little girl so savagely? And no one ever told you, I suppose, that there is such a thing as compassion, for nowhere in that mountain of words of yours did I hear one hint of human feeling for a child in this condition."

Again she grabbed my hands and held them out.

"You may have managed to convince yourself that there was just cause for this, but you'll not convince me."

The Reverend stiffened and her hands shot rigidly inside her sleeves. A dull red spot appeared upon her cheek. Her intention, she said, had merely been to help. Mother scoffed. She could have done that best by not letting her see so plainly what she thought of her, she said. Something in her voice brought my eyes to her face. How small and insignificant she looked before the dignified nun. Never before that moment, and never after, would I feel the pride for her that I had felt then. She turned away disgusted, pushed open the heavy door and ushered us outside.

These events had taken place on Friday. That Sunday morning our home was favoured with a visit from none other than Canon Cavanagh himself. Monday morning saw all four of us sitting at our desks, no questions asked. Mother had won a victory, one that would be remembered not only by ourselves but by many grateful children. For never again would a hand be raised against one of us, and much consideration would be given before it was raised to others.

And so the months had flown away and I had somehow made it to preparatory. In those days there were no public high schools, not in our town at any rate, and a person could go directly into college from grammar school if they met the requirements. My heart, once set on acceptance to the Gaelic college of Donegal, was no longer hopeful.

I cannot remember exactly when I decided that I disliked nuns, but I am sure it was sometime after the scholarship exam. So resentful had I become of their stubborn ways that a question from the lips of any one of them wiped away what little knowledge I did have from my head. Every day was burdened with reminders of the past, of challenges met and overcome, of prizes won but not received, the reward given to someone else. Favourites they gathered around them like flowers from the fields, but I was never one of them. Except in the light of bringing glory to the school I had no relevance. And in that, too, I had let them down.

How much more could a young girl suffer? Wasn't it enough to be thirteen, ugly and freckled and my home life brimming with worries and disgrace? I had given up the fight. Now I wiled away the hours, paying small attention to my studies and waiting for the day of my release. Until that day I knew I would never allow one of them to influence my convictions. It was on a Saturday evening one year later that my father informed me I had been enrolled for the coming year in the only alternative school he could afford, the local Technical School.

20

Some weeks after the ambulance came for him, Madge and I decided to visit Mr. Bourke at the Sanatorium. We made up our minds to go the following Sunday after Mass. Nobody, we agreed, should be told about our plan, for fear they might prevent us. Children were not always welcome at the Sanatorium, and seldom accompanied their parents there. "T'isn't right for them to see such things. Their minds are so impressionable," they said. As if we could not see for ourselves the death notices on doors, and the constant funerals parading through the streets.

The night before we were due to go, I lay awake thinking about what it would be like inside the San. Images of the Dowling boy in that little hut behind their house kept passing through my mind, as I remembered the day that Jane and myself had peeped through the tiny window and had seen him lying there alone, coughing, bleeding and gasping for breath. I wasn't sure any longer that I wanted to go, but I had promised Madge.

When morning came she called for me as we had planned, and without a word to anyone we climbed over the garden wall and crossed the Green to the Friary Chapel. I waited until Mass was over, then, still apprehensive, I suggested to Madge that we postpone our visit. She became annoyed.

"A fine friend you turned out to be," she moaned. "Well, if you don't want to come, I'll go alone," and she strode through the chapel gates and headed off along Friary Lane. Just before she turned the corner out of sight I called out that I would come. She stopped and waited. We continued up Lower Patrick Street to the Ormond Road, then crossed the road and continued up the hill.

Madge began to chatter nervously. Her mother, she told me, would wipe the floor with her when she found out where she had been. It was the ideal moment for me to suggest again that we turn back, but I held my tongue. When we got to the top of Patrick Street we stopped to arrange ourselves in the window of Dwyer's shop. Madge, pulling her hair tight around her ears, pinned it to a bun behind her head and assumed an elderly expression.

"What do you think?" she asked, and I assured her that she could pass for at least fifteen. We continued on to the iron gate at the entrance of the hospital yard and crossed the yard to the front door.

"Wipe your feet," Madge whispered as we stepped into the entrance hall.

The heavy odour of disinfectant rose from every corner as we passed inside and found ourselves in a long open room flanked on each side by neat rows of white iron beds. Except for the dark wainscotting and wooden floors every item in the room was painted white, even the chairs beside the beds. Nearly all the beds were occupied and the few that were empty were stripped bare, right down to the metal slats. We stepped into the centre of the room, keeping an eye out for Mr. Bourke. At that precise moment a buzzer rang and a door opened somewhere behind. A patter of hurrying feet fell across my ears and I heard somebody call out to us. A nurse no taller than myself, her skirt too tight for her expanding hips, came bustling up.

"And just where do you two think you are going, walking brazenly by the office door and not stopping to check with anyone?"

Madge immediately began to stammer something about her first time there and wanting to see her father. The nurse cut her off. There was such a thing as protocol, she said, and Madge was surely old enough to realise that. She would let us in this time, but the next time we took it upon ourselves to enter there, she would toss us out on our impertinent ears. We thanked her and moved along the aisle.

I was beginning to wonder whether Mr. Bourke was there at all until we spotted him in the very last bed. He was sitting up and looking every bit as healthy as ourselves. I had expected to find him grey and drawn, with eyes weak and watery. But he didn't look like that at all. A powder puff of red glowed upon his cheeks and his eyes were bright. Even his laugh sounded healthy.

Madge made a curious whimpering sort of sound and rushed to him with outstretched arms.

"Hello Dad," I heard her say, as her arms enfolded him. She hugged and hugged until I thought he would surely die from suffocation. I stood at the bottom of the bed, not sure exactly where to put myself, until Madge suddenly remembered I was there. Mr. Bourke sat up straighter then, the newspaper he had been reading falling to his lap. He took my hand in his. It felt warm and natural. I expressed my sorrow at his illness, but could not hide my surprise at finding him so well. It was all the good food and lying around in bed, he told us merrily. Seeing that I hesitated to sit upon the bed he beckoned me to a chair at the other side. Madge remained seated on the bed beside him.

An empty bed, devoid of its mattress but covered with a thin white sheet, was squeezed into the space on my other side. Next to it stood a table with a glass of water and a jar of

coloured liquid in which floated upright a solitary ther-
mometer. Behind that in a stemmed glass stood a few wilted
flowers, the used-up petals almost hiding the circular stains
etched into the white paint of the table.

Leaning to the cupboard beside his bed, Mr. Bourke drew
out a large yellow bottle. LUCOZADE, it said on the glassy
wrapper. He twisted the squeaking cap while Madge went over
to a nearby shelf and got some glasses. Then, at her father's
bidding she poured some Lucozade into one and offered it to
me. I averted my eyes, pretending not to see her outstretched
arm, for deep down inside I was frightened to drink for fear of
catching the disease myself. Madge persisted, calling out my
name in her loudest voice.

"Come on," she coaxed, taking my reluctance for shyness.
I knew that Mr. Bourke was watching me, and I wondered if he
had seen through my deception. But if he had he showed no
sign of it. Finally I took the glass and began to drink. The
Lucozade tasted cold, not warm as I had expected, and it fizzed
like lemonade. The taste was pleasant, but I did not thoroughly
enjoy it then because I could not rid my mind of worry.

I sat back in my chair listening to Madge telling her father
all that had happened in the weeks since he had left, and doing
my best to contribute to the conversation. After a while
though, I began to look around the ward. Across the floor from
where I sat, in a bed isolated from the rest by a curtain and
protruding wall, a man lay spent and probably dying. I guessed
that from the grief on the face of the woman standing over
him. He had been thrashing about when we came in and
coughing violently, his head slightly raised on the woman's
arm. Now the coughing had passed and he had fallen back
silent and exhausted, his eyes half closed.

My sympathy went out to the little girl standing nervously
at the bottom of the bed, waiting for somebody to notice her.
Obviously she had that very morning made her First

Communion and was eager, I could see, to parade her dress, yet afraid to leave the mother's side. She had smiled at me when we arrived wanting, I supposed, to be with somebody her age. I was just getting up the courage to go and have a chat with her when the man started coughing dreadfully, and the woman, seeing that I was watching, leaned over and drew the curtain completely around the bed. Her action disappointed me, but I was not offended. What else could she have done? It was the little girl I was thinking of, fate having cast such a shadow on her life. Why was it, I wondered, that people were always dying and leaving so much sorrow? Supposing my own father were to die? What would happen to all of us?

No one ever seemed to have an answer. Not even in the Bible was an answer to be found. It seemed ironic to me that just beyond the windows of this room where a man lay slowly dying, the city life was going on as usual. Somewhere I could hear the strains of St. Patrick's Brass Band getting ready for its afternoon recital. And out in the fields I knew the farmers were working to replenish the earth that would bring forth new life in the spring.

I felt Mr. Bourke's eyes watching me.

"A penny for your thoughts," he said, his tone casual but curious.

"Oh, it's nothing. I was just listening to the band," I answered.

"Ah, the band!" His head went up; his ears strained to catch the sound of it. The last chords of *Let Erin Remember* went floating out around the town as we listened. In common with thousands of others, Mr. Bourke was a staunch supporter of the gallant little band which had become a symbol in our town because of its support of three young Fenians, Allen, Larkin and O'Brien, who had been hastily hanged in England for the attempted rescue of a comrade already en route to an English gaol.

"Twenty years in silent clay, their memory lives as fresh today," Mr. Bourke began reciting, and I thought for sure there was a story in the offing. Usually I loved to listen to old tales, but now I longed to be outside in the cool clear air. Something in my manner may have told him this, for he stopped speaking, his eyes moist. He slipped one arm about Madge's shoulder and drew her close. Self-consciously he wiped his eyes, and I watched in silence until the nurse came and told us it was time to leave.

The gloom was gone from Madge's face when we got outside, and she announced that her father would be home at the end of two weeks. This surprised me more than I let on, though I had to admit that he had not looked in the least bit sick. It was just as well that neither of us understood the nature of tuberculosis and the different stages it went through before it either left or liberated its victim.

Back we ambled the way we had come, chatting gaily about everything we had seen and feeling quite proud of our accomplishment. We both remembered the sad little girl in her First Communion dress, and Madge said that she had overheard her mother telling Mrs. Brennan that it was a family from out on the Ballycallan Road, and that the man had been admitted that Friday afternoon. How sad for the little girl, we thought, comparing the circumstances with those of our own special day.

Madge began to tell me all about hers, and all the time she was talking I was thinking about mine. How I had gone with Chris to the Monster House only days before to pick out my clothes. "Choose anything you like," Mrs. Duggan had said, and so I did, probably the most expensive in the store. I remembered the effusions of oohs! and aahs! and beautifuls! as I joined the ranks of waiting children. How happy and free of sadness the day had been, so unlike that of the little girl in the Sanatorium.

21

When we left the San, we had not planned on any other outing, but neither of us wanted to go home. So we decided to hunt for blackberries in the nearby lanes. Our search led us out onto the Castle Road, and before we knew it we were at the quarry. The Black Quarry it was called, because of its ebony marble. Kilkenny in those days was famous for its marble, black, green, and otherwise.

Scattered about the lanes where the road ran right up against the wall were a number of tiny cottages, their gardens a profusion of brightly coloured flowers. We filled our lungs with the sweet scent of wallflowers hanging in bunches about the walls. A little farther on the opposite side of the road was the quarry.

At a point high above the quarry was the blackberry patch where we knew could be found the biggest juiciest berries ever seen. Not everybody knew of its existence, and because of its close proximity to the quarry edge it was seldom frequented by children. The quarry floor itself was a stopover point for vagrants, tinkers and the like travelling the road to Dublin, but as the corporation had put up prosecution notices all around the place we were not likely to run into them. As far as we could see the place was empty. If there had been anybody here they were not here now. Drawing near to the opening of the narrow path that led up the side of the quarry, Madge saw something move behind the bushes, and both of us were sure we had heard the snort of a donkey. In alarm we hurried off along the path beneath the overhanging branches. After walking ahead a little way we stopped again to listen. We heard nothing, only the chirping of the birds in the broad-leaved trees. All went well until we reached a section of the path that widened to form a bend.

Here our way was obstructed by a pair of squatting boys amusing themselves and their two companions with a pair of angry roosters. The roosters must have been battling for some time, because the grass around was showered with tiny feathers. The birds were tied by one leg to a piece of string wound around the wrists of the owners. This prevented them from locking in serious combat, but allowed them ample room to move, at times coming together with fierce intent, stabbing at each other's eyes, their beaks clacking noisily. I had heard of this sport but never witnessed it. Without stopping to consider, I marched up to them.

"There's a law in this country against that," I said.

They all turned to look at me. The lad closest to me half stood up.

"And what law might that be, little girl?" he asked in a jeering sort of voice.

What law indeed? How did I know what law? I had no particular name for it, but I felt sure there had to be one.

I had a sudden thought.

"A legislative law against cruelty to animals." My voice had just the right ring to it, conveying that I understood precisely what I was saying. The lad was upright in a minute.

"Did yee hear that lads? A leg-is-lay-tive law. Powerful words from a pint-sized Paddy. What do you say Barley?" He drew out every syllable.

Barley, who up to now had remained squatting, rose to his feet and circled me audaciously, his thumb latched in the armpit of his vest in the manner of a barrister. "Begging your ludship's pardon I am sure," he drawled, "for I fear we are ill-informed in these matters. Tell us, me lud, to what law exactly are you referring?"

The sepulchral intonation of his voice brought a guffaw of laughter from the others. Was it possible, one of them asked, that her ludship had never heard of Charles Dickens? I had no idea what he was hinting at.

"I beg your pardon," I replied with equal arrogance, "but I fail to see the connection." This brought on a second guffaw before Barley moved beside me, his face almost touching mine.

"I dare say me lud would recognise an ass if she saw one all the same?"

An ass! What did an ass have to do with anything? I looked at Madge, but her face was blank. By now the boys were beside themselves with laughter while I, filled with dignified anger, found myself grappling with the cord connecting the rooster's legs. One part of it disentangled instantly, and a moment later one bird was free. It fluttered off into the bushes with the owner swearing and sprinting after it. Now that I had done it I was itching to be off and had shifted my limbs into moving gear when Barley, releasing his right hand from the bird he was still holding, reached out and grabbed my arm.

"Not so fast my girl," he said, tightening his grip and threatening to dislocate my shoulder should I make another move. I had every reason to believe him and thought for sure he meant to injure me. At that precise moment the tall one reappeared, the recaptured rooster safe beneath his arm.

"Now that wasn't a nice thing to do," he said. "A nice little city girl like you. What made you do a thing like that?"

I thrashed about for an answer. "Well, how would you feel if someone tied a string to one of your legs and forced you to fight?"

"She's got you there," said Barley, who on a nod from the
lanky one released my arm. They moved aside then to let us
pass. All the time this had been going on the two younger lads
had said nothing, but I noticed one of them watching me with
an unmistakable look of interest in his eyes.

"If you are going up for blackberries," he said, coming up
behind us on the path, "you won't find any."

They weren't ripe yet, he told us, too much cloud and not
enough sun. He moved ahead and without a word his companion rose and followed. When we reached the blackberry
patch he pointed to the half-ripened berries. Another week or
so, he said, and they should be ripe for picking.

"Why don't you come back then?" he asked, looking
pointedly at me.

"We will," I answered, with a casual smile that I hoped
would conceal my pleasure at the frank look of admiration on
his face. Without ceremony we went on walking. As we
walked, we talked. He told me his name was Seamus, and I
told him mine. A lad of about my own age he was, very sound
and stocky, with a nose as freckled as my own and a head of
wavy hair. The notion that he favoured me gave me a thrill,
and when we stopped by the gateway to a field to take a drink
of water from a pump, and he held the cup for me, I was
ecstatic. I had never had such attention lavished on me.
Besides, he was the first country boy with whom I had ever
chatted, and I wanted to know all about his home and family.

He had one brother and a sister, he told me, describing
each. "Maybe you'd like to meet them?"

He stopped abruptly, taking hold of my hand. The spon-
taneity of his gesture embarrassed me, and I drew my hand
back quickly, calling to Madge that we should be getting home.

"You will come again, won't you?" he asked shyly, and I
told him that I would. He stood quietly watching as we crossed
the road, and somewhere farther down I looked back, but there

was no sign of him. Disappointment swept over me, for I had wanted to see his face again. I had so much liked the look of him. Liked the way he said my name, and the serious way he talked about things.

"I will go to England when the war ends," he had said, "but maybe we can be good friends until then." I never did return to the quarry, so I never saw Seamus again and would often wonder what became of him.

Madge had gone very quiet, not saying much, and I guessed it was because we were nearing home. We had been gone all day, and we didn't know what to expect when we did get home.

As it turned out we need not have worried, for we found Mrs. Bourke in an excellent mood. "Sure 'tis perished the two of yee must be," she' said, when we told her of our adventure, leaving out the part about the Sanitorium. She hurried to the scullery to prepare some food. With gratitude I accepted, for not only was I hungry, but her invitation provided me with an alibi should Mother demand to know where I had been. Never before had Mrs. Bourke been so talkative.

When I left the house at nine o'clock, she was still telling us about her youth. Yet, as I hurried through their garden to our house, I thought it strange that never once had she said a word about her husband. Surely she had been to visit him that day? Ah! but they were a strange lot, our parents, always trying to keep secret from us the things we already knew.

22

Mr. Bourke came home from hospital before the new year as Madge said he would, and every sunny day on my way home from school I could expect to see him sitting on a chair outside their door. Then the Yuletide holiday came, and Jane, having finally persuaded Mother, left school forever at the Christmas break. But the thing outstanding in my mind is Christmas Day, for not only did it mark the beginning of the end of my special friendship with Madge, but also the last Christmas either of us would spend as children.

We were standing on the street outside our house displaying our Christmas presents. Madge had a game of Ludo and a pretty wooden cart. I had a black china doll. Neither of us had ever seen a black doll before, much less one with real hair and lashes. I was excited and happy. Madeleine, we decided would be the doll's name, and we both took turns holding her.

Madge was disappointed that she had not gotten a doll, and wanted to hold mine for longer than I was willing.

"Well, only for a minute, mind," I said, as I handed her over for the last time. This seemed to satisfy Madge, and she caressed and fondled Madeleine as though she were her own.

But as the minutes passed and I reached out to reclaim my doll, Madge hesitated. Then, suddenly I saw her fingers open, and I saw Madeleine fall through them to the ground below. Horrified, I stared at the shattered pieces. No toy, no doll especially, had captured my affections the way this one had, and I was inconsolable. I lashed out at Madge with offensive names, threatening to have my father pack her off to gaol. Her face, unreadable until then, dissolved in fear and she raced off to inform her mother, while I with equal speed hastened to report to mine.

Hardly had I time to get the story finished when Mrs. Bourke came knocking on our front door. Mother went to speak with her, and when she returned her face was glum. She refused to say in front of me what had transpired, but later I heard her tell my father that Mrs. Bourke was furious. I couldn't understand why, seeing as it was my doll that had been broken and her Madge who had broken it.

Nothing could persuade me at that time that Madge had not broken it on purpose, but by the time the week ended and my sorrow dissipated, I had forgiven Madge and went as usual to call on her. Mrs. Bourke answered the door. The usual smile was missing from her face. I asked her if Madge was coming out and she gave me a sort of bitter look, her eyes more than anything conveying it. She replied that Madge was not coming out and said nothing more. Yet it felt as though she had said a whole lot more. Like, I'm surprised you had the nerve to come calling at this door. Go away and don't come back.

I could see Madge peeping through the opening and she looked as though she wanted to come out, but when her mother turned her head to look at her she walked back inside. I had never seen this bewildering side of Mrs. Bourke before, and I can think of few things in my childhood more unpleasant to remember than the times after that when I called at Madge's door and got turned away. In the end I stopped calling altogether. Especially after Mother, noticing Madge's absence from our house, asked if we had had a fight, and when I told her what had happened she told me not to go near their house again unless I was invited.

I don't think Madge ever realised the part her mother played in our separation, or if she did she never spoke of it. Many times, though, I sensed her uneasiness, with her mother always watching at the door for signs of our being together.

"I'll have to go now, Tess," Madge would say apologetically and hurry off.

The days when we could chuckle and find excitement in almost anything had gone forever. At times I felt such anger toward Madge, thinking she was being deliberately vague, concealing her activities and unwilling to tell me everything as she used to. But then I would remember her mother's face that day outside their door and realise it was not her fault.

We still spent certain times together, but they were usually spoiled by constant interruptions of "Madge, did you show Daddy your new skirt and cardigan?" or " Come on in Madge and see what I bought for you," while I remained standing by the door. I went on loving Mrs. Bourke in spite of it, for though I felt she had done a cruel thing to me she had never caused me hurt in any other way, and maybe I had hurt her too without knowing it. Years later she softened toward me and tried her best to bring Madge and me back together, but it was too late. Our lives had taken different paths, the capacity of our enjoyment together killed by too much interference and a senseless childish rivalry that neither of us wanted. By the time we reached fourteen we had become estranged; still friendly but no more an essential part of each other's day.

Alienated from Madge and with Jane preoccupied elsewhere, I began more and more to turn to the Old Man for comfort. In no time at all we had become great friends, with him doing me the honour of telling me things he would never tell to others. He was an excellent provider of sympathy and care, listening to my countless complaints and offering whenever possible his grandfatherly advice.

"Hush alana, hush an' listen t'me now, t'morrah ye'll see it different."

Youth and age, he used to say, saw different meaning in the same things, but each of us had to learn to take the bitter with the sweet. A feeling of guilt came over me when I told him about Madge's mother, for I felt I was betraying her and I knew he hated taking sides. His face was grim but compassionate.

"I don't know what t'tell ye child. I don't faith. Th'poor woman thinks she is doin' th'right thing."

If we couldn't find something nice to say about her, the best thing we could do was to say nothing, he said. Besides, it was a mother's duty to stand up for her child and a nice thing to see. In his day the only compassion a child ever got was the back of the hand or the sole of the boot, be they innocent or otherwise. It would be nice all the same, he said, if mothers would stick to cooking and let the children do the fighting.

"I dare say th' cud work things out among themselves without help from anywan."

It was nice to be able to tell him things and not have to worry that he would tell them back. The problem of my mother I kept to myself, too ashamed to mention it. When in the end I did confide, it was only because I couldn't keep it to myself any longer.

23

The summer of my fourteenth birthday found me installed at the Technical School, and from the moment I stepped inside its door I knew I was going to like it, so different was it from anything I had known. There were no nuns, to begin with, and we had male and female teachers. Questions and one's own interpretation of ideas were not only tolerated, but also encouraged. Hope began to grow again in my half-starved brain as each day brought new successes. Once more I began to imagine myself in an institution of higher learning.

But then one day the arguments began again. The war had brought economic hardship to Kilkenny as it had to other towns in Ireland, and though my father had managed to keep us free from too much want, by the end of the war he had little savings. Mother was soon complaining that tuition fees were a luxury they could ill afford.

"Why can't she go to work like all the others? It's time she was bringing home a wage." And when that argument failed, "It's off to England she'll be when she finishes there, and you'll not see a penny farthing out of it."

Father would argue that it didn't matter, that I deserved a chance at something better. Mother couldn't understand that rationale, for why should I have something she never had?

"Better than what I was is what you mean! Domestic work not good enough for her?"

And so it would go on until I grew sick of hearing it. I wanted to stay at school more than anything and I knew my father wanted that too, but the constant arguments and attacks on me when he was not present began to weaken my resolve. One morning I awoke with the feeling that something was about to happen. That same afternoon Mother came to a decision while I was still at school.

I came home at four and found the house empty. Soon after, I heard her coming. She walked into the kitchen and took off her coat, and before she began to speak I knew there was something on her mind. I asked if there was anything I could do for her and she said no. She removed a pot from beside the fire and began pouring water into it. Then without looking up she said, "When I was on the town today I ran into Auntie Janey."

"Oh!" said I, wondering what was coming. Janey was her younger sister who had moved to Kilkenny some years before.

"Her Kitty is making good money in the factory."

The boot factory she meant, and my heart sank for I knew what she was going to say next. "I never liked that place," I put in hastily, hoping to make my position clear. But it only served to reinforce her argument.

"And why not, I'd like to know? The money is better there than anywhere."

Money! Money! Money! That's all she ever thought about. I wished for once she would talk about something different. I understood about the high cost of everything and how she was tired of having to make ends meet, but I disagreed that she had less to manage on than others. If anything she had more. My father was bringing home a decent wage, Sheilagh and Jane were working and she still had Uncle's contribution. How much money did a person need to support a shrinking family?

I didn't have the heart to argue anymore. It was true that jobs in the boot factory were coveted, but mainly because of the money paid. Women who went to work there were looked down upon and considered unintelligent. The work was hard and sometimes dirty—tantamount in my mind to a term in gaol.

"Kitty isn't there because she wants to be," I cried. "She's there because she has no choice."

"And neither do you," Mother retorted. "Either you get yourself in there too, or you can leave this house."

I was enraged by her ultimatum. The boot factory of all places! I didn't want to end up there, not now when I was doing so well in school. Besides, I knew it would kill my father.

"I want to make something better of my life, and it has nothing to do with airs and graces," I argued, close to tears. For a moment her expression softened and she turned to me looking as though she understood. But then her face went hard again and she spun away.

"Well that's too bad, my girl, because that is where you are going."

It was a waste of time to argue; her decision once made was final. My father of course would have some say in it, but at this point I dreaded telling him. To find a job was the thing to do. But where besides the factory? There was little choice, since there were no other jobs available except in other factories. I knew of no one who could help me, except maybe my father's sister Mary. Possibly she could offer me an alternative, or at the very least persuade my mother to change her mind.

The following Sunday afternoon found me sitting in Auntie's parlour sipping yellow lemonade from a Guinness glass. Auntie was sitting opposite in her usual chair, her feet resting on the fender. There was no fire in the grate since the morning had been too hot for that, but now, as the day was cooling, Auntie held a lighted match against the bars to get one started. The newspaper stuffed beneath the kindling began to smoke, then flickered to a sturdy flame. Soon the wood began to crackle, and the flames began licking hungrily at the corners of the turf.

Next door Mrs. Mooney was cavorting with the Barber of Seville, the music drifting through the walls. Auntie leaned her head against her chair with eyes closed and listened. I listened too. Her husband Willie, shirtsleeves rolled to the elbow and rattling bottles in the bar across the hall, imperilled his lungs in an effort to compete. Unfortunately he had no ear for music.

Mrs. Mooney was Auntie's only friend, and had turned up her gramophone especially, one of the little niceties they extended to each other, like knocking on the bedroom wall of an evening to let each other know that they were well. The music stopped finally and Auntie opened her eyes and looked at me, saying that it always put her in mind of her own poor dead father. Her face now assumed that woebegone look that told me she was about to take a leap into the past, and I would have to listen to her tell about teaching in Tramore, her friends there and the years they had spent together. I had heard the story many times before, looked at all the pictures, and absorbed the fact that children then were more obedient, more considerate, and less demanding.

I listened as attentively as any fourteen-year-old could to every detail of every day, from the moment of glory of her very own class to the moment of glory of her very own school, and I doubt if she could have had a more unwilling ear. I should have been more understanding, but all I knew about Tramore then was where it was, that people called it the Golden Strand and that in summer the rich made it their paradise. If only she had talked about something more exciting. But then I suppose she had nothing more exciting to talk about.

"Don't gulp that lemonade dear," she interrupted herself irritably, suspecting, I suppose, that I was barely listening. I laid down the glass and sat up straight, observing the proud tilt to her head, her hair like a robin's nest on top. So Victorian she looked in her high-backed chair. Her lace blouse, lavender in shade, was held beneath her chin by a cameo brooch. If she was beautiful once she was not so then, her features full and flabby. Yet her eyes had the blue of a mountain mist and were large and round.

Tall and impressive she had been in her maiden days and still was in spite of the added weight. A woman of superb development a gentleman might say, with a bosom that rose and fell like a ship on the sea. Yet there was a fragility about her that used to fascinate me, like the feeling of porcelain or a China vase. She could not bear the sound of profane words and usually paled in their presence.

Like her brother Jim she had been blessed with the gift of total recall and had excelled at school. As early as was possible she had begun to teach, and like most proper Irish girls of her time had married well. No children had resulted from the union, and I had many times heard it said that Auntie didn't care, that she had neither the patience nor the understanding to be a mother. But to this day I believe that story to be false. At times, I will admit, she invited gossip, with her grandiose ideas and her la-di-da ways, but she never engaged in idle gossip, and except for the occasional chat with her friend next door she kept to herself.

A victim is what she was, of that special kind of gentry in the Kilkenny of her day, the English influence everywhere. Her life had been carefree and protected, untouched by poverty or dirt, so it was not surprising that she held on to certain habits.

Uncle of course was the opposite, small in stature with big brown eyes and sallow skin. He loved to talk and chatter. His great enjoyment was his morning walk to work along the city streets meeting and greeting everyone. The courthouse, where he worked as senior clerk, was situated in the heart of town, a good way from his home in Barrack Street. It was never fully decided which job he was better suited for, sitting at his desk behind the courthouse walls or leaning on the counter of his little pub.

The pub had been his own idea when they got wed. Auntie had wanted no part of it, but Uncle with his quiet courtly manner and doglike eyes had managed to persuade her. He loved the pub and the pub loved him, and I had often heard my father say that it might have been the most prosperous in the city had it not been for Mary. She hated the locality, its proximity to the soldiers' barracks, and didn't want anything to do with its inhabitants.

"My Willie should have been a barrister, and not catering to the likes of them," she would say to us, and maybe she was right. For I remember well the respect and admiration people had for Uncle and his knowledge of the law, calling often at his door for the benefit of his advice. When he was delayed at the office, however, Auntie opened and attended bar, though she never enjoyed doing it.

The lemonade fizzed in the back of my throat, causing me to cough and splutter. Auntie sighed and looked as though she were about to cry. She allowed me a moment to recover and then said, "I told you so. I told him too but he would not listen." She was referring to her earlier warning to Uncle about allowing me a drink too near her precious furniture. She stared fixedly at the polished surface to my right.

"Wipe that liquid from the table now before it leaves a stain." She passed across her handkerchief.

Uncle, hearing the commotion, appeared in the door. He opened wide his arms and held them out to me. "Come here to me darlin' and let me look at you." I went to him dutifully, and to my embarrassment he picked me up.

"Put her down Willie, put her down," Auntie chuckled, aware of my discomfort. They exchanged a glance which I understood, and a few minutes later Uncle handed me a shilling. Then he asked how I was getting on at school, I quickly told him everything.

"Dear, oh dear!" wailed Auntie, beginning to look pale. "We must not let that happen." She passed a weary hand across her forehead. "Willie dear, the factory! It will mean disgrace."

Uncle agreed, asking what Mother could be thinking. How she could even consider it? He had always thought her so sensible, he said. Surely she must realise how it would affect my father?

"You'll have to talk to Tommy, dear. You'll have to talk to him, that's all. We cannot allow this to happen."

It dawned on me then that neither of them knew anything about my mother's drinking. I felt guilty concealing it yet did not like to mention it for fear they would consider it improper. What their reaction would be when they did find out was something I did not care to ponder.

"Well!" said Uncle, throwing up his arms. "The best laid plans of mice and men." He shook his head and walked across to the window where he stood looking out.

Auntie waited for him to speak, and when he did not turn around, she said, "You might as well tell her now dear," and began herself to inform me that Uncle had hoped to secure a place for me in the courthouse when I finished school. She must have seen the excitement on my face, because her hand went up immediately.

"Not a word to anyone, mind," she made me promise. Nothing further was said about it then as Auntie grasped the edges of her chair and began to rise. Her eyes had a look of pain in them and she made groaning sounds. Rheumatism, she told me was what was ailing her, and hoped I would never suffer it. She dragged herself laboriously to the door and disappeared along the hall. Uncle shook his head worriedly. Any other day, he said, he could have managed the bar quite nicely on his own, but not today. Not with a match at Nolan's Park, a stone's throw from the premises.

"Perhaps I could help," I offered, but Uncle didn't think it a good idea, and even if he did, he said, Auntie wouldn't agree. It was almost four o'clock and the sound of voices in the street told it was time to open. I called goodbye to Auntie from the bottom of the stairs, kissed Uncle on the cheek, and left for home.

24

Sadly, Uncle's plans for a job for me at the courthouse would never come to pass. One Saturday evening later, I was standing on the steps outside Smithwick's shop, waiting for my father to finish work. I had decided to tell him about Uncle's plans, or to find out whether he had heard anything. As a rule, he finished work at five o'clock, but because the last cartload of spirits had arrived late, it was now past five. Through the glass window in the door, I watched him fold the invoice and stuff it in the pigeonhole beside the office door.

The rest will wait until Monday," he said, coming through the door. He took my arm. "Come on pet," he said, hurrying me down the steps, "or there will be wigs on the green if I don't get home."

He was referring to Mother's anger at his being late. Somehow she had a fixed idea that he was always late when in fact he seldom was. Today she would have a legitimate complaint. I hoped for his sake she would not be in one of her miserable moods. We walked a little way in silence before Father said, "A man can't win in this world, pet, not when the odds are stacked against him. He's damned if he does and he's damned if he doesn't."

I looked at him quizzically and he explained.

"Take that cart, for instance. Helping to unload it had never been my responsibility."

It was the duty of another man, he said, but once or twice when the cart was late he had offered to stay and help the man unload it. Then one summer the man took ill and never returned to work, and before Father knew it the job was his. Now every time the cart was late he was expected to stay and help unload. He had tired of the struggle of trying to get ahead, he said, working like a dog with nothing to show for it. To make matters worse, earlier that year the company had hired a young lad to assist at shop, and more and more he was taking over Father's duties while Father found himself doing less important things.

"Could you not find a job somewhere else?" I asked, and he shook his head. The idea was forever present in his mind, but the task was easier to think about than to accomplish. At forty-eight there was little chance of anyone willing to hire him.

I made several attempts as we walked along to tell him what I had learned at Auntie's house, but was prevented each time by a passerby wanting to speak to Father. Just when it seemed the moment had arrived, something else took our attention—a man lying face down in the gutter.

A drunk most likely, I thought, and was prepared to hurry by, but Father said no, it was a man he knew, an epileptic. He bent down to investigate. It was indeed, and I stood quietly by while he helped the stricken man. The seizure passed and the man rose shakily to his feet, thanking Father. Some words passed between them and the man left. Father shook his head.

"The world is an ugly place at times," he said, and began to relate some of the sad experiences he had had. Before I knew it we were at our house.

"Late again," Mother scowled, as we came through the door. Father explained about the cart and our encounter with the man. He then went to the scullery to wash his hands, picking up the newspaper from a chair on his way back.

"Now put that down," Mother said, "and eat your dinner while it's still hot."

She laid his plate in front of him and sat opposite.

"Why don't you talk up for yourself and not let them walk all over you?" she asked, and Father sighed, repeating the fact that he had done so many times already.

"You're not bold enough, that's your trouble. You've got to assert yourself, and let them know you won't put up with it."

"What? And get myself sacked?"

"Ah! you have no gumption," Mother taunted. She wouldn't mind, she said, if they would offer to pay him extra, but they never did—or so she was led to believe.

"Now what is that supposed to mean?" Father asked, adding that she knew full well what his wages were.

"Oh! do I indeed?" Mother scoffed. She knew only what he chose to tell her, she said, or what she managed to stumble on herself, like the money hidden in the trunk beneath his bed.

"Thought to hide it from me, did you?"

Father, disbelieving, attempted to explain that there was no deceit intended, but Mother, on her high horse now, refused to listen. Nothing he could say would make any difference, she said. She had known all along that the money was there and felt justified in taking what she needed. Father leaped up from the table, his hands in fists above his head, and my stomach tightened. Then, with a sigh, he sank back down in his chair, defeated.

"I don't believe it," was all he said. "I simply don't believe it!"

"What don't you believe?" Mother asked.

"That you would stoop so low as to steal from me, and feel justified in doing it." He shook his head. Mother replied that she didn't see it as stealing, that she had a right to share in whatever money he brought home.

"You had no right, no right at all. It was all the money I had, every penny of my savings. And what am I to do now? How am I to meet my obligations?"

Mother shrugged. That was his affair, she said, and he could meet them the same way she met hers, labouring night and day to keep a home together. At this Father lost his temper.

"Home! You call this a home?" he shouted, and the argument began.

I stood in the scullery listening as their words became mean and rapid, with each one trying to outdo the other, until neither of them cared what the other said. The house swelled with accusations and sounds carried outward through the windows to the street. Even the younger ones playing in the yard were too frightened to come in. Eventually, however, the anger died. Father left the table and Mother brought his half-empty dishes to the scullery. I thought by the way she looked at me that she was sorry now, regretting the whole incident. But maybe it was wishful thinking, that she simply had enough of quarrelling and was longing for a drink, because a short while later when Father left the house and she heard the front door close, she got ready to go out.

The silence between my parents grew deeper and more bearable as time went on, but only because Mother was seldom home when Father was. On Sundays he shut himself away from her, the knowledge he could no longer trust her eating at his heart. Besides the money missing from the box beneath his bed, his small collection of coins and stamps was also gone, among them his precious Penny Blacks. One terrible row behind closed doors had followed his discovery of the missing coins, with Mother claiming to have used the money for food and clothing, and Father for the first time since they married not believing her. The fact that she would stoop so low as to steal repelled him.

Gradually he became a changed man, the once open malleable mind becoming closed and suspicious. All along he had thought her drinking confined to the privacy of home and not exposed to the prying eyes of Kilkenny, but now he knew that he had been mistaken.

Several weeks had passed since my Mother's ultimatum to me, and I had hoped somehow that she had reconsidered or that Auntie had spoken to her. But soon I began to realise the futility of the situation, with Father's savings gone and Mother's constant nagging.

"You know as well as I do that your father can't afford to go on paying for your schooling. Be sensible," she would say. She had had her big ideas at my age also, she said. That was only natural, but a person had to face reality. There were bills to be paid and mouths to be fed, and she couldn't handle it by herself. The sadness in her voice when she spoke like this always bothered me.

Maybe going to work wouldn't be so bad. At least a job would bring me independence, and there were worse things than working in a factory. Besides, the chances of my finding work anywhere other than in a factory were virtually non-existent. Woolworth's was the only place besides the factory where a girl might find employment, but the wages there were less than half to be gotten at a factory. If one had to be humiliated, I decided, one might as well be well paid for it.

Padmore and Barnes the company was called, but people simply referred to it as the Boot Factory. It was situated on the other side of town. I dragged myself across John's Bridge in its direction, wondering as I did what awaited me and how my father would react when he found out. As I walked along with spirits low I tried to think of working as glamorous, a more exciting life. At least I would have something to look forward to on Friday nights when I got paid and for the first time in my life I would have money of my own. That thought alone was encouraging. I began to walk faster through the busy streets until finally I turned the corner to Wolfe Tone Street and found myself outside the factory.

A few months later I was working there.

25

The streets of our town, with names like Wolfe Tone, Emmett, and Parnell, were history lessons in themselves. A few bore the names of churches they had grown up around, Friary, Canice, and Abbey. You could stroll down any one of them and roll back the centuries to some medieval happening. Of all of them, Abbey Street, with its quaint thatched houses and great stone arch, was my favourite. Half-hidden under water when the river rose, and scarred with the boots of the Black and Tans, a street of many sorrows one could have called it, every corner with its ghosts and its reminders of the past. Residents here had known great suffering and had survived.

Mostly old people were living there when I was growing up, and those children that did live there had gone before I left the city. I used to wonder how they all fit into such tiny houses, yet the cramped space hadn't seemed to bother them. Some had no gardens front or back, and the children played their games on the cobbled streets and sang as we had done before them.

Most of the games we played had been handed down, the oldest ones invariably with some bearing on the past, though we didn't know this at the time. One game, a favourite of most children, had found expression from the shameful outcome of the famine years when mothers had been forced to give away their children. "The Old Woman from Bantry," it was called and it went like this:

There came an old woman from Bantry Tide,
With all her children by her side,
She asked to know if you'd take one in,
Please, take one in.

One child, usually a girl, would skip around from door to imaginary door, six children in tow begging their acceptance and calling out their attributes.

This can knit and this can sew,
This can make the Lily White grow,
This can dance and this can sing,
This can't do anything.

Some kindly souls would show pity and take one in. Others would slam their imaginary doors. But no matter what the outcome, the youngest and least qualified usually got left with the mother. Ah yes! It was a noble street and I loved it well. In one of the houses near the Great Arch my grandparents had lived, and my parents for a few years in the house beside. Grandmother's house was a little larger than the rest and older too, smelling, my mother said, of obvious decay. And she was probably right, for it was barricaded up after my Uncle Jim left and allowed to fall into ruin.

Beyond the Great Arch was a row of smaller houses, one of which was Farrell's, and outside whose door a bicycle stripped of all its pieces could be seen most days naked on its saddle. The family, there when I was born, remained long after I had

164

left the town. The Farrells' friendship, one that lasted all our living days there, was not as much perpetuated by the parents as by the ongoing friendship of their children. By the time we reached our teens the house had become part and parcel of our lives, and we could never pass its door without going inside.

Mr. Farrell, a small friendly man with bloodshot eyes and hardly any teeth, wore the same pinstripe suit most days of his life. He had a large gentle wife and six children, three of whom were girls. He was a man of many talents and loved to play the fiddle, the accordion or any other instrument one cared to offer him. At certain hours most days of the week Joe, as he was known to us, could be found outside his door mending someone's bicycle or sitting by the window in his kitchen repairing clocks and watches. At any time of the day or night he could tell a visitor what hour it was by the numerous clocks about the room or by the heaps of watches on his window sill. Any spare time he had he spent fishing.

The best fisherman in the county, some people said, and judging by the cap upon his head you might well believe it. In all the years I had known him I had never seen him take it off. I supposed it was glued to his forehead, a shapeless mass filled to every fibre with fishhooks and flies. What he didn't know about fishing had little need to be known. Everybody I knew loved and respected him.

Mrs. Farrell died before I had a chance to know her well, but I recall her standing by the small front door, her large frame filling up the opening. A soft-spoken woman I barely remember, yet for whom I had a fondness.

By the time I was old enough to frequent their house without the company of an adult the family had gotten smaller. Dick, Paddy and Birdie were the only ones at home. It was Birdie mainly that kept us going there. A diminutive girl in her middle teens whose hands were forever flying to her face in some dismay, she was best friend to my sister Chris. Seldom was one seen without the other. Birdie was an intensely shy and weak-sighted girl, obliged to wear thick glasses all the time. Her two top teeth protruded, and her hair, as limp as a rag doll's, fell down around her forehead. Naive to the point of ignorance and steeped in superstition, she was drawn like a magnet to anything bizarre.

We youngsters had great fun with her, absconding with her glasses and leading her into ridiculous plights. In a way she had herself to blame, because she was older than we and should have known better. I remember well the last prank Jane and I played on her. Both of us standing by our garden gate had seen her coming up the street and fled inside to alert Sheilagh, who sprawled herself out on the kitchen floor pretending to be dead, her face smeared with the juice of red berries.

"Oh hurry, Birdie, hurry," Jane called, as though just catching sight of her. We all reached the kitchen door together, whereupon Birdie, catching sight of Sheilagh on the floor, promptly fainted. By the time we revived her completely we had scared ourselves. She forgave us as she always did, but the incident taught us a lesson.

Times were changing, and before we knew it we had all grown up. Chris had gone to England, and Birdie had finally married though she still lived at home. Dick, the eldest and not yet married, also wore thick glasses. Like his father, he had a flare for music and could play any tune. A likeable shy sort of chap with a ready smile, he was intensely religious, fasting and drinking black tea during the weeks of Lent and sleeping on bare boards with chains around his body in the manner of Matt Talbot, the Dublin docker. We younger ones thought he was daft for doing it, but the older ones respected him. Dick had been friend to my brother Joe, as Paddy was now to my sister Jane.

I found Birdie in the kitchen one day peeling new potatoes beside a great blazing fire. She was flushed and damp with per-spiration. She looked up when I entered, seemingly annoyed at my sudden appearance, and I guessed she had not heard me knock on the open front door. "Where is everybody?" I asked, and she pulled a frown, looking tired and touchy and loath to speak.

"I was supposed to meet Jane here," I said, and asked if she had seen her. She answered no, and why didn't I go and ask Mary Hayes? It was Birdie's way of telling me I wasn't wanted.

Apologising for my intrusion I left the room. Passing through the outside door again I heard their back door open, and glancing over my shoulder saw Dick standing in the hall, a strange expression on his face. He headed for the stairs midway along the hall and went up without even seeing me. I found that strange and wondered if he had seen an apparition. On tiptoe I backtracked to the bottom of the stairs and peered up after him. It had been at least ten years since their sister Babby had died in a room above, and we had heard tales that she appeared from time to time to members of the family.

Whether it was true or not I couldn't say. But I could never forget what Babby had once told me. I had gone with Chris to visit her. It was the first and only time I had been upstairs, and I remember well the cold unpleasant feeling that had travelled up my spine, the smell of death on everything. With one leg already missing and the other soon to go and consumption eating at her arms and face, Babby had managed to be cheerful, smiling when we entered and allowing Chris to prop her up so she could chat with us. The prospect of death didn't worry her at all, she told me, because her own dear dead mother was waiting invisible by the door and watching over her. To this day I remember her telling me that, and I often wondered if she had made it up or actually saw something that we couldn't see.

I heard Dick move about quietly overhead, and when he didn't come down again, I left.

26

Outside in the street I heard someone shout,
and hurried down the hill expecting to find
Jane around the corner, but she wasn't there.
The shouting was coming from a man riding
on a donkey in the middle of the road, a gal-
vanised pail in one hand, a long-handled
broom in the other.

R oll up! Roll up! Roll up! and see, a horse's head where his
tail should be."

I knew immediately the carnival had arrived. Every lamp-post and shop window had a poster advertising it.

LINDBERGH'S DEATH DIVE—DARING AND UNNATURAL, the one pasted to Kieran Conway's pub window said, and it featured a tiny pool at the bottom of a metal tower reaching to the sky. One could barely see the figure of a man standing on a plat-form at the very top. From the poster I learned that the car-nival had come to the Market Square and I wished that it had not. For years it had come to the Fair Green, where all we had to do was climb over the wall to get to it. With barred walls and iron gates surrounding the Market Square we would be obliged to pay.

A small crowd of people had gathered at the gates watching the proceedings going on inside. Among them I recognised my sister Jane standing with Maizie Dooley, and Billy Bood beside them. I walked over to them and a few seconds later Paddy Farrell arrived. All of us had changed since that day beside the river, but none more so than Maizie. Immediately on reaching her fourteenth birthday her myopia had disappeared and seldom now, if ever, was she seen out with glasses. Her freckles, too, had vanished and her cheeks heightened with a dab of Rebel Rouge gave her eyes a voluptuous expression. She had also managed to control her hair, which was red and used to stand out from her head like electric wire. You couldn't say she was pretty, mind, but close to being attractive, which was a shock to us because none of us expected her to turn out so well.

As far as I knew she had lost most of her nasty habits, though I still wouldn't have trusted my fingers to her care. Paddy, of course, had matured at last and grown more level-headed, though he still possessed an innocence. He and Jane had remained good friends.

Billy Bood McGuire was the one who had changed the least, his black shiny hair still plastered to his head. He had left the hero-worship stage, but still adhered to his George Raft image. Chewing gum had become his habit when he ran out of fags, cracking it between his teeth for everyone to hear. As usual he was out of work, finding it hard or not trying hard enough to keep a job. The arguments were endless.

"I'll go next week," was his usual reply when he heard of one available.

"Next week? You'll be there by ten o'clock the day before tomorrow," and his mother would push him out to apply.

The amazing thing was that he would get the job but always fail to hold onto it. One couldn't help liking him all the same. He was a gentle lad for whom I sometimes felt great pity for the way he stored his dreams deep inside his heart, extracting miracles from them whenever he was down yet knowing full well they would never happen.

Polite amusement and mixed approval were expressed at my arrival.

"Speak of the devil and he's sure to turn up," from Maizie, a casual nod from Billy and a barely audible salute from Jane, who was either out of sorts or worried about something, judging by the way she kept looking at me and turning away abruptly. Evidently she had changed her mind about coming with me to Auntie's house, because she was careful not to mention it. I hung around with them for a little while, observing Maizie peddle her charms to the fellows from the carnival, sashaying about in her tartan skirt, her eyes filled with promises. But promise is as promise does, and Maizie despite her common bearing was thought to be a decent girl. Though I had my doubts at times, laughing and joking with the boys as she always was, herself and Nuala Brannigan.

Unlike Nuala though, Maizie lacked that amplitude of flesh so vital to the female form, and the means by which she compensated Mother Nature's deficit was a much-debated topic. We all knew of course that she was stuffing her bra with her mother's nylon stockings, but short of physical molestation we had no way of proving it. She had become more voluble since I arrived, managing to shock the rest of us by strutting over to the market gate and chatting with the carnival lads inside, all of whom were dressed in soiled work clothes and looked as though they needed shaves. One of them sauntered over to her, his eyes on hold.

"And what's a lovely girl like you doing in a little town like this?"

We saw Maizie giggle and glance shyly at us. A few more compliments and she was inside the gate, forgetting us entirely.

"Oh, that girl," Jane hissed, looking around hurriedly.

"Well, what do you expect? You know what she's like," Billy said, enumerating all of Maizie's indiscretions and getting Paddy so charged up as to take himself over to the market gate to order Maizie out. The result, as I recall, was comical, with Paddy pacing back and forth calling to Maizie to come outside.

"Have you no pride at all?" he asked, pressing his face against the bars while Maizie, responding with a lewd expression, sat herself down on a concrete slab in the manner of a model. He should have walked away then and let things be, but diplomacy was never one of Paddy's virtues.

"If ya don't come out this minute, I'm going in there to get ya." A ripple of laughter sounded from the lads inside the gate, but a few supporting voices on our side gave Paddy courage. He opened the gate and stepped inside. Seemingly from nowhere a tall blond lad with shoulders wide as the Khyber Pass stepped in front of him. Something resembling a skirmish followed before Paddy, looking dazed and choking with embarrassment, hurried back to us.

He looked at Jane and threw a venomous scowl at Billy and myself, who were trying to hide our laughter.

"I'm not afraid of that yoke, if that's what yeer thinkin'," he said.

"You did the right thing, Paddy. Don't mind them," Jane said, adding that Maizie had no shame and needed to be told. "Honestly," she sighed, "there are times when I could murder her. Just look at the way she's sitting!" All of us looked across at Maizie sitting with her skirt above her knees, her body braced upon her palms.

"Oh, she's just doing that on purpose," Billy said. "You know what she's like." He turned to Paddy. "Give us a fag, man," he asked, in an effort to put things right between them.

Paddy obliged, lighting it with a wooden match, then with his nail tossed the match stub halfway across the square. They peered at us through a haze of smoke before Billy, with unbelievable casualness, remarked, "I wouldn't mind, but all those fellows want is to feel her diddies, and have her up the pole before she knows what happened."

Jane, whose head had been averted, whirled around. "Billy Bood! My God! May I remind you that there is a young person present. Do you have to be so crude?" Her eyes went wide. Billy began to apologise when Paddy, shooting me a scornful look, prevented him.

"Ah! she knows more than she lets on. Don't kid yourself." Paddy whispered something into Billy's ear, whereupon the two of them began conferring openly about the male physique and using various euphemisms to express their coarsest thoughts and indecent observations of the filthy things boys do to girls.

Contrary to Paddy's claim it was a subject I knew little of, having started life in a cabbage patch, so I listened in a twilight of interest and disgust until finally they stopped.

"You girls are far too innocent. It's time you grew up and faced the facts," Billy said.

"And what facts are those?" Jane asked indignantly, regretting instantly that she had, for she now learned of something that she would rather not have known.

It concerned a girl called Mary Lonnigan who we all thought was married and living happily in Dublin, but who according to Billy was in Clonmel in the home for wayward women.

"I don't believe it," Jane said. "Not Ladybug!"

It was the nickname Mary had earned at school in response to her educated notion that God's Cows were ladybugs. So obsessed had she been with this little bug in her early days at school that she carried one about in a matchbox everywhere she went. Ladybug, she insisted was the proper name, to the merriment of everybody present. She knew, she said, because she had seen it in a storybook. And so she had, as we found out later, though we did not believe it at the time. God's Cow was the name we had always given to the little bug, and considered Mary silly.

"Poor Ladybug!" Jane said, recalling the times she had walked to school with her; crossing the creamery yard in winter, her coat pulled tight around her and Mary with hers wide open, flapping in the wind, her black sleek curls scattering on her head. A Viking, Jane said, was what she looked like, her face the face men carved on ships but her manner always modest. She couldn't bear to think of Mary being locked up, she who loved to walk bareheaded in the rain, who had every lad's attention but had eyes for none but Jimmy Gallagher. How could he have disgraced and then deserted her?

Billy was right. We were too innocent. We had no knowledge of animal desire, that destructive chemistry that unites people's minds and flows like electric current through the contact of their hands. Sex is what they call it now, but what did I know of it way back then? Even the word was a mystery to me and it would be years before I would discover for myself the biologic urge that moves young men to mindless acts and renders women impervious to the thousand shocks that flesh of ours is heir to. I knew what it meant to be pregnant, mind, and that it happened to women who allowed men to do certain things to them. But what these things were and exactly how they caused you to be pregnant was never clear. That such a thing could happen to a gentle girl like Ladybug was frightening, and it would keep me from getting close to any boy for years.

Billy insisted that he only told the story for our own protection, because if it could happen to Ladybug it could happen to anyone. His words brought our minds again to Maizie. Jane called and called to her but she wouldn't come, nestled in the arms of her sent-from-heaven worshipper.

"Brazen thing," Jane muttered, and vowed never to associate with her again. Billy gave her a fishy look as if to say he had heard that before.

Inwardly I thought the same, and felt though I didn't say that her annoyance stemmed not merely from the fact that Maizie had deserted her, but because she yearned for a little of that attention too. She watched Maizie for a little while then turned away. It was the excuse I had been waiting for, and I used it to talk her into leaving. Some moments later we were on our way to Auntie's house.

27

It had been over a year since I had been to Auntie's house, partly because I was ashamed to go, and partly because of Mother. Somehow Auntie had learned about her drinking, and had made it understood that she wanted no connection with the family, except for my father and Uncle Jim. My working at the factory hadn't helped matters either, and in that respect alone I felt responsible, for I knew she had meant well by me.

Auntie came to the door in a flurry of surprise, glancing up and down the street before admitting us. But once inside, embracing us, big wet tears falling down her face, she was so palpably distraught she could hardly speak. We followed her into the front room where we all sat down, she not saying anything, just staring at the fire and waiting for one of us to speak. I looked to Jane beseechingly, but her face was blank. I did my best to start a conversation, beginning with an explanation as to why I had taken the factory job. Auntie nodded her acknowledgement.

"You should have warned us all the same, dear. If you had warned us," she said, "all that unpleasantness might have been avoided."

I had no idea what she was talking about, but the look on Jane's face told me that she understood.

"Your mother is a disgrace to all of us," Auntie moaned, then looking pointedly at Jane, "You know what I'm talking about, you were here."

Jane's face went crimson as she glanced at me before lowering her eyes. I was fired with curiosity and resolved to question her when we got outside. Auntie went on to say that Uncle had suffered embarrassment arranging things for me, not knowing I was working in the factory.

Even if he had managed to arrange an interview, she added, she was doubtful that I would have been given the job. "All this business with your mother," she said, flicking her fingers.

I thanked her for any effort she had made on my behalf and asked if I might speak with Uncle who was serving in the bar. She nodded and I left the room. I found him leaning on the counter reading the *Free Press*. I told him that Jane was in with Auntie and explained the reason for our coming.

"I'm sorry for all the trouble I've caused," I said, very near to tears.

He looked at me with his melancholy eyes.

"Not at all, pet. Not at all. You have nothing to be sorry for." His strong arms went around me, his heart close to mine, and I felt the urge to hold on to him as he loosened his grip and stepped back to look at me. His face was pale and drawn, I thought, with more grey hair than I had ever noticed.

"You look tired," I said, a transient fear passing through my mind.

"Exhausted!" he corrected jokingly, pulling a haggard expression.

It made him sick, he said, to think about what had happened. But things would take a turn for the better yet and as time went by it would all work out.

"I hope so," I told him truthfully.

The pub door opened and some customers came in.

"It was good of you to come," he said, "and don't mind your Auntie grumbling, she doesn't mean it. She feels the same way I do about all of you." He kissed me gently on the forehead and went back into the bar.

"Well, if we are going to go, we had better move," I said to Jane some minutes later.

"Oh! you didn't come all this way to leave again," Auntie protested lamely, already out of her chair and halfway to the door.

When we got around the corner I turned to Jane.

"I know what you're thinking, but I couldn't tell you before," she said.

Then she explained that some months earlier she had been visiting with Auntie when Mother arrived unexpectedly. It was obvious she had been drinking, and Auntie, shocked, ignored her request for another drink and offered tea instead. Mother, insulted, became coarse and abusive.

"One drink. One fecking drink is all I ask," she had argued. Auntie remained adamant and a torrent of insults followed, ending with Auntie asking Mother to leave.

I was doubtful. "I don't believe it. Mam would never swear like that in front of anyone."

"She would when she has drink in her," was all Jane said. I felt sick with anger, for I had believed my mother when she told me she had taken the pledge. My heart was heavy as we headed home, thinking about all that had gone before.

IT HAD TAKEN ME ALMOST two years to settle at the factory. From the moment I put my foot inside its doors I hated it. It wasn't that the factory itself was all that bad. The building was agreeable with no gothic overhangs or iron bars. There were no rats inside, and the roof, a mixture of wire and heavy glass, was tinted green in the summer. Unlike other factories and mills it was bright and clean.

However, the very fact that I was working there was demeaning, isolating me from the groups of friends I had known before. Some would scarcely talk to, much less associate with a factory hand, no matter how well we had once got along or how many games we had played at school. Girls whom I had known since childhood began avoiding me, some never speaking to me again. Others, wanting to be kind but not wanting to be seen with me, would smile and hurry on. Though I made new friends at the factory I found myself subjected to the constant taunts and spiteful acts of certain supervisors there. Yet even to them I owe a small measure of gratitude. Their persecution helped to strengthen my character in a way that no amount of schooling could. All in all my life at the factory was bearable.

At home, too, things were peaceful. Mother argued less, and her attitude toward me had changed completely. Now, instead of being "too smart for my own good" I had, to anyone who cared to listen, "a good head on my shoulders," and might have gone far had the Good Lord willed it. That it was *her* will that kept me in the factory was never mentioned. After one or two futile attempts to change her mind I had given up.

My independence also turned out to be a fantasy, for Mother kept a watchful eye on me, making sure I handed up my pay envelope unopened every week. Initially she gave me back one shilling, increased to two and sixpence by the end of two years. From that I had to dress myself and pay for any luxuries I might desire. Yet I was content, the thought that I was helping Father a compensation. I did my best to make things up to him. His disappointment at my leaving school seemed to go on forever, but as time went by he resigned himself to my betrayal and like myself clung to the hope that things might change. I should have realised by then that I could never change the situation in our home any more than I could stop the sun from shining.

Many families besides our own made swift descents from positions of comparative affluence to ones of relative poverty, but most made it back up the ladder to security. So, too, might we have done had we not had to wrestle with the ultimate disgrace of Mother slipping in and out of pubs around the city or being seen in the company of women known to be found drunk in doorways.

There were no secrets in Kilkenny. For a time Mother had tried, had taken the pledge, had paid all her debts and for weeks the house had been happy with her laughter.

All that changed very quickly. Mother yielded again to temptation and was once more riding a merry-go-round to disaster.

28

Winter came with driving rains and cold winds that swept down from the hills and roared across the valley, and on the day my Uncle Willie died it was still lashing. I had seen him earlier that day, bumping into him by accident on my way home from work. He, huddled beneath his huge umbrella, and myself, head down against the sleety rain, almost passed each other in the street. I had looked up at the last moment and recognised his coat. We stood for a moment chatting.

A re you all right Uncle?" I asked, noting the greenish colour of his face and the weariness in his manner.

"I'm fine, pet," he answered, smiling, and told me not to worry.

"Well, if you're sure," I said, lingering. "Only you look a little pale." Still concerned, I looked back when I reached the corner of the street, but then continued home.

A few hours later Uncle was dead. I didn't hear the news until dinnertime next day and as soon as I finished work I hurried over. The house grey and gaunt against the fading light looked as though it, too, had died, the curtains closed across the windows and a black crepe hanging from the knocker. I tapped lightly on the door and when no one came to open it I tried the knob. The door opened easily and I went inside.

Voices were coming from a room upstairs and I stood in the hall listening. Then on tiptoe I started up the stairs. When I reached the top I saw my mother standing talking by an open door. She seemed surprised, saying nothing at first, then shaking her head in sympathy she beckoned me along. There was no sign of Auntie. The bed I had expected to find Uncle in was fully dressed and heaped with flowers. A lone candle flickered on a table in one corner and in the centre of the room I saw the coffin. It was already closed with a purple ribbon draped over it and a red devotional lamp on top. On a wall behind was a large picture of the Sacred Heart, his eyes pained and sorrowful, looking down on it. It didn't seem to me like a wake at all with people standing chatting. Except for the heavy odour coming from the flowers there was no other smell.

I walked in and stood alone beside the coffin, wanting to see poor Uncle's face and wondering why they had closed the lid. Nobody came to enlighten me, so after a decent interval I crossed myself and went downstairs. In the kitchen I found Mother drying glasses by the sink.

"Stay for a while," she said, thinking I was leaving, and I pulled a chair over and sat beside the table. A kettle simmered quietly on the range nearby and she walked across to it, asking if I would like some tea or maybe something stronger? I told her that I wanted nothing

"Never mind girl, never mind, he's gone," she sighed, and answered the question already on my mind. The coffin had been closed because Auntie had no stomach for a long exposure.

"He died peacefully at any rate," she said, explaining about the heart attack.

"I would like to have seen him all the same," I said, and she nodded.

"Well don't get het up about it now," she said, and continued talking. I sat quietly and listened, giving her a chance to say some things she had wanted to and complain in a gentle voice about others. Little was said about Auntie as memory led us back along the road to yesterday, with Mother recounting old tales of yore and bringing Uncle back with a sigh or smile.

"He was different altogether from her," she said, her voice cracking. "There'll never be another like him," she choked.

I knew what it was she had wanted to say—Uncle, a man who had loved the poorest creatures on the earth and served them all, had to be the one taken. Only on one occasion before had I seen my mother crying. It made me feel uncomfortable and for a few moments we said nothing, staring at our hands. Then we heard the hall clock strike and Mother spoke.

"Sure you won't change your mind and have a sherry?" she asked, and I shook my head, not wanting to provide her with an opportunity to drink, yet at that instant realising that she was cold sober, her eyes only watery from crying.

"Have one yourself," I blurted guiltily.

She shook her head and said nothing, but a queer expression passed across her face as though she had guessed what I was thinking. I felt a terrible sense of shame. It had been a chance for me to speak with her about her drinking habit, but I had let it pass. So tired she looked and so downtrodden, her work-worn fingers spread out in front of me. Seeing them there reminded me of the years she had spent in servitude, the hardships she had endured. How could I bring myself to mention her failing, force her to admit that she was a drunk or extract from her a promise that each of us knew she could never keep? And though I longed to know the origin or nature of the secret pain that drove her to destruction I couldn't bring myself to question her or interrupt this moment of intimacy, for she had gripped my hand in an effort to convey her deep and inner feelings.

Suddenly I found myself resenting Auntie. Was she truly lying in her bed exhausted or just avoiding Mother? A peasant was all that Mother was to her, rough-hewn and tempered by the harshness of a class cursed with grinding poverty, while about Auntie and her kind there was always a subtle quality, a gentility that even in the most trying situations remained unchanged. That gulf between them had always been there, would always be, bridged only by the fact that Mother was married to her brother.

Yet here Mother was as usual, single-handedly taking care of everything. She had washed and laid out Uncle all by herself, and arranged the funeral and the flowers. The slice of bread set out in front of her was the only meal she had had all day. Outside the latticed window the wind battered furiously and rain slapped steadily against the panes as she looked around the kitchen sighing.

"The light has gone from this house forever girl," she began, but then someone called and she rose wearily and left the kitchen.

I followed her into the next room where whiskies and brandies were being handed out amid the smell of pipe tobacco. Mourners stood about in groups whispering, some a mite unsteady, some staring into space and one or two weeping. A few clustered around Mother, saying what a good man Uncle was and how they were going to miss him. I felt a scream rising in my throat though I wasn't sure why, so I made my way into the small front room where I sat alone in my usual chair, remembering. The room felt cold and empty with a slight musty air, the result of too much rain. Had Uncle been alive there would have been a great fire burning and music coming from the gramophone. I laid my head against the chair, remembering how he liked to sing along with it, always out of tune.

I did not attend the funeral—we were not allowed and I never found out why, though I remember hearing that the cemetery was crowded. As the weeks and months went by

Uncle's memory began to fade. Auntie sold the premises and went to live in a private home for ladies of her class, where she clung to her privacy like a barnacle to a boat. She made no friends but was always happy with a visit from us. My mother's kindness at the time of Uncle's death had made a sort of truce between them and she welcomed Mother, but only on the Sabbath when she was certain to be sober.

Life continued on at our house as before, except that now Mother could be seen coming and going openly from pubs around the city. Many of her friends were common drunks, careless in dress and coarse in tongue. Relations with my father had deteriorated to a point where constant rows were commonplace with things reaching a fever pitch on Saturdays, when he was compelled to grapple with the truth. A perpetual air of depression hung over the house and I waited impatiently to be twenty-one.

One day a year or so after Uncle died I came home from work to find the house and larder empty. There was no fire in the grate, and no coal or wood with which to light one. Little Jack and Jim waited in the kitchen, hungry. For months I had been aware of a scarcity of food—some days with nothing but an egg for dinner—but the larder had never been totally bare. When Mother came home that evening I had it out with her. It was the beginning of a long and painful series of arguments, our emotions driven like the tides.

The situation was made worse by my father's inability to interfere. Every day he floundered in a bog of indecision, seeming utterly unable to accept the truth of Mother's conduct and too fearful to agitate an already volatile situation. Occasionally he would lose his temper and threaten some dire action, but mostly he refrained from doing anything. His pride was overwhelming, and that pride, so characteristic of people fallen down the social scale, was intensified by fear. More than hunger, cold or even death, he feared the loss of his respectability, of being talked about by others. More and more he withdrew into himself, seldom saying anything and ceasing to be of any comfort to the family. This angered me, because I could see no sense to it and we had no one else to whom we could turn.

As time went on a cruel and vicious rivalry developed with each one doing their best to overrule the other. We children were caught like minnows in the middle, pulled from one side to the other. To make matters worse Father's supervision over us became excessive, his rules regimental, as too often we were summoned to account for our activities or penalised for imaginary offences.

Life became intolerable and it wasn't long before Sheilagh, having reached a point of desperation, decided to leave home. Her departure left a lesion on my heart, because for months she had filled for me the vacant spot left by my mother.

It seems a harsh and bitter thing to say, but I had the impression at the time that Father often viewed *us* as the enemy and Mother as but an innocent bystander. As time passed an estrangement grew between us, its presence affecting everything I did. I had loved him more than I had ever loved my mother, and everything I had done or ever hoped to do was with him in mind.

Yet I remember at times almost hating him, and I can close my eyes this minute and picture the scene on a Friday night: me sitting at the table by the window waiting for Mother to come home and give me my allowance from my unopened pay packet, and Father emerging from another room, ceremoniously donning his glasses. Then, tight-lipped and officious, he would examine the details written on the packet. There was nothing said, no word of praise, no kind remark about my contribution. The rift between us widened.

29

As the weeks passed, I hardly noticed that the harsh winter had softened into spring, until I saw the first snowdrop. The year was 1947. Rarely did we see snow in Kilkenny, but that winter had been memorable, the snowfall heavy. Now, with the onset of mild weather, melting snow, still heavy in the hills and driven by torrential rains, began to fill the streams and rivers. Many fields upcountry were already flooded, and tales of small disasters began to seep into the town. Not everyone believed these stories, mind; most of them were second-hand, and possibly spun from over-imaginations. Whatever the truth, as I hurried down the lane to the Old Man's house on Kenny's Well Road, I gave no thought to them.

The sky this day was glorious, not a cloud in sight, the kind of day for a stroll along the river. I had not seen the Old Man in months, mainly because I was always busy and seldom had a chance to go look for him. Today however I saw smoke coming from his chimney, and I stood for a moment outside the house gathering the courage to approach the door. We Irish, you see, are a funny lot. Famous for our hospitality, we will do anything for anybody, but don't ask us to go knocking on someone else's door unless we have an invitation.

I had never been inside the Old Man's house. I stood outside a moment, looking up and down. Then I passed inside the gate and gave the door a thump, for it had no knocker. It was opened almost immediately.

"Well, be th'hokey pokey!" He was so pleased to see me.

"Come on in, why don't ye? And don't mind them," he added, referring to whomever might be watching. He was heartily glad to see me and brushed aside my apologies.

"There's tea in th'pot," he said, when he had closed the door.

"I'll pour ye some." Then hesitating. "Or milk if ye'd prefer?" I told him that I wanted nothing.

"Sit down then, sit down." He pointed to a chair beside the fire and sat in the corner opposite.

"Faith an' 'tis grand t'see ye. Yer lookin' well."

I thanked him and asked how he had been, aware of his cough and his loss of weight, the way his shirt hung loose around his neck and the light stains on the front of it. He had aged since I had seen him last.

"Ah! sure I'm not too bad at all considerin'. I do me best."

A quick glance around the room confirmed it. For an Old Man living by himself the room was spotless. There was little furniture, just two chairs and a table in the middle, a sideboard taking up one wall and a bookcase the other. The red linoleum covering the floor was worn in several places but had recently been polished. One tiny window looked out to the back and another to the street out front. Through an opening in one wall I could see the corner of a large brass bed and a scullery close by. The room was warm but very damp, with small beads of water trickling down the walls. Some pictures hanging near the chimney were stained brown with moisture. No wonder he spent the winters up at Mickey's house.

Behind the closed front door I noticed Meggie's bell and collar, but saw no sign of the little goat.

"Where is she?" I inquired, and his face went sad.

He nodded toward the yard out back. I walked to the window but couldn't see her anywhere, and was just about to say so when my eyes lighted on a fresh mound of earth alongside the geraniums. I looked back at him in disbelief.

"Aye!" he sighed, without looking up. "'Tis her there. She's gone." For a moment I was too stunned to speak.

"What happened?" I managed finally. He cleared his throat.

"It had t'be done child. There was nothin' I could do. I couldn't see her suffer. Some sort iv growth she had all along." My mind flashed back to that lovely sunny day when we walked along the riverbank with Meggie limping on the path in front of us.

"But that was so long ago," I said.

"I know, I know, t'was me own fault. I should've taken better care iv her. But what with wan thing an' another..." His voice trailed off and he turned quickly away. When he turned back he seemed calmer.

"Th'funny thing was, th'limp disappeared, so I thought she was okay. But all th'time she was sufferin', 'til in th'end she was whimperin' all times iv th'day an' night. I couldn't stand it." Clearly he was fighting his emotions as he continued to speak, blaming himself and saying that he could have done more for her.

"You did all you could," I told him. "How could you have known?" Hot tears were sliding down my own throat now and I kept my head averted. After a while he came and stood beside me.

"She's out iv her misery now at any rate, and God grant it won't be long before I'm out iv mine."

I looked up at him. His eyes were large and empty and I felt at once that I had let him down, that I had not been there when he needed me. Even when Mickey had died some weeks before I had not found time to visit him. His grief about Meggie must have been unbearable. If I could feel such sadness now, how must he have felt alone here in the house with her? I felt his hand upon my head.

"Don't let it worry ye child," he said, and walked back to his corner.

I followed, but hardly had we sat our bottoms down again when we heard a stamping of feet outside the door followed by a banging. The Old Man looked at me.

"Now who th'divil can that be?"

It was Chief Constable Barney Callaghan, muffled to the brows in a heavy coat and scarf. He stood outside the door for a minute then came inside and made directly for the fire, turning a pair of watery eyes on me but saying nothing. I expected the Old Man to show surprise, having heard many times of the feud between them, but he showed no emotion, just waited for Barney to say something. Finally he did, but not before explaining he had just returned from a fire scene at Willoughby's.

"One of the barns went up in flames," Barney said, "and took the cowshed with it. Lord, what a mess! You could hardly breathe, and cold, my God!"

He tightened up his shoulders in a shiver. The Old Man asked him how it happened and Barney said he didn't know.

"I'll have a cup of tea if there's one going," he said, walking to the table and cupping his hands around the warm teapot. The Old Man moved to get a cup and saucer, putting them down on the table with a clatter.

"Anywan'd think 'twas in th'Arctic ye were. 'Tis not that cold out surely?"

Barney sniffed.

"It is when you're standing out in it. That wind up there is woeful."

He took a slurp of tea, lit a cigarette and looked at me again, this time with more deliberation.

"You're not lost for company, I see," he remarked, and the Old Man grinned at me but said nothing. It occurred to me then how strange my presence must have seemed to Barney.

"I have just arrived myself, Mr. Callaghan," I said. "I needed to speak with Mr. Dempsey."

Taking the cigarette from his mouth he looked hard at me, his eyes narrowing, smoke trickling from his lips. Uncomfortable I glanced at the Old Man, who was obviously amused at my dilemma, not to mention Barney's curiosity. Not a solitary word did he contribute as he sat there drawing on his pipe and coughing.

"Look at you," said Barney, "sitting there puffing your head off, and with a cough like that. You smoke too bloody much, do you know that?"

"An' I suppose you don't? What is it now, twenty fags a day, or more maybe?"

Barney scoffed.

"It's not me I'm talking about, it's you. You'll go on until you kill yourself."

The Old Man pulled a wicked face.

"An' is that what ye came t'tell me?"

"No, it is not," said Barney, sipping at his tea. "As a matter of fact, I'm not here on a social visit."

"No!" came a surprised response from the Old Man, with a look that said "you could have fooled me."

Barney fiddled with his coat before continuing. He had come, he said, about the current situation, not making his point specific yet wanting to know if he had heard.

"About the floods ye mean?" said the Old Man. Yes, he had heard something on the wireless but hadn't paid much heed.

Barney groaned and said that he should take more notice, for there had been reports all day of people barely managing to get out with their lives. The situation in town was getting serious, he said, what with the floodgates at the brewery open all week and the water in the Breagagh River rising dangerously. He jerked his thumb to the back window. "That wall out there will be of little help if the river rises. You should take precautions. Go stay with someone until the danger passes."

The Old Man looked at him, incredulous. Who in heaven's name did he have to stay with? He shook his head. "Not a'tall. Th'wall'll hold. 'Tis been there long an' stood many a flood."

"Maybe so," said Barney, but nobody could say what the river would do. He got up from his chair and headed for the door. "Well, you know best," he said. "Don't say I didn't warn you. It's best not to take any chances." The Old Man thanked him and said he wouldn't.

We listened to Barney's footsteps going down the street. Then the Old Man turned to me. "Did ye hear that? Wants me t'leave th'only house I have." He made his way to the room beyond, where I heard him muttering to himself before coming back out with his coat and scarf.

It had struck me funny to see Barney Callaghan in the house of one I always thought to be his enemy. So, when the Old Man came back out of the room I said, "I didn't know you and Mr. Callaghan were such good friends."

His grey eyes held mine as he drove his arm through the sleeve of his coat.

"Did ye not? Well, maybe 'tis better ye didn't. But since yer eager t'know, I'll tell ye." Sorrow, he told me, brought folk together. Ever since Mickey had died, it seemed, Barney had been showering him with kindness. He heaved a great sigh and shook his head.

"He means well, I suppose, an' I shouldn't grumble. 'Tis a pity, though, that he's such a clown."

We headed for the door and some minutes later were standing on the bridge looking at the river. Barney's fear had been well founded; the river was rising dangerously. A small group of men had gathered at the corner and I could hear fear and caution in their voices. The Old Man raised his arm in a salute then stepped onto the bridge, crossing from one side to the other and looking down into the water.

"'Tis bad," I heard him mutter as he leaned over. Below, the river was greatly swollen, the current swift. Even large objects were being swept downstream—whole trees, wooden crates and bits of furniture. The space beneath the arches had grown quite small and water sucking in beneath made an ugly sound. Over on the meadows side two men trying to cross the Green could find no way. The shallows that had once been there at the widest part and where we children had loved to play were no longer visible.

The Old Man turned his gaze to the stone wall behind his house. That and a small divide were all that stood between him and the river. The ground around his house was higher, however, and so far was not affected. We stayed on the bridge for a short while, then made our way to Kenny's Well. From up there on the hill the scene was no more encouraging; miles of land all underwater and the little bridge to Mickey's farm barely visible.

"Maybe Barney was right after all," I said, beginning to see the danger.

"Ah! 'tis hard t'know at this p'int. Ye don't know what t'make iv it."

He began to descend the steps leading to the well and stopped. Partway down the grassy incline was a great oak tree and we walked across to it. From there the view was wider and we could see the river rushing through the woods around Kilcree. Here and there an animal stood stranded or struggled gallantly to reach high ground.

"What do you think?" I asked, when we reached the road. He shook his head. "'Tis hard t'tell. If th'weather holds it may

go down. If not..." He raised his hands. "There's no tellin'
what might happen."

If the weather holds, I thought with scepticism, looking at
the sky. Most of the blue that I had seen there earlier had
already vanished and great dark clouds were gathering. We
threaded our way past Daly's Hill and out around the little
roads, but prospects didn't alter. All the streams were flooded,
the water brown and muddy. A dead horse floated in one of
them. The Old Man made a sound beneath his breath and
turned back. He had seen enough.

It wasn't the first time we had seen floods in Kilkenny.
Every seven years or so the rivers rose and flooded certain sec-
tors of the city. The Abbey area was usually the hardest hit,
because it was situated low like the bottom of a bowl with hills
on every side, and because the Breagagh, the second largest of
the rivers, passed close to it. The Nore, our largest river, which
flowed through the centre of the town, was more contained,
set deep inside its basin and restrained by sturdy banks. Yet
even it could flood at its weakest points. The more I thought
about Mr. Callaghan's suggestion the more my conviction of its
merit grew, but I didn't tell this to the Old Man for fear of putting more worry his way.

It was late afternoon by the time we got back to his house,
and all the way back he had been coughing. As we neared the
house he handed me some coppers and asked if I would run to
Denny Waldron's and bring him back some peppermints. More
than willing I hurried to the shop, selecting Bullseyes, his
favourites. But when I got back I could see no sign of him. I
noticed the side gate ajar and walked around to the back. I
found him there inspecting the yard for any signs of water.

Everything was dry except for a small patch near the wall
where the grass was sodden. The wall must have been about
four feet high, but we could see the river clearly. It had not
flooded its banks, but huge globs of water were being thrown

up over the edges, covering the rocks and broken branches. Worse still, far away lightning bolted out across the valley and we could see the rain moving toward us in a sheet. A few minutes later thunder rumbled through the heavens, and the rain crashed down upon the house like a giant hammer. The windows rattled and ran with water and the wind began to wail through the eaves and attic.

We sat beside the fire sucking on our mints, he telling me some stories from his past and I interrupting every now and then to remark upon the wind and the rain pelting down the chimney. The house began to groan and grumble and it frightened me because I had never heard a house make a noise like that.

"Ach, now!" the Old Man said, "'tis only a storm, 'twill soon pass." His face took on a comical expression.

"Yer not afraid iv it are ye? A bit iv rain dancin' on th'roof, an' th'wind singin' in th'shingles."

To him I suppose that was all it was, but to me it was something different, like something on the outside wanting to get in, some kind of monster riding on the wings of a demon wind and shrieking through the rafters. Despite the Old Man's outward calm I sensed the uncertainty inside him and I saw his eyes slip across the floor to the scullery where the back door creaked and rattled on its hinges. He got up and bolted down the shutters, then drove the bolt on the scullery door.

"There now," he said, "th'house'll hold. 'Tis as strong as Fionn MacCuhaill."

About an hour later the storm passed though the wind remained, and he pushed his face against the window trying to see out into the yard where a thin film of shiny black water was creeping up the path.

A little while later when I left for home I went to look at the river. Full darkness had fallen and the small crowd that had gathered earlier had gone. A few men holding lanterns remained, and I guessed they would linger into the night. Except for the lamppost on the corner there was no other light, but I could hear the river thundering and see the angry swell of water as it passed beneath the lamppost light, solid tons of water squeezing between the arches spewing spray and gravel. The wind howled out of the blackness and I shuddered inside, thinking of the Old Man alone in his little house nearby.

As I climbed the steep hill up Motty Lane to home I thought about telling Barney Callaghan, but when I reached the barracks and learned that he had already gone I left without speaking to anyone.

Not until the next morning did I learn of the disaster when news of the flood began to circulate, and rumours of the Old Man's death to spread around the neighbourhood.

30

A fair crowd of onlookers had already gath-
ered at the scene by the time I arrived. Most
of them had gloomy faces, except for the
younger ones, happy at the prospect of not
being able to get to school, as all routes
beyond the Water Barrack had been cut off. It
was certainly a grim scenario, with most of
the street submerged in dirty water. Dead cats
floated among bits of broken furniture, and
only the tips of the chimneys on the small
thatched houses were visible.

I could see the slates on the Old Man's roof glittering in the sun, the water almost touching them. From some of the upstairs windows in the larger homes people leaned precariously, calling out requests or instructions to the rescuers below. Across the street from Denny Waldron's I saw Jane and Maizie Dooley. I made my way over, hoping that they would have some fresh news about the Old Man. He had not been seen since the night before and stories of his having drowned were prevalent.

In the doorway of Dick Ring's shop Paddy Farrell and Billy Bood were arguing. I could hear Billy saying, "In the chimbly? Don't be daft, an auld man like that. He'd need to be a bloody monkey."

Paddy answered. "'Tis where he is all the same."

I walked the few feet past to where Jane and Maizie were leaning lazily against the wall, both with pained expressions. Jane looked up when she saw me coming and shook her head to let me know she had heard nothing. Nobody seemed to know anything, she said, but Maizie insisted that the Old Man was "drownded."

Jane raised her eyes to heaven. "Don't listen to her, she doesn't know that."

"I do so," Maizie said, repeating word for word what she had heard. "Why can't you just face up to it?" she asked.

"Because we don't know for sure, and until we do you shouldn't go around saying it."

"Well, who else can it be? No one else is missing." Maizie snorted.

Maizie's conviction resulted from a story we had heard earlier of two bodies being taken from the river. One was a tinker fellow whom it was assumed had been lying drunk in some farmer's field. There was nothing they could do for him. The other was an older man whose body had been dragged ashore near Fryers Bridge with so much mud and dirt on it that it was difficult to say whether he was alive or dead. He had been taken to the County Hospital. The men who rescued him didn't know his name, but as far as they could tell it was not the Old Man. Yet the rumour had taken hold somehow, and with nobody to dispute it was becoming fact.

I clung to Paddy's theory of the chimney in the hope that the Old Man might have climbed up into it, as Mickey Evans had done in the last great flood. But Mickey Evans had been a younger man and the circumstances altogether different. Nobody knew exactly what to think and stood around in groups discussing it. One such group was close to us, with Gabby Hayes and Statia Donovan doing all the talking, a pastime that Statia spent her days perfecting, barely taking time out to feed herself, let alone to wash. The only time her face saw water was before Mass on Sunday. The rest of the week she went maggoty. An enormous woman with hips so wide they could stop an army at a mountain pass and fingers thick as sausages, she had little sense and loved to gossip, leaning outside her door for hours.

Ag an doras was the name that we attached to her, meaning simply "at the door."

Gabby, on the other hand, was everybody's pet, spic and span with nice careful manners. Unlike Statia, he was well-informed and had what he considered a scholastic background. This consisted of a few weeks at the local college when he was a lad, yet to hear him speak you would think he had spent his life at Trinity. Gard Sweeney wandered over with his pad and pencil and Gabby told him everything he knew. How he had been standing on the bridge around twelve midnight, himself and Matty Flannagan, when he caught sight of the Old Man by the lower wall. "He was by himself, at that spot there." He paused to point out the exact location.

"Did you speak to him at all?" the gard asked, and Gabby said he hadn't but had seen the Old Man stop outside his own gate before crossing the road in the direction of the barracks.

"Faith, I saw him myself at that time. I was there when he came in," said Seamus Slattery. "He was looking for Barney Callaghan, but Barney had left, and he practically knocked down Paddy Corcoran going through the door in his hurry to get out. He had his old grey coat on and seemed upset."

"Did he not tell you why he wanted Callaghan?"

"He told me nothing. I asked him where he was going in such a hurry, but he wouldn't say."

"Poor man," said Gabby, sympathetically. "Sure he was very old and not at all himself since he lost the goat."

Statia sighed, tut-tutting.

As they were speaking a boat with two men in it caught everyone's attention. They had been trying to reach the Old

Man's house, but each time the boat rocked and swirled violently. "Look out lads, look out!" everyone cried as the boat capsized. Great excitement followed as it was righted and the men, giving up the attempt, were helped ashore. With nothing left to keep me there I started back up the hill. I heard Jane call and looked around to see her following.

"Where's Maizie?" I asked.

"I don't know," she said. Maizie, it seemed, had been acting weird all morning and had walked away without telling her why.

"Weird? In what way?" I asked, remembering that I had thought the same thing earlier. Jane said she couldn't explain it, because it was nothing physical. All she knew for certain was that Maizie was acting different lately. I had not seen Maizie since the carnival, which due to cold and rainy weather had stayed in town for only one week. She and Jane had been riding in the bumpers and I, wanting to take the next ride with Jane, waited excited on the platform. Maizie, seeing me, had taken Jane's arm and pulled her away, leaving me standing there alone. Long ago I had grown accustomed to her treatment, accepting it as part and parcel of her personality, her jealous ownership of Jane.

Today she had greeted me with her usual glum expression, but her eyes had that look I had seen many times at school, like that of a frightened child or animal.

"I wonder why Maizie didn't say anything?" I said, and Jane shrugged.

"Who knows what goes on in Maizie's mind? I have no doubt we'll find out soon enough." Little did we know that something terrible was taking shape in Maizie's head.

TWO DAYS LATER I WAS ON MY way home from work when I saw Jane waiting at the corner. "They found him!" she called excitedly. "They found him half frozen in the attic."

We rushed down the hill to the Old Man's house. Outside we saw a small crowd on the road and two gards in possession of the gate. They were talking with Barney Callaghan. Once or twice we saw him look in our direction. I thought of going to ask him what was happening but didn't dare for fear of giving rise to gossip. Few people knew of my friendship with the Old Man and that was how I wanted it; I can't say why. I suppose I was afraid of ridicule or of my father finding out.

In very short time we saw an ambulance approach and come to a stop outside the house. Everybody moved aside to let two men in with a stretcher and a few people came and stood close to us. We listened eagerly to everything being said but learned nothing. Gradually we inched our way along the path to get nearer to the gate. From the door a man called out to Barney Callaghan. He was leaning backwards in the hall as though holding onto something and we could hear the Old Man yelling.

"Gimme back me mattress, give it back t'me." Two big arms appeared around the door tugging at a bundle.

Barney sighed, left the gate and disappeared into the house. A moment later Doctor Fennessy emerged, followed by the men carrying an empty stretcher. They said a few words to the gards outside the gate, then drove away. We knew then what all the commotion had been about. The Old Man had obviously refused to be taken to the hospital. This came as no surprise to me, for I recalled him telling me once of his fear of becoming ill, being removed from his home and not being allowed to return to it. It was a fear many old ailing people had.

Jane and I waited until the crowd dispersed and Barney Callaghan came out. "I didn't know you were a friend of his," he said to Jane, ignoring me. But halfway to the barracks he looked at me and said that none of us need worry, because the Old Man could live through anything.

"I don't like to say this," he added, "but I told him so. He has only himself to blame." Addressing me, he said, "You know the truth. You heard me telling him. But would he listen?" I made a face, not knowing what to answer, stunned as much by Barney seeking someone else's opinion as by his outburst.

WHEN WE GOT BACK TO OUR street we saw Madge and Nuala Brannigan talking at the corner. Madge was looking like her usual self, but Nuala, buzzing about like a fly drunk on syrup, her hair like dandelions gone to seed, was dressed for an occasion. Madge rolled her eyes at us.

"She going somewhere special?" I asked, and Madge said no, but that it was her birthday.

Nuala tugged at Jane's arm. She had something to show her, she said, and dragged her across the street. Curious, Madge and I followed, and when she reached their door Nuala made a dive into the hall and pulled Jane in after her. We pressed ourselves against the wall outside and peered around the door just in time to see Nuala showing Jane her new underwear, a blue satin slip with a paler blue lace border.

"Don't you love the neckline?" she was asking excitedly, her jumper in a roll beneath her chin.

We heard Jane gasp. "It's a bit low, isn't it?"

Nuala giggled, lifting her enormous chest for emphasis.

A few minutes later they came out, and it being mild and sunny after all the rain decided to walk around a bit. Madge and I tagged along with Nuala keeping a close eye on us, her head swivelling around every now and then to see if we were following. We cruised around the streets for a little while, stopping here and there to chat with friends so that Jane could spring the news on them that she was going away. She had finally talked my mother into letting her go to Youghal. She had found a job at a hotel there.

But why Youghal? they asked. Why not England, where everybody went? And why not indeed? For it was Ireland's great loss that most of her sons and daughters were obliged to work in England, where jobs were more abundant. Furthermore it had become the accepted fact that people overseas could make more money in the space of one year than could be made in Ireland in a lifetime. Boys and girls from every village left their homes to go there, but not our Jane.

"Why not Youghal?" she answered. At least it was clean and free from crime, not to mention fog, unlike the land of Jack the Ripper where a person couldn't see a hand in front of them. People only went over there, she said, because they were told the streets were paved with gold, but the only gold they ever found were the nuggets dropped by horses. Then Nuala, not to be outdone, proclaimed that she would never go to England, because even dogs were not safe there. This information she insisted she had obtained from an uncle who lived in Battersea and had witnessed them being slaughtered. Madge and I had nothing to add, but I knew what Madge was thinking. She would never leave her home. Predictably, she never did.

Nobody mentioned America, not wanting to embarrass Jane. At least Youghal was not a world away, though it might as well have been from our lack of transportation.

I tried to talk Jane out of going, not wanting to be left at home the eldest. But the following week she was packing her bag, her face flushed with happiness.

She decided to go and tell the Old Man that she was going to Youghal, thinking it might please him, he being a native of County Cork. We went together but found the house empty. All over town people had been busy sweeping mud and dirt into the gutters to be cleared away by the Corporation lorries. The Water Barrack had returned to normal and the river was calm.

Smoke was coming from the Old Man's chimney. We stood by the garden gate looking up and down and after a while we saw him coming up the street, his back bent and walking with steps so slow we thought for a moment he was someone else. I couldn't believe the change in him. He was leaning heavily on his cane, his body shrunk and skeletal.

"Oh, the poor devil!" Jane said, going ahead to speak with him. I heard her ask him how he was and why he was out walking. He raised his head to look at her with a quizzical yet appreciative expression. He was leaning on his cane with one hand and holding something in the other.

Jane bent to take the parcel. His expression changed immediately and he began to smile, thanking her for her thoughtfulness.

"Will yee not come in an' stay awhile?" he asked, and we shook our heads explaining that we didn't want to be of any trouble.

"Trouble! No trouble a'tall! An' even if 'twas itself, wouldn't I only be too glad iv it. Come on in for a minute now, can't yee."

We followed him inside and found the house as cold as ice, despite a blazing fire. Dampness hung on everything and a noxious smell seemed to emanate from every corner, yet we could smell the disinfectant and could see the place had all been scrubbed. Nevertheless, light traces of mud and sludge still lingered on the ceiling and all the windows lacked curtains. Beyond the scullery door something had pushed right through the ceiling, damaging the wall, and the back door was missing, a gaping hole where it had been. An army blanket had been draped across it.

Except for one chair, a table and a makeshift bed beside the fire, the room was bare and the floor filled with cavities. The scene out back was even worse, a shipwrecked beach with mud and boulders everywhere. A huge tree stump had lodged itself in Meggie's grave, making me wonder if her body was still under it. I sighed to think how he must feel and heard Jane ask if he might consider living somewhere else, to which he replied that he would not, that he would patch it up.

Jane glanced awkwardly at me but I turned my head away, not wanting to agree with the impossibility, any more than with the probability, of his being forcefully removed. Every effort would be made to get him out, of that I was certain. All this and more, Jane's eyes were saying, and he knew quite well what we were thinking.

"I don't want t' go, but I know they'll try t'make me," he said. "No wan except meself would want t'live here now." A look of pure despair came over him. "An' where would I go but t' th'poorhouse?" Thomastown, he meant, and I flashed an angry look at Jane, furious that she had made him think of it.

"Surely this can be repaired," I said, going toward the wall. "We could ask Billy Evans to take a look at it!"

Jane said this was a good idea, because if anyone could put it back to normal Billy could. That seemed to please him and he brightened.

"In any case," I added, "what makes you think they'd want you at the poorhouse?"

He laughed at that, saying that maybe they wouldn't, but that there was always the wild chance they might. He settled himself into his corner, his pipe between his lips, and told us what we had come to hear. How as the water seeped steadily under the scullery door he had toiled long after midnight, dragging everything he possibly could up to the attic. Even the bedclothes and the mattress he had managed to drag up, and all of his books he had moved to higher shelves. He had been about to sit down to rest, he said, when the back door had flown open on its hinges, knocking him against the wall. The water had rushed in a whirlpool to the room beyond. The table he had stacked with furniture had been sucked into the narrow hall, blocking the street door. With one great heave he had flung his body through the swirling flood and had grasped the ladder hanging free from the open trap door, pulling himself to safety. No sooner had he crawled onto the mattress when a flash of pain had shot through his head as a heavy beam crashed down on him, robbing him of consciousness.

"It was well for you that you had the attic!" Jane put in, and the Old Man agreed. It was just a small storage space he had designed himself, he said, but it had saved his life.

The river was what had caught him by surprise, the terrible might of it and the speed with which it had cornered him.

"I could've had th'arms an' legs iv a centipede, an' t'wouldn't have made any difference."

We had passed a half-hour or so when he began to yawn, saying he was very tired and hadn't slept in days. Just as I was thinking that we ought to leave he pulled himself abruptly to his feet and shuffled to the door. Jane clasped his outstretched hand and wished him well. She told him I would be back to visit him and bring him all the news. He smiled and let his eyes rest on my face a moment, then closed the door.

31

The weeks went by as they had before, with the outlook at our house becoming grimmer. Mother's drinking had worsened. No longer was she stealing in and out of pubs around the city, but doing it openly. It became quite common to see her staggering home each evening, and once or twice she had fallen in the street.

On one such occasion Madge and I were coming home from someplace, the wind tearing at our clothes, the sky pelting us with rain. We turned the corner into Kickam Street and could hardly keep our heads up from the driving rain. Midway along the street we saw something in the road ahead of us and hurried to investigate. Madge got there first and bent to look, then she looked at me in disbelief. An awful feeling came over me and I knew instinctively that it was my mother. I looked at her huddled figure on the ground, the rain soaking into it, and all the fury in the world washed over me followed instantly by shame. As I stood there motionless I feared for an instant that she might be dead. Then I saw her begin to stir, trying to struggle to her feet, and I could not make myself bend to help her.

Madge moved to help.

"Leave her there," I said, my throat tight with anger. Madge looked at me, incredulous.

"Oh! I don't know Tess. I don't like..." she began, and I took her arm and dragged her away. She looked back once but didn't speak.

Sometime later Mother was shuffled through our front door by none other than Father Chapman. I lied for her, maybe because of my shame, saying that she had not been feeling well all day and should never have gone out. For days I could not bring myself to look at Mother, and every attempt at conversation erupted in an argument. She in turn avoided Father, who drew into himself, a certain sternness always present in his face.

Unable to do anything about restraining Mother he tried to compensate by restraining us, making our lives even more miserable with his discipline. It was inconceivable to me that he could be so rigid in his supervision over us yet so weak when it came to Mother. By the time I reached eighteen I had begun resenting him and challenging his dictatorial regimen, yet my heart was driven by the need to go on loving him. For months after I had started work I thought and worried about nothing else. I tried in every way to make things up to him, to be around when he came home, to encourage conversations and try to keep normality in the house.

But things were never normal. More and more it seemed that Mother hated him, her venom like a snake's. Their quarrels were constant, the talk of the neighbourhood, and we were ashamed to put our heads outside.

"Some marriages were never meant to be," Paddy Brennan said to me one day on hearing them. He meant it kindly and without malice yet for months after I avoided him, too proud to admit that he had spoken the truth. A kind of silence fell between my father and myself, and years would pass before either of us would understand its presence.

BY THE FALL OF THAT SAME YEAR Mr. Bourke had died and Maizie Dooley taken to the lunatic asylum. The first shock—the death of Mr. Bourke—came while I was standing in our kitchen wondering why the house was empty. I had found the front and back doors open but nobody at home. Then I saw my mother coming through the garden crying. Mr. Bourke had died and she had just been in to help lay him out.

"Sit down," she said, and pulled a chair out from the table. She sat down opposite and wiped her eyes. "He was very fond of you," she said. "I didn't know. He told me I should be proud of all of you." She started to cry again.

It was the only time I had ever heard her admit to any such thing and I can't remember what I answered, my mind numb with shock. Cruelty comes in many forms, ignorance being one of them. The fact that Mr. Bourke was still tubercular and not expected to recover had been kept from us. We younger ones all thought he was getting well and given time would recover. That his illness beginning all those years before had taken so long to assert itself was unbelievable. We had always known that he was not strong and at times became exhausted and had to stay in bed. But then he would get well again. For us the announcement of his death was totally unexpected.

The second shock came about two weeks later. I was walking home when I heard somebody calling. I turned around and saw Nuala Brannigan racing up the street. Out of breath and brimming with excitement, she reached my side.

"Did you hear the news?" she panted, grabbing hold of me.

"What news is that?" I asked in a slightly choppy voice, still vexed with her for telling Billy Meagher that I wouldn't have him. Not that he had ever asked me, mind, not openly at any rate, but several times he had hinted and quite often he would linger at a corner when he saw me coming and walk along with me.

"You're never going to believe this," said Nuala. "Maizie Dooley is in the Lunatic Asylum."

My mouth dropped open. Could this be another of her fantasies?

"Are you telling me the truth, Nuala Brannigan?"

"I am, I am. Oh, honest to God, I just saw them taking her away!" She didn't rightly know what had occurred, she said, but had been coming home by way of Abbey Street and saw the men bring Maizie out. Her mother, she told me, was standing by the door crying, and when Nuala asked her what had happened she just shook her head and went back inside.

"Are you sure they were from the Asylum?"

"Positive. The whole street was out."

"And did nobody say anything?"

"Not to me, they didn't. But I did hear a neighbour telling someone else that Maizie went for somebody with a hatchet."

"Oh my God!"

I dropped my arms down by my side, my purse sliding to the ground. Nuala picked it up, suggesting that we go back down to Maizie's street and see what we could learn. We found the street deserted with no signs of anything unusual having happened. Nuala said she couldn't understand it, because when she had left only minutes earlier the whole place had been buzzing.

"Somebody must know something," she insisted, but we couldn't find anyone who did. Disappointed we headed home.

"It couldn't have been anything serious," I said to Nuala, recalling that I had seen Maizie myself only days before. It had been our first encounter since Jane had left and I couldn't believe the change in her. She was like another person. The modesty of her appearance had astonished me, no frills or artificial bulges, just a plain red skirt with a navy sweater. Around her neck she had a silver chain with a little cross attached to it. She had no makeup on and her hair though still frizzy was neat and groomed. I had asked her how she had been and she had said she was fine, but that she missed our Jane. No, she wasn't working and was still at home, a fact that had not seemed to bother her. I had never seen her look so nice and I told her so.

"Well, I'll swear to God," said Nuala, "those men were from the Asylum."

And they were indeed, as we found out later. Rumours sprung up everywhere—Maizie disembowelling Bridie Murphy's cat, and ripping Jamie Cantwell's ear off with a billhook. That evening we decided to go and see her mother to see if we could learn the truth. She looked at us with pure contempt and told us to be off. Her Maizie had never hurt anyone who didn't hurt her first, she shouted after us. This caused me to wonder—who it was that might have hurt her Maizie.

Jamie Cantwell came to mind immediately. I remembered that Maizie had told our Jane that he was trying to fondle her and always calling at their house when he knew her mother would be out. A civil servant whose job it was to monitor the care of poor and foster children, he was seen by most as a decent man and respected member of the community, which only goes to show that not everything that happens in a small town is known to all its residents no matter how sharp their ears or pliable their tongues. For Jamie Cantwell was a proper scamp, a Dr. Jekyll and Mr. Hyde skulking about in alleyways watching for a chance to shock us girls with a glimpse of his naked member. Most of us were too shy to tell and those who did were not believed.

Jamie Cantwell left town before anyone had a chance to question him. Oh! I know Maizie had always been a little wild, inciting us to joke about her sanity, but we never seriously imagined her a lunatic or wanted to see her in that terrible place. Nuala, as I remember, showed great concern over Maizie, a side to her I hadn't known existed. Parting company that evening we exchanged kindly words, each of us vowing to go and visit Maizie first chance we got but knowing full well we wouldn't. Just the very thought was enough to send us running. Too many were the stories we had heard about that place—raving lunatics everywhere, some in cages screaming to get out, some chained to walls, some assaulting visitors. It was a place where many people were sent simply to be rid of them or for anything other than an injury. Those who didn't want to go there were often tied with ropes to the backs of carts and hauled along like animals. Some, to be sure, were mentally ill, but not all were raving lunatics. Yet we thought they were because we had never been told any different. The outcome was an unnatural fear of the Asylum.

Many were the nights I laid awake thinking about poor Maizie. She never did come out. Years later on a visit home to Ireland I plucked up the courage to visit her. But when I got inside the building I wished I hadn't.

"Maizie Dooley?" they exclaimed, looking at me as though I had six heads. "But that woman is in the Tower!" Not wanting to show my ignorance, I spluttered some excuse and left.

I never did find out what the Tower was and I never saw poor Maizie. The years held fast to her solitude as her condition worsened. To this day I do not know what became of her.

32

Life went on, each dreary day followed by another. It had been three years since I had started at the factory, and though I had never grown to like it, I had settled in. By now my wages were comparable to Father's, and still I passed my pay packet unopened to my mother.

Nevertheless I managed to acquire a bicycle of which payment was my responsibility, and I had little money left from my allowance for anything else. In all fairness I should mention Mother's part in the acquisition of my bicycle. Having come along as promised to act as my security, she rewarded me by paying the first instalment. "There now girl," she said, looking mighty proud, "nobody can say you haven't earned it." The pleasure on her smiling face was genuine.

Yet all I could think about at the time was, Where had she got the money? And no sooner did that thought pass across my mind than I was filled with guilt, wanting to put my arms around her neck and wash away the terrible thoughts I harboured. It was a gesture on her part that I would not forget, in spite of her eagerness to hurry, as I suspected, to the nearest pub. I remember for the first time feeling sorry for my mother, of watching sadly as she disappeared around the corner and not being filled with my usual disgust. I went home alone with my new bicycle.

Jane was right, Mother couldn't help her nature any more than I could help my own. Whatever the reason, I made up my mind that very day to try be more tolerant and in the months following I succeeded. Short of going to the pub with her, I did everything she asked. Yet by the end of summer, with her drinking worse and she arriving home each evening quarrelsome, I was near to madness. Every weekend found me on a trip alone to somewhere, leaving, as I thought, my troubles behind. But troubles have a way of catching up with you or travelling steadfastly alongside, new ones cropping up where old ones die.

Before I knew it I was miserable again, the tension tearing me apart. It hurt me to watch Mother squander money on drink. Every week found someone knocking on our door demanding payment for one thing or another. Each Monday saw Mother penniless with a whole week in front of her. Then would begin the borrowing. Food became a rare commodity, and at times I found myself wondering what the younger ones were eating. Plain bread and butter?

And that was how it was when December came, with Jack Frost feathering the windows and dressing up the hedges with webs of dew. Puddles that had lingered on the streets for weeks had now turned to ice and had young boys busy skating on them. Inside our house the rooms were cold. The only fire was in the kitchen and all of us fought for a place by it. Old coats were strewn across the beds at night to help keep us warm and fleas soon gathered in the hems and seams. Scabies, we were warned, were everywhere, and I was scared to death of catching them. Day by day little Jack and Jim were running wild, in trouble with the law and heading toward the Reformatory.

Each day found me more depressed, and once again I turned to the Old Man, but I found him melancholy and slow to talk, the absence of Meggie pulling at his heart. "Did I tell ye Meggie died?" he always asked me. It occurred to me that his mind was slipping.

"Why are ye always so sad alana?" he inquired of me quite suddenly, on one of these visits.

"I'm not," I answered hastily, not knowing what else to say. Never once in all our conversations did I tell him of my mother, and never once did he inquire. Yet I'm sure he must have known. A dark horse Mother always said I was, one whose right hand never learned what the left one was about, for I seldom showed my feelings and had always found it difficult to confide in anyone.

December found me miserable. Christmas was the loneliest I had ever known. Jane had not come home as I had hoped and Madge's reluctance to leave her mother alone in an empty house kept her indoors. Try as I might, I could not shake off the mantle of depression that had settled on my mind as I trudged alone through the empty streets. It was Christmas Eve. A light snow had fallen, its soft clean carpet draping the roads and rooftops in a blanket of pure white. From every household chimney trails of blue smoke curled upward to the sky. An atmosphere of stillness had settled on the town, not a sound or movement anywhere. Yet all the little shops were bright with decorations, the light from their windows spilling in a yellow wash across the path.

Outside Brown's shop window a lone boy was standing watching the jolly cobbler in his red and green attire tap-tapping on his last. He shot a startled glance in my direction and darted into the nearby lane. Overhead I heard a window open and a woman's voice exclaim, "For God's sake Billy, will yeh come inside before yeh ketch yer death." Then the sound of a closing door and all was quiet again.

In Barrack Street I found my uncle's house still empty, the new owner in no hurry to move in. I stood for a moment in the hallway door and then leaned my head against the parlour window, straining to see in. It didn't seem right to leave a place so empty.

"Could you spare a penny, miss?" a voice behind me whispered.

I spun around to see a man with a two-wheeled cart stacked with scraps of wood and holly, standing by the curb. He was tall and thin and poorly clad in a ragged overcoat and cap. I thought he might be a tramp, but something about him told me no, for his face had a gentle quality. He set the cart down heavily and looked around, cupping his hands around his mouth and blowing into them.

"I wouldn't trouble you at all only that I'm famished," he said, seemingly ashamed of his need to beg. Moved by his predicament and without time to think, I thrust my hand into my pocket and pulled out a coin which he accepted with alacrity and joy.

"Oh! the blessings of God on you," he gasped, staring unbelieving at his palm.

He hunched forward more, his hand still open, and only then did I realise what I had done. I had given him my precious florin. Whether he realised my error I couldn't say, and I had neither the courage nor the will to ask it back.

The man grasped my hand and shook it silently. Then with a heave he raised his cart and hurried off along the road. Perhaps it was the atmosphere or the wonder on his face, or maybe it was just my own interpretation, but suddenly I felt more happy than I had felt all day.

"Merry Christmas, sir!" I shouted after him and he turned to wave.

"God bless you, child. God bless you," his voice drifted back.

By the time I reached our street again the bells were ringing for midnight Mass. Madge's house was all in darkness and I wondered if she had gone to Mass without me, but passing through our garden gate I heard a noise behind me and turned and saw her running toward me.

"Come on," she called impatiently, "or we'll be late." My heart leaped eagerly.

"Madge!" I yelled excitedly, and we raced together to the Abbey Chapel.

33

When Jane arrived home at Easter, she found the house much changed. Gone were all our precious ornaments and china, and our chairs, the leather fireside ones, replaced by mismatched calico. Even the old walnut coat rack by the door had vanished. The cupboard, once filled with homemade bread, meat pies and sausages, was empty. There was no fire in the grate, and Mother, not expecting her, was out.

A sense of dismal isolation hung over everything. As Jane looked around her in disbelief at the bleak surroundings, she began to regret her decision to come home. "Why did you come?" I asked of her when she told me all this later, for her decision made no sense to me, considering her eagerness to get away. She gave a short embarrassed laugh.

"Homesickness I suppose," she answered. How could she have forgotten how things were before she left? I didn't say this though, because I didn't want to hurt her.

"I'm glad you're back," I said, and meant it. "Mam was right," I told her laughing. "She said you wouldn't stay." Jane laughed too, and said she hoped to God she would not regret returning home. I was certain that she would. And sure enough, less than five weeks later I was proven right.

It was a typical Saturday afternoon and we had just come home from our usual promenade about the town. Mother had gotten in ahead of us and was in the kitchen taking off her coat. She was in a genial mood, talking freely and unimpaired by alcohol. Jane helped her put away what few groceries she had brought while I made the tea. Then we sat around the table chatting, Jane telling of her experiences in Youghal and Mother telling of hers in Rathmines. It was something of a novelty for me, for not since the day that Jane had left had I been party to a chat with Mother.

Somewhere between Jane's adventures on the seafront and Mother's rude awakening in Rathmines we heard the front gate opening. All three of us looked up in time to see a tall man wearing a three-piece suit and carrying a briefcase coming toward the door. I went to open it. He hesitated, unsure, as though he had expected someone older, and then he cleared his throat and unclasped his briefcase.

"This is the Lennon residence?"

I nodded that it was, whereupon he withdrew something from the case. "I'm here to speak with somebody about this," he said, holding up a folded sheet of paper.

From inside Mother called to him to enter, and he stepped past me through the door. She rose to meet him and he shook her hand, giving his name as Carmody. Mother showed no sign of recognition, her face as blank as a pane of glass.

I glanced at Jane.

The Rent Board, I mouthed to her, for the name if not the man was well known to me.

Carmody took a quick glance around the room, then handed Mother the paper. "This is not a task that I enjoy, but I could see no other way around it," he said, and I knew right away that it was something serious.

Mother remained calm. Inwardly I knew she was angry with herself for being found at home. There was nothing for it now but to bluff her way out and hope to gain more time. In mock surprise she held the invoice out in front of her, claiming some mistake. A few pounds maybe, she admitted, but never that amount. She suggested Mr. Carmody go back and check his records.

"Come now, Mrs. Lennon, you know as well as I do that our records are accurate." Should the account not be discharged within the time allotted, it would be necessary for either she or Father to appear in court, he warned.

Jane groaned, and two red spots appeared on Mother's face as she adopted an air of injured pride and insisted that she always paid her debts. Then in a gesture of supreme disdain she tossed the notice to the floor. I bent to pick it up, the red figures in one corner jumping out at me—ARREARS, SEVEN POUNDS, SEVEN SHILLINGS AND SIXPENCE, and in large black letters underneath, FINAL NOTICE. Mr. Carmody shook his head resignedly, then rose to leave.

After he had gone we sat back down at the table, this time subdued. "What else could I do?" Mother finally wailed. "And what am I going to do now?" She picked up the notice and stared at it. "When your father hears of this, it will be the end of him." She put her head down on the table, near to tears.

"No it won't, Mam. No it won't. Don't worry," Jane exclaimed, going to her side in a sudden gush of feeling.

Mother raised her head. "He'll have to be told, girl. I can't pay all that alone."

Jane looked at me and I should have stopped her then, for I knew what she was going to say before she even said it. "We'll help you, won't we Tess?" Her eyes pleaded above Mother's head.

I made no reply, but if I had had a razor blade I might have slashed her tongue. How in the name of Bethlehem was I supposed to help with so little money of my own? Together they scrutinised the notice, before Mother with a grateful look handed it to me. Somewhere inside of me an angry knot was forming, and I had to pull my breath in deeply to control it. It was all very well for Jane playing the Good Samaritan, but where were we to get the money? Besides, I was sick and tired of Mother's promises. And little did Jane know what was going on. I had not told her of the overdrafts all over town, of the shops we dared not enter, of merchants seeking payment at our door. But that evening after Mother had gone out I told her everything.

By the time the evening ended, Jane was wishing fervently that she had not come home and that she was back once more in her cosy room in Youghal, with nothing more to worry her than her chilblains in the winter. Now she was beginning to have real doubts, for she had only a meagre sum put by with no immediate means of augmenting it.

"What are we going to do?" she moaned.

"Don't ask me," I answered. "But I'm sure we'll find out soon enough."

And so we did when Father arrived home one evening later with a face like Quasimodo and a temper to match, demanding that Mother tell him why the rent had not been paid. Mother gave as explanation her usual complaint about never having enough money.

"But where does all the money go?" Father asked.

"All what money? The few meagre shillings you give me every week? You try managing on it."

Of course there wasn't just Father's wages. There was mine and Peg's and Jane's contribution as well, not to mention the odd pounds from the family in England every now and then. But realising the futility of even mentioning it Father held his tongue.

"You told me all the bills were paid, and now I find that they are not."

Whether he was referring to other bills outstanding or simply the rent bill we didn't know, and hoped for his sake that he did not know of them. Most of us at age seventeen are too young to fully grasp the severity of any situation. Yet the crisis that filled me with most dread was the threat of poverty. This prospect I feared above all else.

The thing about poverty that had always frightened me was what it did to people, destroying every atom of their self-respect, turning their natures callous and their habits foul. Mother's promise to try to put things right with the Rent Board was of little comfort to me, for I knew full well that the problem would crop up again as soon as she felt safe. Feelings of shame and inferiority were already gnawing at my vitals. This fact, even more than Mother's image in the gutter, compelled me to find a solution.

So it was that on the Friday following Father's admonition I began to formulate a plan.

"Jane," said I, in a becoming voice after we had finished washing up the dishes, "what would you say to you and me taking over the management of the house?"

"I'd say you were crazy, that's what," she answered.

"Just hear me out a minute now," I said. "It's not as crazy as it may sound. I have given it a lot of thought, and I think it will be to your benefit."

"Oh!"

Her eyebrows lifted and she sat down by the fire and waited. Excited, I pulled the spare chair close to her and outlined my plan.

I had worked it all out, I told her. Instead of handing all my wages up to Mother every week I would give her only a small part of it. The rest would be used to pay off bills and to purchase what small comforts as were needed for the home. Mother would have to be responsible for the upkeep of the rent and for what few groceries as was her habit to provide. The rest would be up to us.

"And where do I fit in?" she asked.

"I'm coming to that," I said. "Just listen. It occurred to me that since you have no job right now, and little hope of finding one, you might like to earn a few bob at home."

"Are you suggesting what I think you are?" she asked.

I nodded. "You stay home and look after the house, and I'll supply the money."

Jane gave a sort of sorry laugh, lit herself a cigarette and blew the smoke out through her nose while I took my time explaining some details. It was a good plan, she said, but with one major flaw—Mother would never agree to it.

"She won't be asked," I answered.

Alarm sprang back into her blue eyes and her palms went up.

"Oh! wait a minute, now. I know Mam isn't going to like it."

She stubbed her half-smoked cigarette against the chimney.

"And what are we going to tell Daddy?"

"Nothing. What he doesn't know won't trouble him."

"But what if he finds out?"

"He won't, not unless you plan to tell him. Mam certainly won't, because she won't want him to know why we are doing it."

"Hmm! Thought of everything, haven't you?" Jane replied, and she agreed.

As it turned out, Mother made no fuss at all apart from one initial burst of temper in which she called me a few choice names. In a way I think she was expecting it and may have even welcomed it.

And so it was that Jane and I settled into our new roles in the family. Neither of us had any training in managing a home, but as time passed we learned, and little by little we paid off the bills and managed to buy new furniture. This we accomplished through a hire-purchase plan with a company known as Cavendish. In time we succeeded in replacing all the shabby furniture with new until the house began to look once more as we remembered it.

It wasn't long, however, until a fresh cloud of misery arrived to hang over us, when the Garda appeared at our front door asking about my brothers, little Jack and Jim. All summer long, it seemed, they had misbehaved, playing truancy from school, loitering in forbidden areas and vandalising property. Despite repeated warnings their offences had continued until, finally, charges were being laid against them. They were ordered to appear in court.

Once again my mother hastened to the barracks to defend her children but this time succeeded in making matters worse when, under the influence of alcohol, she collided with a wall. My father, disillusioned and shocked by the charges, washed his hands of the whole affair. With nobody to vouch for their behaviour and Mother's credibility in ruins, the boys were sent to the reform school in Clonmel. Though the torment of that dreadful day did eventually fade the images did not. Over and over through the years I have gazed upon the scene of two confused and frightened boys being taken from their home. Should I live through all eternity I could not forget my feelings as I watched them go, tears streaming down little Jimmy's face.

When I went to work the next day, questions were being asked of me and what was I to answer? My shame, like a cancer in my throat, was too enormous to conceal.

"I do not blame your mother, and I ask you not to blame her either," Father said with a sorry face, when I spoke with him days later.

I could have hit him.

"Oh! Mother of God, what have I done to deserve this," I remember him saying when he first learned of the affair.

And on the day of his sons' departure, so forlornly, "They have taken them away."

Yet he had not used one ounce of his supposed influence to prevent it happening. Could he not have bent a little to their pleading instead of sending them away, instead of cloistering himself behind closed doors, too proud to run the risk of pity from his friends?

My confidence in Father was the growth and habit of years, and anything he did or said seemed always to be right. At the time I felt I understood his action, and though a dark thought as to his motive passed across my mind, it suited me to blame my mother. Over the years I have regretted this. For was it not she who had suffered most, albeit through her own default, fettered as she was by intemperance? With the departure of the children the house fell quiet. Mother looked as white and crushed as a broken lily, and apart from some sharp words on that fateful day she had no further words with Father. It was as though he had ceased to be a part of her environment.

He in turn accepted her attitude and did his best to adjust to it. Every now and then his old bitterness returned, but never once did he ask of her whereabouts and stopped watching for her at the window. More and more he spent his leisure hours away from home, serving bar for Smithwick at the Mayfair ballroom, or walking little Timmy, his terrier, by the river.

For a while I resumed my former habits of solitude, Jane having found herself a boyfriend. In personal expenditures I was rigid as with a miser's care I counted out my money, and it wasn't long before my goals were realised. It might be said that Jane and to some extent my father got the better of the bargain, but I was never cheated. I had enough money to do all the things that I wanted, and each payday Jane hugged herself with happiness.

The house, too, seemed excited, with glowing embers in its grates, a new radio to liven it and electric lighting in its rooms. What more could I have wanted? By now my brother Tom was working, his contribution going to Mother, of whom it must be said never again allowed the rent to lapse. So, gradually but honestly, we rose out of debt.

34

The current of life flows quickly by, bringing changes as it goes, and one condition altered by its passing was my relationship with the Old Man. Whereas the affection I had always borne him had not diminished, my dependency on his guidance had. More and more I found myself neglecting him, leaving him to his loneliness, and relying on street gossip for news of his affairs. Not once in all the weeks since Jane and I had started our routine had I been to visit him. It was my fault, and mine alone, that I had missed so many weeks of his companionship. So when I saw him coming up the hill on that bright and sunny afternoon, I was delighted.

He was wearing the same old coat and carrying the same stick, tapping the edge of the curb with it as he walked along. Excitedly I ran to meet him, half expecting some rebuke, but there was no reproach on his beaming face, no malice in his greeting.

"Ah! there y'are me little wan. Ye had me worried. Where have ye been?" He let out a long breath, as one might who has been searching for a missing thing and just found it. So ashamed was I about my thoughtlessness and eager to retain his confidence that excuses spouted from my lips like water

from a fountain. And though he listened graciously to everything being said, I was not entirely certain that he absorbed it,
for he looked at me for such a long time without saying anything. Then he turned away and started down the hill.

"I'll walk with you a bit," I said, stepping after him, and
thinking as I did how changed he was. Not in a merely physical sense, but in the resolute quietness of his manner, that
quietness I had often seen in aged people or those depleted by
an illness and losing hold on life.

We walked in silence to the bottom of the hill where he
took my arm and led me toward the little path that wound by
the river. The recent rain had made deep puddles in dips along
the way which he avoided with great care, reminding me of
stories he had told me long ago of when he was a lad and used
to leap right over them or land with shameful teasing in the
middle. On the remnants of the old wall by the river the sun
had spread a blanket of warm rays, and here he sat looking up
at me. Though he was smiling his eyes were sad.

"Th'family is what matters child," he said, as though I had
just that minute finished speaking. "An' your family, along
with many others, has not been blessed with total harmony."

So he had learned of our misfortune! And by whose wag-
ging tongue? Barney Callaghan's, I suspected, though he
might have seen it in the paper. I felt miserably ashamed and
found myself saying ridiculous things in an effort to hide my
embarrassment. In the end I told him everything.

"Ah, child!" he said with a heavy groan, and I sank down
beside him on the wall.

"'Tis not yer fault. Put it all behind ye."

Life, he told me, was like one of those newfangled har-
vesters. It ploughed and stubbed and harrowed the field of a
person's character but its nature never changed.

"Me own fathur did everything he cud t'change th'way he
saw me mother, but it did no good."

226

It was only after people left you to manage your own affairs that you really learned how to live with them, he said, and nobody desired the company of a person constantly trying to convert them to their own ways. I suspected he was speaking of my mother though he did not say.

"And how have you been keeping?" I asked, when he had finished speaking.

"Ah sure! Not bad a'tall. But I've no life t'speak iv now. No life a'tall. Not a soul t'speak to. All th'lads are gone."

It was true. Most of the boys who had been his faithful audience had gone to England, Paddy Farrell being the last to leave. And poor Milo, of course, who had died.

"Billy Meagher is still around," I said.

"Billy! Ah! ye can't depend on Billy anymore. He doesn't come down here like he used to. He's a grown man now an' busy with th' girls."

This remark set my mind to wondering, for only two days earlier I had walked with Billy on the Castle Road, where he told me he had no girl and had asked if he could take me to the pictures. I had refused, of course, not only because of the three years difference in our ages, which to my mind put us into different worlds, but because of the constant innuendoes surrounding Billy's reputation. A proper scamp, the girls said. And the boys though noncommittal seemed reluctant to defend him. Yet to be admitted to his friendship seemed a coveted honour, candidates from both sides vying for attention. Why was that?

While thinking up ways of finding out, I heard the Old Man say, "He's very fond iv you alana. He's often told me so."

The admission pleased me, but could Billy have put him up to it? Certainly not if the Old Man was aware of any questionable behaviour. Not knowing what to say I made no comment, and from the corner of my eye I felt his eyes regarding me.

"D'ye not believe me then?" he asked, and I shrugged and said I didn't know.

"But why wouldn't he be fond iv ye? I'm fond iv ye meself. Yer th'most sincerest little girl I know."

Quite suddenly I felt his fingers trace the edges of my face.

"Well, ye know best I reckon. I'll not attempt t'sway ye."

He lit his pipe, his fingers cupped around the bowl, and he was soon sucking like a honeybee from a flower, his eyes blinking with the pleasure.

"Ye know," he said, after a little while, "ye remind me a lot iv poor Mickey. Always ready t'believe what people tell ye, but shy t'believe when it concerns yerself. 'Tis a great pity he didn't live for ye t'know him better. The dearest little fella in the world, he was. Yet, look at th'way things happen! For there I was, lookin' for him t'grow old with me, an' th'minute I turned me back he was gone."

He paused in sad remembrance, and I was about to answer something in response when he began to cough, a deep dirty cough from somewhere in the bottom of his stomach. Uncomfortably I waited until the seizure passed.

"Should you be smoking with that cough?" I asked, and he looked at me with a wry expression.

"I dare say I shouldn't," he responded carelessly, and went right on doing it. But after a while his breathing became impossible and he laid the pipe beside him on the wall, fumbling in his pocket once again. This time he drew out a Baby Power of whiskey which he placed without ceremony between his lips, and shivered as he drank.

"Aaah! better than any medicine," he gasped. "Here, take a sup," he teased, holding the bottle out to me and laughing when I frowned and turned my head away.

"'Tis all that keeps me goin' now," he said, and began to reminisce about the past, about things that he had told me long ago and things I had told him. It all came back to me in a scene so clear, the place, the time, the feeling of the moment when I first laid eyes on him. How awesome he had seemed, how grand his stories.

Suddenly I forgot about my mother, my father and all the problems surrounding them, everything but those evenings in the past when I had raced to meet the Old Man and we had sailed the sky in our silver ship and crossed the mighty oceans to uncharted lands where tigers roamed the forests deep and angry, fierce bull elephants stamped crocodiles to death. "Look there! Look there!" I could hear him call. "The stars are coming out," and in my mind I raced to beat him at the count of them, and leap before him to the waiting moon.

And so we talked, or rather he talked, finding me an eager listener. And while he spoke the sun went down and the breeze became quite chilly. With a shiver he rose to leave, and as he did so the cough began, tearing at the lining of his lungs and causing him to scurry for his handkerchief.

"You ought to have that seen to," I said, in a tone of some authority, as he dropped back down again.

Seconds later he stood up again, passed his hand across his face and with slow careful steps started back along the path. Halfway along he lingered, caressing the bark of an old oak tree, and with a deep sigh looked back around the fields, his eyes drinking in the misty outline of the hills and the blue sweep of the horizon.

"Come. Come alana," he murmured finally, grasping my arm in his clawlike hand and pushing me gently in front of him.

"Will you be all right?" I asked, as I left him at his gate, his face still buried in his handkerchief.

He looked around at me.

"Don't worry about me child, I'll be fine. Go on home with ye now an' have yer supper."

And so I left him, happy to have spent the time with him and looking forward to our next meeting.

35

In most provincial little towns, I suspect, life goes forward in a chain of accidents, shocks and averted catastrophes. Kilkenny, in my day, was no different. Its citizens, still reeling from the result of one disaster, were often brutally confronted with another—a small boy crushed beneath a lorry, another burned to death, a little girl drowned in a stagnant pond, an infant scalded by a drunken midwife. The list goes on, and I can scarcely convey in written words the whirling emotions in my mind when I learned of Billy Meagher's accident.

It was threshing time in the country and a beautiful Sunday afternoon. As was their custom, several of the local lads had gone to help the farmers. Even we city girls loved the sights and scents of threshing but few of us attended, not because of any aversion to the work involved but because of the dangerous nature of the thresher. Too many accidents had been known to happen when some girl's hair or clothing made contact with its parts.

It was a monstrous machine with a wide belt that ran in snapping revolutions between the engine and the separator. The noisy rattle of the sheaf carrier and the shrill blowing of the whistle could be heard for miles. Special precautions were observed to avoid being struck by the flapping belt and drawn up into the waiting jaws. Yet such was Billy's fate on that dreadful afternoon. The scene described to me over and over left a scar forever on my memory. For weeks I could almost see him in the hospital, pleading that he didn't want to die as they gave him extreme unction. Could they not have spared him that misery?

Barely a week had passed since we had walked together on the Castle Road, he teasing about my innocence and I declaring jokingly that he was too old for me. "I'll wait until you're my age so," he had laughed, and kissed me on the cheek. Then off he had dashed in a whirlwind of spirits. Hardly the actions of a proper scamp, who from the moment of maturity had resolved to conquer women.

Now that he was gone I missed him. For days I could not escape that sense of desolation when every sigh, every sound, every minute act so vividly and painfully recalled his memory. Regretfully the world rolls on, and before the year was out that tragedy, too, had been forgotten and another chapter in the book of life completed.

Spring arrived, as always, with a blaze of wild flowers all along the roads and through the fields. First the snowdrop, then the crocus, followed by the daffodil, the tulip and the hyacinth. It was almost June and the mayflower was still blooming, its scent filling the air. I had reached my nineteenth birthday and had started as had every teenage girl before me to frequent the main thoroughfare at night, parading up and down its streets in pursuit of boys. Usually a few of us would band together, stopping every now and then to chat with others but never losing sight of our objective, always with the hope of meeting someone new in town. It was a fruitless ritual, however, since most of the lads our age had left the town and those who remained never had money enough to take us anywhere.

We usually ended up down the canal strolling arm in arm along the gravel path or reclining on the grassy bank staring at the river. The canal was a place of ancient beauty where people liked to walk on summer evenings. Where young boys fished or paddled in the water or sat with smirks on low stone walls making eyes at girls. Where men with sniffing dogs chased rats along the river. And where certain sights and smells seemed to be eternal, like the ancient drinking well with its heavy iron cup from which a thirsty traveller might drink of the purest water. Or the reek of rotting vegetation from deserted mills, where once the wheels of industry set the pace for the shawled women and ill-clad men who streamed through the iron gates.

Halfway down, the gravel path became a lane with grass-banked hedges and low stone walls covered with honeysuckle and sweet briar, the aroma of which was heavenly. Many a courting couple found seclusion in these hedges, occasionally interrupted by overzealous priests prodding the hedges with their canes. Here Jane and I were sitting on a beautiful after-noon, humming spoony songs and listening to Henry Parrot reciting from the local paper.

"Having strugg-elled to his feet again, the injoored man began to leave, when sudd-ent-ly he coll-ap-azed. A doctor was called to the skene, but arri-ved too late."

He looked up suddenly.

"What the blazes are yee laughing at?" he asked. "It's no laughing matter. The man died didn't he?"

He shook his head.

"Jaysus Christ! Bloody ignoramuses. Skitting and laughing at everything."

He took a sudden swipe at Jane, who screamed and dodged sideways, her shoulder scraping on the wall behind. Jane cra-dled it and whimpered, but Henry was too mad to care.

"Buzz off, the two of you. Go on buzz off."

His eyes were angry behind his glasses.

Repentant, I tried to humour him.

"Ah, come on, Henry. We were only codding. We weren't laughing at you."

"I may look stupid, but I'm not," Henry replied.

He threw us both a dirty look and said he had better things to do than to sit there listening to our lies. He rose and stamped off. Jane dropped her head.

"I wish we hadn't done that," she sighed, as we watched him disappear along the path.

I, too, was sad, for Henry was one of the nicer lads and we had not meant to hurt him. In all the years we had known him we had never seen him lose his temper, except when Joey Fahey broke his glasses. Not that he had no reason to be angry, mind, living with that whining mother.

Henry had told me once that the only time he had seen his father sober was when he saw him dead. A terrible man by all accounts, constantly finding fault with Henry and picking fights with everybody, until one evening in a drunken rage he picked a fight with a tinker man who struck him on the head with an iron bar. Henry was only thirteen then, but remembered going to the barracks and seeing his dead father, his clothes all rumpled and caked with mud. It was the face, Henry said, that affected him. So angry and hate-filled in life yet so calm and gentle-looking in death. It was a face he had never before witnessed, and Henry Parrot, who had hated and feared his father all his life, found himself sorry at his passing.

Why he cherished books so dearly we could never understand, since it took him an hour to read one page. Yet, as Henry said, he was not stupid. Somewhere in his genes there was intelligence, for he could hold you spellbound with his explanations and had an analytic kind of mind that put the rest of us to shame. A genius in reverse people said he was, though we never knew what they meant by that. And it was always a source of some annoyance to myself that God could have been so merciless to have given him a face to match his name.

"God can be cruel sometimes," said Jane, lifting the thought right out of my head, "for there's poor Henry with all that nose, and old Mr. Doran with no nose at all. Lord, when I think how we used to torment that man! What was it we used to sing?"

Nosey Doran was a fool,
He left his nose upon a stool,
A great big cat came in one day,
And took poor Nosey's nose away.

"You had to remind me, didn't you?" I said, trying to look sad.

But Jane wasn't fooled. She gave me one of her silly looks and prodded my side until I, too, was laughing. Soon we were both hilarious, staggering all around with Jane grabbing at my arm and hugging her belly. My abdomen tightened painfully and I began to groan, at which point Jane laughed all the louder. Finally I blundered off to find relief in a derelict mill. Minutes later Jane arrived. She had stopped laughing, though a little grin kept playing at the corner of her mouth.

"Don't start again," I begged, and she pulled her face to serious.

"I couldn't help it. It wasn't my fault. You were laughing too."

"It doesn't matter, it's finished now," I said, and we both laughed some more.

"May God forgive us is all I can say. As though the poor man wasn't cursed enough."

"What happened to his nose, in any case? Did you ever know?" I asked.

Jane said she didn't and we both fell to wondering. Maybe he was born without it? Or lost it through some painful misadventure? Either way he went through life without it. He married and had several children, all equipped with perfect breathing apparatus.

"Now that I think back on it, I feel ashamed. Don't you? Henry was right, we are ignorant, and when I see him I am going to tell him so."

We sat silent for a while then, listening to the drip-drip of the old mill wheel outside the crumbling building.

"That's where they found poor Bridie Murphy," Jane said, "out there beside that wheel. Let's have a look."

We leaped across a narrow channel to an opening in the wall that must have been a window or a door at one time. A shiver passed through me at our closeness to the wheel, the water sucking at its paddles. Tendrils of green slime hung from its arms. I pulled my head in quickly. Jane laughed and leaned forward more, her fingers reaching for the paddles.

"Don't!" I cried. "It's dangerous," and pulled her back.

We stayed inside the opening looking across the river to the grounds of the Asylum where human shapes were moving in and out between the trees. We wondered if one of them might be Maizie but the shapes were too far away to tell.

"I hate to think of her in there, and I feel guilty not going to visit her," Jane said, suddenly emotional. "It's strange when you think of it. There's poor Maizie, who couldn't bear to be restricted, ending up in there.

"And poor Bridie Murphy with such a fear of water, and that wheel, ending up out there. She wouldn't even come in here alone, you know. I remember Paddy Farrell teasing her and trying to get her to come in here, but she wouldn't come past that boulder." She pointed to a granite slab just inside the door. "It's awful when you think of it. It was bad enough that she drowned, without ending up there."

"Most likely she fell in farther up," I said, "and the current carried her down."

Jane looked at me puzzled. "Fell in? What do you mean, fell in? Bridie committed suicide. I thought everybody knew that!" Her statement, so unexpected, angered me.

"Everybody knows nothing of the sort," I spat, for I certainly did not and believed that story to be gossip. But Jane was adamant. She knew better than I did, she said, and it wouldn't hurt for me to take her word sometimes instead of thinking that I knew it all.

"Oh! you don't know anything more than I do. You only know what other people told you. You weren't there. And nor were they for that matter. They're just making up stories to suit the situation. You said yourself that Bridie was terrified of water, so it's hardly the place she would go to do it, even if she did, which I don't believe. Nobody knows for sure what happened except poor Bridie, and she's not here to defend herself."

Jane rolled her eyes. "Now don't be a stupid cow," she said. "Nobody is running Bridie down. She drowned herself and that's all there is to it. Why do you think she's buried in unconsecrated ground? What's more, I know for a fact that Bridie was pregnant."

In shock and still smarting from the insult of being called a cow, I glared at her.

"So conveniently you forget. I was working and couldn't go to the funeral. Not like some people, home all day."

"There was no funeral to speak of, I told you that. It was all kept very quiet, so don't go getting mad at me because you didn't know. Anyway, I don't want to get into a fight over it."

She walked away. A few minutes later she came back.

"All I can tell you is I went to the graveyard after Mrs. Hanley told me, and there was Bridie's grave, all by itself in that empty patch of ground behind the chapel, and only a small iron cross with her name on it."

We sat down again and she put her hand upon my shoulder.

"I'm sorry I called you a stupid cow," she said.

I was thoroughly depressed. Not because Bridie was a friend of mine, for she was older than myself and moved in a different circle, but I had always found her a friendly soul despite her dull and dowdy appearance. Her accident I believed to be just that, and until now no one had told me otherwise.

"I wonder why she did it?" I said, and Jane shrugged.

"Who knows? Probably because that fellow jilted her."

"What fellow was that?"

"Well, I'm not exactly sure, but Billy Bood thinks it was Eamon Devlin."

"Eamon Devlin! I don't believe it! Not with Bridie Murphy!"

The picture of Bridie with any man, much less a handsome lad like Eamon Devlin, was too much to imagine.

"Surely she didn't think he would marry her!"

"I don't know, I can't imagine it," Jane said. "But apparently they were seen together on more than one occasion, with him wrapped around her like a blanket. And Billy Bood told me that his mother saw Bridie's mother leave the Devlin house one evening in a woeful temper, so it must be true."

My mind boggled. How could Bridie have been so foolish when every girl knew that Eamon Devlin was a scamp? True, he was handsome and exciting, but he had no respect for girls and believed they existed for his pleasure only.

"She had to have known he wouldn't marry her." I said.

"Who knows what pressures were brought to bear on her," Jane said. "Or why she even went out with him. On the other hand, I can see how she would be flattered by his attentions. I could fall for him myself. And I'm sure it wasn't every day she got an offer of a date."

"I don't suppose it was, poor thing. And don't think that scoundrel didn't know it. The thing that bothers me is the way men get away with it. It isn't fair. They do the dirty deed and leave the woman to worry about the consequences."

"That's how it is, though."

Jane sighed at the unfairness. She picked up the stick that she had trodden underfoot and tossed it through the opening. It hit the wheel and lodged there for a fraction of a second before dropping out of sight. We heard it plop into the water as we rose and started toward the door to home.

36

*November came with its usual fog and drea-
riness. Halloween had brought a minimum of
excitement. The table, set as usual with a
large barmbrack, apples, nuts and oranges,
seemed bare without the children. Unlike
larger cities where children trick-or-treated, it
was customary for our younger ones to
remain indoors playing games and telling stories, for it was a night unsafe to be abroad, a
time of evil and disruption when keening
spirits roamed the earth, and the slightest
invocation might arouse the dead.*

Myself and Jane, with nothing better to amuse ourselves,
decided to stay home. Madge came in as usual, as did
Paddy Brennan with his accordion. We listened courteously
while he played his repertoire, then we settled by the fire to tell
our fortunes from the saucers on the hearth and listen to
Paddy's stories. Peg, who had arrived home while the music
was still playing, spread hazelnuts around the hob to see who
would be married first. The nut belonging to Madge exploded.

"Ah! I was sure it would be mine," lamented Jane, who had
found the ring in the barmbrack earlier.

Paddy laughed and said we were ridiculous, that those
were old wives' tales, while admitting that when his sister May
was young she used to do all sorts of crazy things. One of them

was looking in the mirror on the stroke of twelve to see the face of the man that she would marry.

"And did she ever see it, Paddy?"

"Begob! I couldn't tell you, because she wouldn't say. But I knew a girl myself once who claimed to have."

Madge's face lit up. "Maybe we'll try it tonight," she cried, looking around at us.

"I wouldn't if I were you," said Paddy. "You might see something you haven't bargained for."

"Like what for instance?" demanded Jane.

"Like the devil himself," said Paddy, pulling his face into a gruesome grin.

"Oh, go on!" said we, laughing.

But Paddy's face was serious. "You can laugh," he answered, and told us a story of a beautiful maid in a silken shawl who despite her parents' warnings had crept downstairs at the stroke of twelve, a lighted candle in her hand, to beseech the mirror for a glimpse of her intended. No sooner had she whispered his name three times when the mirror changed and a terrifying head with horns looked out at her. The girl screamed as the mirror broke into smithereens, and when the parents rushed downstairs they found her unconscious in the hall.

"She was never the same again," Paddy said.

"Oh, that's a lot of nonsense! Don't believe him," chuckled Jane. Then whispering to me, "We'll try it tonight before we go to bed."

At eleven o'clock Mother came home drunk and picked an argument with Father, who had just come in ahead of her. Jane and myself sat in darkness in our bedroom listening, waiting for them to go to bed. When finally we heard Father slide the bolt on the back door we undressed and waited. When the Tholsel clock began to strike we hurried to the mirror. Jane lit a candle and we each peered in, willing our future husbands to appear. But all we saw was our reflection.

"I knew it," Jane said, disgusted, and blew the candle out.

The next night, All Souls', we watched Mother leave a bowl of water and some bread upon the table for the benefit of spirits who might chance by. Through the previous night they had been descending from the skies all over Ireland, allowed to wander for a little while on their beloved land. It was a ritual Mother rigidly observed despite her constant criticism of the custom. As a child I had lain awake on many a Halloween listening for their rap-tap on the window, but I had never heard a thing. All Souls' Day found the weather mild, but a heavy mist had fallen, and though the streets were clear enough, pockets of fog were everywhere.

"I can't see a thing, can you?" Jane asked, clutching at my arm as we peered into the mist.

"I think we should have stayed at home," I answered, for all around great billows of fog were gathering, leaving only minor openings to show the way. All along the quayside it lay in heavy folds, shrouding the edges of the river and obscuring it from sight. One false step and you'd be in the river. Having trudged a lengthy distance of our usual hunting grounds, I was ready to go home, but Jane insisted on hanging around in the hope that some exciting male might chance along. We lingered, shivering on John's Bridge, looking at the river slide quietly by, black glassy spaces between grey balls of mist. There was an odour of rotting vegetation rising up from it and I could feel the dampness creep inside my bones.

Finally, Jane conceded.

"This town is dead. I'm going home."

Through chattering teeth I readily agreed. The town *was* dead. Apart from the activities of the night before there was no excitement anywhere. Outside of two mischievous boys who had bumped into us, and one courting couple, we had not met a soul.

"I'll never believe that prophecy again," Jane complained, glaring at the ring she had found inside the barmbrack.

"I never believed it in the first place—only idiots believe that finding a ring in a currant cake assured them of a man. Most likely it would do the opposite. Look what happened to Eileen Byrne. Engaged for two whole years, she was. Then found the ring in the barmbrack, and the next thing we knew the engagement was off and her boyfriend marrying someone else."

"Oh, yeah," said Jane, taking off the ring, "I forgot about that."

She held it out as though to throw it in the river, then hesitated.

"Maybe I'll keep it just in case," she said, and slipped it into her coat pocket. Passing the Friary Chapel on our way home we noticed the men's bicycles outside the gate. "So that's where they all are," Jane cried excitedly, intent on loitering.

I threw her a warning look. "Don't even think about it," I said. "Both my feet are frozen and I'm perished from that bridge."

"Oh, you," she moaned, "you have no endurance," and followed me reluctantly across the road to home.

And so the weeks slipped by. The year was rapidly coming to an end and Christmas once again around the corner. The fog which had lingered in the fields and narrow lanes for weeks had finally dispersed, replaced first by lashing rain and then by bitter cold. Soon the white frost clung like marble to the iron railings and lay like carpet on the roads. The roofs of houses gleamed with it and people cursed and slid on every corner. Discouraged by the constant fear of falling, Uncle Jim stayed indoors hunkered by the fire. With Father seated on one side, Uncle on the other and Timmy the terrier in between, there was little room for us. So despite the constant fear of falling, we went out.

Mother, as well, determined to go out no matter what the weather. But one night she came home injured, having attempted to negotiate the steps leading up to Mary's Lane, a popular shortcut to the streets above. Had it not been for two young lads who were walking in the street below she might have stayed where she had fallen. Luckily they heard her cry and ran to her assistance at the foot of the steps down which she had fallen. The two lads succeeded in reviving her, helped her to her feet and brought her home.

All of us were shaken, for Mother's face was ghastly with one eye badly swollen and rivulets of blood drying on her cheeks. Her upper lip was split in several places. One of the lads who had helped her home offered to go and fetch a doctor, but Mother, making light of things as usual, laughed and said that she was fine now that they had brought her home. She thanked the two of them and came inside.

Jane clicked her tongue.

"You should have had more sense, Mam, taking those steps on a night like this. You could have killed yourself."

Mother smiled. She had taken those steps a thousand times, she said, and never had an accident.

"It was foolish all the same," Jane continued, and Father agreed, scolding Mother for her foolishness. He insisted on attending to her wounds in spite of her objections. For a few short hours that evening the house seemed blessed, with no harsh or hating words between them. The next day Mother's eye was frightening, the wound black and ugly. She remained indoors all the following week to satisfy us about her safety. It was nice having her home and not be worrying over her where-abouts.

A state of peace settled on the house and for a little while our hopes were raised by what seemed like Father's efforts to bring things back to normal. A spark of love seemed to be igniting. What we didn't realise was that there had been many stages in the ebbing of Father's love for Mother, and the tolerance he was showing now was not because he loved her but because he loved her less. Indeed, as the days of that week drew on, Mother surely sensed it, for suddenly her heart seemed closed again, her manner withdrawn. The silences began all over, the atmosphere charged again. Then on Saturday morning, with Father having left for work and Jane out doing the shopping, Mother announced she was going out.

37

No sooner had Mother left the house when Uncle Jim returned from his morning walk. He passed me in the kitchen without saying a word, and then, on the point of opening his bedroom door, he turned and asked if I had heard any news of the Old Man lately. He only asked, he said, because he had heard he was doing poorly, and wondered if I knew.

Poorly in Uncle Jim's estimation meant dying, which frightened me. And maybe it was that that prompted me to say the terrible thing I then said, coupled with resentment at Uncle's sudden interest in a man he had never liked. "An old fool!" he had always called him.

Too hastily I retorted.

"Why ask me? What makes you think I'd want to know?"

Then, spurred by the venomous expression on his face, "He's no friend of mine!"

The words were out before I could restrain them, and Uncle, shaking his head with obvious disgust, disappeared into his room. I stood in the kitchen motionless, a Judas. In one awful moment I had denied the closest kindest friend I had ever had. I cursed my wicked temper!

Why did I always allow my emotions to control my mind? My only consolation was the Old Man's voice telling me,

"There's no wrong or right emotions, child. We feel what we feel an can't help it."

Conscious of Uncle's mutterings from beyond the wall and fearful that he might come out, I grabbed my coat and left the house.

A SHORT WHILE LATER I STOOD outside the Old Man's house, not caring who might see me. I knocked loudly but there was no reply. I knocked again.

"Mr. Dempsey. Are you in? It's me," I shouted. I heard a shuffling inside, and called again. The door creaked open and his face peered out at me.

"Ah! 'tis you at last. Come in. Come in." His voice sounded weak and distant. I hesitated a moment, then followed him in.

"Did you not hear me knocking, then?"

"I did," he answered. "I'd want t'be deaf not to." He eased himself into his chair, an old grey blanket thrown around his shoulders.

"I won't stay," I said, alarmed at his appearance.

He either did not hear, or did not care to answer, for he made no reply. On the hearth I saw a glass with something in it, a medication I assumed. He picked it up and sipped at it, then looked at me. Only four months had passed since I had seen him last, yet the face staring at me across the fire had aged by ten times that. His eyes were tired and lifeless, his hair, though still plentiful, clung to his head like a withered vine, the brown skin on his forehead as wrinkled as a prune.

For the first time since I had known him I was lost for words.

"Have you not been well?" I managed, finally, not mentioning my uncle. At first he said that he was fine, but then he gave a little laugh followed by a sigh and admitted he was lying. Poor health had come to roost with him, he said, had kept him indoors, too weak to venture out. Then as bad luck would have it, a few days ago he had felt well enough to chance it and fallen—or been knocked down by a bicycle. It had given him a fright, and now he lacked the courage to go out again.

"Who knocked you down?" I demanded. As usual he knew what I was thinking.

"Arragh, sure there's no blame attached. 'Twas me own fault. I had no business in th'road."

He explained how it had happened. How he had gone to Waldron's for his peppermints and, on his way back, impatient with his progress on the narrow path, had stepped out on the road in front of the bicycle.

So that explained the limping.

"You were lucky you weren't hurt more," I said, and told him of my mother's accident.

"Aye, I have that much t'be thankful for," he answered, straightening his back. "But God in heaven! Will ye lookit what 'tis done t'me. Afraid t'stir out now I am."

He placed his fingers to his head at a point above his ear and only then did I notice the ugly bump on it. I asked if it still hurt and he said no, not exactly, but that it bothered him at night, keeping him awake.

Ever since Mickey had died, he said, he had known nothing but misfortune, with one thing following another. First the pleurisy. Then Meggie. Then the dizzy spells. And after the ordeal of the flood, bronchitis. Now it seemed every bone in his body ached all the time.

"You'll feel better when the warm weather comes," I said, attempting to make light of it.

He looked at me with a dreadful seriousness but didn't answer. Then he turned his gaze upon the fire. The minutes passed with neither of us saying anything, until my eyes fell on the glass he was sipping from.

"Are you taking that for your cough?" I asked. He nodded, his face twisting in a grimace. "What is it, Buckley's Mixture?"

It was some concoction John O'Connell made up for him, he said.

"I was afraid t'ask what was in it."

I noticed the absence of his pipe. "You're not smoking, I see. Don't tell me you're finally taking your own advice!"

He chuckled. "Go'way with ye now. T'was more a matter iv not wantin', than any prudent decision t'resist."

I didn't ask why he had not seen a doctor because I knew what he would answer. Most people of his generation preferred to rely on their own remedies or the counsel of their druggist.

He put the glass to his lips again, but as he did so his hand began to tremble, causing the liquid to overflow and trickle down the glass. It ran along his fingers to the back of his hand, then dribbled down his wrist. And as I watched it disappear beneath his frayed old sleeve I couldn't help but notice his emaciated hand, the sinews showing through the skin. It hurt to look at it. His hands were once sleek and sturdy with strength enough to lift a plough. Busy industrious hands, I thought, not like the useless lazy ones wrapped around beers in the local pubs.

An urgent need to be away came over me, but the sudden movement of his chair delayed my action as the Old Man stood up and cocked his head as though listening to something. He leaned on his walking stick a second to get his balance, then hobbled to the window where he raised the curtain slightly and looked outside. A smile lit up his face.

"What is it?" I asked. "What's out there?"

He beckoned me across. "Peep out," he said, "but don't let him see ye."

I did as he directed, peering at the garden, then at the hanging branches of the Rowan tree, but I could see nothing. Then something stirred on the window ledge and moving closer

I distinguished the shape of a little bird. It had its head back in song, though the sound was muffled through the leaded glass and I wondered how the Old Man could have heard him.

"It's a robin," I exclaimed.

I remembered a story he had told me once about his little robin friend having breakfast with him every morning. "How do you know it's the same robin?" I asked.

"Ah! sure he's there at this time every day," he said. "Can't bring himself t'leave me."

"But how can you be sure it's the same one?" I persisted. "All robins look alike." He was probably mistaken, I told him, and that this was a different bird.

He grinned and shook his head. "Not a chance iv it. 'Tis him all right. I know 'tis him, and he knows I know."

"But how? How can you tell?"

An expression of amusement spread across his face. "He won't like it if I tell ye," he teased. "It's our little secret. Ye'll just have t'take me word for it." He hobbled back to his chair chuckling to himself.

"Okay then," I said, stepping back across the room. "I believe you. It's the same robin. But tell me why he is out there sitting on your window."

I wished I had never asked, for suddenly his face, so happy and excited only moments earlier, went grimly serious and he looked at me for the longest time without answering. Then in a mournful voice, he said. "'Tis a mystery t'me. I've tried me best t'discourage him. T'make him feel unwanted. An' for a while there I thought I had succeeded, when th'weather got so bad. But here he is again, th'little rogue, in spite iv every-thing." A look of total misery came over him and he looked directly at me. "D'ye think maybe he knows?" he asked. "Can he feel it comin'?"

The question, so unexpected and so out of character, shook me.

"Know what? Feel what coming?" I asked. But I knew quite well what he had meant. He was sure he was dying.

A feeling of deep sorrow crept over me. Seeing the sadness on my face, he buried his head in his singed old hands. There was silence in the house.

I wished I could think of something nice to say to him, something that would make him happy. Oh! I had many things I would have liked to say, things that I knew he would have loved to hear but which I couldn't bring myself to say. What was it about myself, I wondered, that made it so difficult to say what was in my heart?

He began to cough, gently at first, then harsher and harsher until his shoulders shook. Groping for his handkerchief he fell sideways in his chair and I thought for sure he was going to collapse. I told him that he ought to be in bed, but he insisted he was feeling fine, better than he had felt in ages and that he would dance a jig on New Year's Eve.

I said, "I think I should be going," and buttoned up my coat. He made to rise, then sat back down. "I'll wish you a Merry Christmas, in case I don't see you," I added, holding out my hand. He grabbed it and held it tightly, forcing a smile but with eyes so sad I hated leaving him. "Is there anything I can do before I go?" I asked. "Can I get you anything?"

He shook his head and thanked me, saying that he could manage, that he sounded sicker than he was and would be fit as a fiddle next time we met. He wriggled his arms and legs to show me he was serious, and just to give him pleasure I agreed. We both knew, of course, that he was bantering, that beneath the guise of gaiety lay a mantle of despair.

38

The weather continued unimproved until mid-December, when finally the sky cleared and the dry frosty mornings came again. On one such afternoon I was strolling down the lane to the Old Man's house when I saw Barney Callaghan coming toward me up the hill. He was walking fast, like one in a dreadful hurry, his overcoat hanging open and his woollen scarf askew. He didn't stop or speak to me, just bent his head and hurried by. That fact in itself did not bother me, it not being unusual behaviour for Barney, who had a repertoire of habits aimed at keeping people like myself at a respectful distance.

As I continued down the lane, reflecting on the grimness of his face and untidy manner of his scarf, a feeling of uneasiness came over me and all at once I knew that something grave had happened to the Old Man. I quickened my pace, then began to run, but by the time I reached the bottom of the hill I knew I was too late. They had taken him away, the ambulance having left only seconds earlier. I watched it disappear up Clooney's Hill toward the County Hospital. At least they were not taking him to Thomastown, I thought. The gate to his house was standing open as was the front door. I waited, deeply worried, until somebody came out.

"Poor auld fellow. 'Tis a shame to see him go like that, but it had to come." It was Tommy Wall.

"What happened? Is Mr. Dempsey dead?"

He looked me up and down. "He might as well be for all the strength that's left in him," he said, seemingly on the verge of an explanation, but stopping abruptly. He gave me a funny look as if to ask what concern it was of mine. Not wanting to betray the least of my emotions I muttered something and left.

Later on that week I presented myself at the desk inside the door of the County Hospital. "I'm here to see Mr. Dempsey," I told the plump red-faced nurse behind the counter, who looked quizzically at me, then at my bicycle visible through the window.

On the desk beside her elbow sat a pair of reading glasses. She picked them up and put them on, her eyes travelling over me. Then satisfied that I looked respectable and had washed behind my ears she offered me a smile. But getting in to see him proved more difficult than I thought, for there were certain rules to be observed which I was unaware of, never having been to that hospital before. But after some persuasion on my part and a little sympathy on hers I was admitted. She glanced up at the clock on the wall behind her head, then stepped out from behind the counter.

"Come this way, please," she said, and I followed her along the hall past some sort of storage space where the smell of iodine and ammonia was overpowering. "In there," she said, stopping outside a glass-panelled door through which one could see into the room beyond. "You'll find Mr. Dempsey that way," she indicated with her thumb. "You may visit him for fifteen minutes only."

I thanked her and went in. He wasn't difficult to find, with few beds in the ward and one or two secluded behind wooden screens. I had a shock when I saw him, however. His head was gaunt against the pillow, eyes closed and sunken, mouth hanging open and skin like polished marble drawn tight across his cheeks. They had trimmed his beard so close against his chin it was barely noticeable. Had it not been for the ugly bruise still evident above his ear I might have passed him by. I thought he must be sleeping, but he opened his eyes the moment I stood beside the bed. He looked bewildered, his eyes confused as though trying to recall my face or understand what I was doing there. After a moment the clouds parted and he smiled.

"So this is where you're hiding," I said. "You had me worried half to death."

He lay still, smiling without answering, his eyes resting on my face. Then, pulling himself up higher on the pillow, he said, "Ye had no trouble findin' me I see." His voice was barely audible and I had to bend to hear him. "'Twas nice iv ye t'worry," he continued, "but ye needn't have. There's nothin' wrong with me."

I gave him a disbelieving look. "So, what are you doing in here if there is nothing wrong with you?"

"I'm on me holidays, what else?"

"Well, you might have said something before you left."

He was more awake suddenly and tried to sit up straight, lurched forward, then slumped back on his pillow. "Is there not a chair for ye t'sit on?" he asked with agitation, turning his head from one side to the other.

"I'm fine. I don't need a chair."

"Did ye walk th'whole way here?"

"No, I have my bicycle."

"That's good."

He looked about him anxiously, taking in the empty bed across the room and the low murmuring sounds from behind a nearby screen.

"What were they thinkin' bringin' ye in here? 'Tis no place for a young girl t'visit."

And why was that? I asked, looking all around.

The room seemed nice enough to me, clean with few beds and bright sunny windows. I was about to mention this fact when I saw the nurse approaching. She stopped a moment by his bed, then seeing that I was standing, went and fetched a chair. She asked him if he needed anything or if there was something she could do. He replied that he was fine and that the best thing she could do for him was to let him die in peace. The nurse laughed and shook her head.

"There's little fear of it. You'll be telling me that on the day you leave." She turned to go, then looked at me. "Ten minutes mind," she whispered, and was gone.

No sooner had she left when he began to grumble.

"I don't know why she keeps on saying that, when she knows as well as I do that th'only way I'm leavin' here is in a wooden box."

I stared at him unable to reply, and seeing the concern on my face he softened.

"Ah child! We can't go on pretendin'. D'ye think I don't know what ward I'm in? Sure every time they put a screen around a bed 'tis because someone is dyin'. Why d'ye think they put me here?" This was said with not the least resentment nor any trace of fear.

"You're not in here to die. You are in here to get well. Maybe they had nowhere else to put you on such short notice. I take it you didn't make a reservation?"

My words sounded lame and ineffectual, and though he chuckled at my remark he made no effort to reply. He just slipped into a silence, lying motionless, his eyes staring fixedly in front of him. The object of his gaze was the empty bed across the room in which, he told me, somebody had lain the night before but which the morning had found empty.

"It'll be my turn next. I'm sure iv it."

"I wish you wouldn't talk like that," I said. "You're feeling low, that's all. People do when these things happen."

But I was frightened now. I knew that there was truth in what he said, that he would not be leaving here of his own free will but would die alone or in the company of strangers. I felt my stomach tighten, anguish pinching up my face. He saw the transformation and with an effort raised himself on his elbow.

"Now listen t'me alana. I don't want ye upset. Remember what I told ye. Yer whole life is still ahead iv ye. Mine is all but over."

He laid himself back on the pillow.

"I've had a long life an' I'm not complainin.' I'm happy t'be goin'. But, there's wan thing I'd like ye t'do for me. Bring me Meggie's bell."

The lump was big in my throat by now, and fearing I might let him down, I rose.

"Try to get some sleep and I'll come again tomorrow," was all that I could bring myself to say.

Smiling, he reached out and touched me lightly on the arm, the misery in his soul pouring through his eyes. Then he lay back calmly, and I hurried to the door.

I NEVER SAW HIM ALIVE AGAIN, because when I came the next day they wouldn't let me in, and one day later he was dead. The funeral took place shortly after, on that kind of sunny day he always loved. More people turned out than I had expected, some of them ones who wouldn't speak to him in life, now begging his forgiveness and praying for his soul.

Alone and utterly dejected I stood behind the gathering, watching Barney Callaghan stare blankly at the grave. As the coffin was lowered into it, he gave a sudden mournful wail, causing the priest to look up sharply. Barney glanced around embarrassed, waited until the coffin disappeared, then slowly walked away. I stayed a little longer, examining the iron cross lying idly by the grave.

MALACHI DEMPSEY 1865-1950 was all it said. There were no flowers on the grave, just one wreath from Barney Callaghan, but I knew the Old Man wouldn't care about that, for he hated to see God's ornaments wasted in that way. Consumed with such a longing to see him just once more yet knowing I would never ever lay eyes on him again, I walked away.

That same evening Jane and I went to his house to get Meggie's bell. I had been unable to retrieve it earlier, having found the front door locked. This time we sneaked around the back, and standing on Jane's shoulders, I forced the bedroom window which had been broken in the flood and never quite repaired. The house felt cold and empty. Remnants of a meal lay moulding on the table and tiny flies were feeding in the sugar. Jane shooed them with her fingers, then covered the bowl with a saucer.

My eyes fell on the empty armchair, the old grey blanket lying in a heap against the cushion. In all my life I had never seen a space so empty.

Quickly I found Meggie's bell and started for the kitchen door.

"I can't stay here," I muttered.

"We'll have to leave the way we came. We can't lock that from outside," Jane reminded me.

With one final look around we passed back through the bedroom door, and just as I was stepping to the window I saw the book. *Porcelain: The Soul of Ireland*, by John Mackay. It was the book he had often carried about with him, reading passages to me. I picked it up and looked at it, then took it through the window.

"Why did you take that book?" Jane asked when we got outside.

"No reason. I just did, that's all."

"Well, you'll have to put it back. That's stealing."

"I don't care. I'm keeping it."

She looked at me with an odd expression, but didn't argue.

I wanted to explain why I had taken it, why I couldn't leave it there, and why the memory it evoked was causing me such grief, but I couldn't bring myself to speak. All I could think about was that day beside the river, when the Old Man had dropped it and I had picked it up—it was his birthday, but I had not known it then. He had cherished that little book, and the least I could do now was to take care of it.

My heart ached for him. He had shown me nothing but kindness and affection, and I had loved him, but never told him so. Why couldn't I have been more understanding, and I so starved for affection myself I could have loved a stone? All the way home I kept thinking about that, and what he had said about having no one in the world to care for him.

Oh! Old Man, forgive me and hear me now. I was young and didn't understand. A child whose emotions were buried under mountains of reserve, and who could have faced a firing squad more easily than have told you that I loved you.

39

The snow that we had hoped for never came that Christmas. Instead, rain lashed the city. The weeks before had seen the weather cold and dry, the air alive with expectation, of people busy with their special preparations, and in homes the warm scent of ground cloves and spices.

D owntown, too, had its own excitement. Shops sparkled with coloured lights, and the smell of ham and poultry above the softer smell of iced cakes from the bakeries was divine. Turkeys hung on skewers in every butcher's window. For several days blue-fingered women had been plucking them in Slater's yard, their voices light with laughter or raised in solemn chorus to the strains of "Silent Night."

Then almost overnight it began to rain: gently at first, like the soft spray from a waterfall, then growing in force as the days wore on, to a driving dreary downpour. The wind increased in strength, and soon the streets, so cheerful and bustling earlier, began to look deserted. Shopkeepers pulled their doors a little tighter, and buntings new with Christmas greetings only hours before lay sodden and abandoned on their doorsteps. Soon sawdust from the butcher's began to clog the gutters while feathers lodged in messy heaps at every corner.

Yet people kept their cheery dispositions, calling season's greetings to each other, while struggling with their soaking

Christmas shopping. By Christmas Eve the rain had eased to a steady drizzle, but the wind still whipped the rooftops. Jane had developed a nasty cold yet refused to remain indoors. "I'll die before I give in to it," she said, determined to go out for holly. "We have to do something with this house for Christmas." We arrived back soaked, having walked for miles in search of it, and had to spread our coats before the fire to dry.

"That's it for me," I said. "I'm not stirring out of this house again today. I have no will for anything. Just look at my good shoes."

"I told you not to wear them. What did you expect? You can't go walking in rain-soaked grass and not get them wet." Her lack of sympathy was galling.

"How was I to know we were going on a route march? I thought we were only going to Kenny's Well. Besides, I didn't know the holly tree had vanished. What happened to it, anyway? I can't believe it isn't there, after all these years. People loved that old tree. They used to sing carols there every Christmas."

"Well, they won't be singing there anymore," Jane said. "It must have perished in the flood."

"Either that, or someone chopped it down for firewood."

"And that wouldn't surprise me either. Especially to learn it was Jasper Hynes. A proper Scrooge he is."

"Well, he'll have no luck for it if he did," she said. "I'm not going to let it spoil my Christmas. Come on, help me put this holly up."

We placed a sprig behind each picture and two above the mirror on the mantel. Then we hung the mistletoe and paper decorations, one chain from each corner of the room held aloft in the centre of the ceiling by a dazzling Christmas bell. We brought out the tinsel to loop around the edges of the ceiling.

"There, that's better," Jane declared, stepping down and surveying the scene.

"At least we got some lovely berries," I admitted, admiring the red reflections in the mirror and pleased with the transformation in the kitchen. "I'm glad we got them now," I said, and Jane smiled.

Peg arrived home at that moment and raised her hands in unaccustomed pleasure, like a child seeing itself for the first time in a mirror. "Oh, the place looks really grand!" she cried, gazing all around. "Who gave us all that lovely holly?"

Nobody gave it to us, we said, and told of our adventure. "Oh! I knew that tree wasn't there," she said, with her usual nonchalance. "It's been gone for months. I'm surprised you never noticed."

Before we could ask her anything more Peg raced out the door in search of her buddy May Blanche, to show her the decorations. Seldom had we seen her so excited, and that alone, Jane said, made it all worthwhile.

She started laying some dishes on the table and I sat beside the window looking at the rain, wondering when it was going to stop and thinking about the year before when I had walked in the snow to Uncle Willie's house. What a difference then! The town had been a scene from Charles Dickens. I had half a mind to go to bed.

There was no use crying about it, Jane decided, and headed to the scullery to put the trifle out to gel. Catching sight of herself in the kitchen mirror, she muttered something about her hair, and plucked the hair oil bottle from the shelf.

I dozed off then, until I heard Mother coming through the kitchen door.

"Merciful heavens what's that awful smell?"

Smell? What smell? Then I, too, caught a whiff of something queer. Mother asked again, looking pointedly at Jane, who was standing by the fire. She didn't answer, just made a rapid gesture with her hand as though annoyed with Mother for even asking. It was then that we noticed her glistening hair.

"In the name of God what's that you have on your hair?" Mother asked, and Jane's face went red.

"Nothing!" she replied.

"Nothing?" Mother echoed, wrinkling up her nose.

Jane sighed. "Well if you must know, it's hair oil."

Mother looked at me with a comical expression.

"Oh, is that what it is! I thought for a minute it was horse manure."

It was clear, of course, that Jane had something other than hair oil on her hair. Goose grease I suspected, for besides the smell her hair looked a mess, limp and matted to her head. She obviously wasn't aware of this and thought we were simply having fun, but a quick look in the mirror soon told her different.

"My God!" She clasped her hand against her mouth.

Mother shook her head, about to make another comment, then noticed the decorations.

"Well, for heaven's sake! Where did all of this come from?" She was obviously enchanted. We related the episode of earlier and she listened with amusement. "Well, it was worth it," she said, "it makes a great difference, and I like the holly." Coming from Mother it was a compliment indeed. "Well, I can't stand around here all day," she said, taking her hat from behind the door.

Jane's smile disappeared. "You're not going out again are you Mam? Why don't you stay and have a drink of sherry?"

Mother smiled and shook her head. She didn't care for sherry, and anyway she had to take a ham to Julia Nevin's Times had not been kind to the Nevins of late, and she wanted to repay them for all the times they had been good to her.

"Why! when you were little, Martin used to mend your shoes for nothing. Now he can't afford to mend his own, poor man. I won't be long, though. I'll just make sure they're not in want for Christmas."

"Do you think she'll come home drunk?" Jane asked, as soon as she was gone.

"Most likely," I replied, certain that she would.

"In the meantime, I suppose I should try to do something with this hair. I wish I hadn't put that grease on it."

"Why did you anyway?"

"Oh! I don't know. It looked so crushed and lifeless from that heavy scarf, I thought a little oil might liven it. There was none left in the bottle, so I used the grease."

"Well, you've made it worse."

"It didn't seem like much when I put it on, and there was no smell that I could notice. I blame the fire. It melted the grease and brought out the smell."

That seemed as good an explanation as any.

"There must be something I can do," she said. "I can't go out like this."

"We could stay home," was what I wanted to say, but didn't, for fear of making matters worse. I knew she wanted particularly to go out and with a bit of luck to meet Jimmy Doyle.

She read my mind.

"It's not so much that I want to go, because I could very well stay home, but the thing is, I promised Nuala." She fetched a comb from the scullery shelf, attempting to put a semblance of normality to her hair, then threw it down again.

"Oh, it's no use! I can't fix it." She slumped into a chair. "It isn't fair. It isn't fair. After all the effort I put into it." She was referring to the night before when she had spent an hour or so shampooing and setting it, then sleeping all night in her metal curlers.

"Do you want me to help you wash it out?" I asked. "We still have time. And you can set it with the rags."

"But I'll never get it dry again."

"Yes you will. You can kneel before the fire and it will dry in no time."

"I suppose I could," Jane said, somewhat encouraged.

"It won't be as nice as it was this morning, mind, but it will be better than it looks now."

"Well, there's no other way. I can't leave it like this, and I would like to have it looking nice for Christmas." Nice for Jimmy Doyle was what she really meant, though for the life of me I couldn't fathom why, since he had shown a marked disinterest in her lately. I took the kettle from the hob.

"Come on then. What are you waiting for?"

We marched off to the scullery where she submitted with gratitude to my ministrations. Shampoo was scarce, but a mixture of carbolic and pure lemon soon brought results. Grease globs spread like lily pads on the water until finally her hair was free of it. We rinsed it well and towelled it, curling up the ends as I suggested. Then Jane sat on the low stool beside the fire, and in no time it was dry again and we combed it out.

"Well! maybe there is something to be said for goose grease after all," I said, pleased with the result. "Have a look yourself." Jane hurried to the mirror and was as pleased as I. She hugged me and said she felt much better.

Peg arrived back just then and May Blanche was with her. They twirled around the kitchen making gleeful sounds.

"The bit of holly makes all the difference," May observed, and we all agreed.

"We almost didn't get any at all," Jane told her, launching into the same tiresome story.

May listened until she had finished, and then, with a certain awkwardness, she asked, "Are you still going with Jimmy Doyle?"

She had obviously expected Jane to answer no and confirm the latest rumour, but Jane lied and answered yes and that she expected to meet him later on that evening. She shot a quick glance at me, worried that I might contradict her.

"Anyone like a lemonade?" she asked, going to the chest beneath the table. She gave us each a bottle, which we opened and raised in a toast.

"Merry Christmas, everyone."

We sat around the table chatting. Then Peg suggested we have some Christmas carols and went to turn on the radio.

"Put it on Radio Eireann," Jane said. "That's where the music is."

Peg fiddled with the knobs, but all she succeeded in getting was Meehaul O'Hare talking about the races.

"Oh! I don't believe it. On Christmas Eve!"

Jane, in the meantime, was back before the mirror, looking at her face and no doubt thinking about Jimmy Doyle. The reason she had no difficulty lying was because she had convinced herself, despite all evidence to the contrary, that Jimmy Doyle still cared for her and that his absence from her life in recent weeks was simply due to his long hours at the creamery.

Peg snapped off the radio disgusted.

"Who needs it anyway?" laughed Jane, lifting the lid of the harmonium.

"Adeste Fideles," she began, her voice soft and beautiful.

Peg and I joined in, but May hesitated, embarrassed. "The only thing I know in Latin is Mea Culpa," she said, when the carol ended. "I like the Latin words, mind," she added, and suggested we sang another. But nobody knew another Latin carol, so we settled for "Silent Night" in English. Then Peg and May continued with their own rendition of "Little Town of Bethlehem." Before we knew it, it was five o'clock.

"We better get a move on if we're going," Jane said to me. "The shops close at six."

"Not tonight, they don't," May told her. "They're open until seven."

"Oh good!" Jane replied, fetching a clean blouse from the bedroom. She put it on, then brushed down her skirt. We both checked our faces in the mirror, applying a little lipstick and some powder to our cheeks. Then I dabbed my ears with perfume, Evening in Paris, my favourite.

"I think I'll wear my green voile scarf," Jane said, and draped it loosely around her head, securing it with a hairpin. "That should do it. At least it should keep out the drizzle and won't flatten my hair." She glanced at her old brown shoes. "I think I'll wear my Cuban heels," she said, and off she went to get them.

We went to the Brannigan house and found Nuala in the hall dressed as one might for a wedding, in a lavender coat, paisley scarf and a dainty pillbox on her head.

"I thought you were never going to get here," she said, doing a pirouette around the hall.

"Well, here we are. So, let's go," said Jane, admiring the new outfit.

"You're not wearing it tonight, surely? It's still drizzling, you know."

Nuala's face fell. "Oh, don't tell me!" As though she had not been aware of it, or that anyone with eyesight couldn't see it for themselves.

"Oh, for heaven's sake! It's been raining cats and dogs all week," Jane said, annoyed.

Nuala replied that she knew that but thought it had let up since morning, as she hadn't been outdoors all day.

"Well, it hasn't. And I wouldn't advise an umbrella "

Nuala was disappointed. She had been looking forward to wearing her new outfit, she whined, "seeing as how it's Christmas Eve."

Jane cut her off. "Wear it then, if that's what you want. It's your coat Nuala, and you must suit yourself. I just think you're foolish, that's all."

Nuala turned to me.

"Maybe you can walk between the drops," I offered. She tightened her lips.

"Oh, you're a great help, aren't you?" She brushed past me to the door. "It can't be raining that hard." First she stuck her hand out, then her head, then her whole body.

"Jesus Christ! You're right. It's still coming down. Feck it anyway." She pulled back inside.

"I do wish you wouldn't swear like that," Jane scolded. "Supposing there was somebody in the street!"

"What of it if there was?" cried Nuala, in no way given to swearing but driven by our sanctimonious attitude. "It's enough to make a bishop swear, this fecking rain. It never fecking well stops."

"Nuala Brannigan!" Jane wailed. "If there's one thing worse than a woman in curlers, it's a—"

"Woman with a foul mouth. Yeah, I know," Nuala finished, and disappeared into her bedroom. She reappeared minutes later dressed like Tommy Wall the fireman, in a raincoat and galoshes.

At thirty minutes to closing time we arrived downtown. Most of the shops were still open. We wandered around the Monster House admiring their displays and watching Father Christmas hand out whistles to the children.

"I have to buy some ribbon for my mother," Nuala said, and went off in search of it.

"Did you not find it?" Jane asked when she returned empty-handed.

"They only have pink, and I need purple. Anyhow, I'll get it cheaper at Woolworth's, seeing as how I work there."

We left the Monster House and headed for Woolworth's, where we wandered around again handling the cosmetics and smelling all the soaps.

"I love this one," Nuala said, picking up the Yardley Lavender and pressing it to her nose. "Maybe you'll get it as a Christmas box," we said, and Nuala laughed.

"With my luck I'll get handkerchiefs." She crossed the aisle to the handerchief display—pink, blue and white, three in every box, some with a little flower in the corner and others with white lace around the edges. Jane pointed to one box in particular and Nuala picked it up and looked at it. "They are pretty right enough," she said, fingering each one, "but when you get them every Christmas!"

"I know what you mean," Jane laughed, and moved to another counter, from behind which Gertie Gallivan was watching our approach.

Gertie, a buxom girl with strawlike hair and droopy eyes in a vague face, was one of Nuala's friends. She worked behind the biscuit counter. How she ever managed that remained a mystery. With nobody home upstairs and rooms to rent she could hardly spell arithmetic, much less compute it. Like Nuala she was fond of mascara, red polished nails and plunging V-neck sweaters.

"Well! look who's here! Trust you to get the day off," she called out to Nuala.

Nuala responded with a wide grin. "Seen anyone I know lately?" she asked, gazing around the shop. Gertie said she hadn't or at least had been too busy with her customers to notice anybody.

Busy stuffing herself with biscuits would probably have been more accurate, I thought, judging by the lack of space behind the counter.

"I do have something to tell you though," Gertie said to Nuala, and they leaned across the counter like a pair of talking parrots, repeating everything they had heard or overheard.

We heard Nuala mention Tommy Murphy of the Metropole Hotel, whom she imagined herself in love with. "Well, I can't help you there," laughed Gertie, "I hardly know the man."

"You'll have to talk to Jane about that." She looked inquiringly at Jane, who was the only one present with a line to Tommy's ear, not through any special place in his affections, mind, or status in the town, but rather through her chambermaid connections.

Jane shook her head. "No, and don't ask me because I won't. She's not using me to set up her liaisons. I wouldn't have it on my conscience."

Nuala laughed. "If there's one thing I can't stand it's a jealous woman. Just wait until you ask me for a favour."

Jane rolled her eyes. "When pigs grow feathers, maybe! Besides, what makes you think that Tommy Murphy would consent to speak to you, much less be seen with you? You're not exactly the type of girl to inspire a man like that."

"And you are, I suppose," barked Nuala.

"I didn't say that. But you think you can have any man you like just by walking up to him. Well, it doesn't work like that. Some men prefer a woman for her qualities and not for her dimensions."

Nuala laughed outrageously. "Will you listen to what's talking? You might try telling Jimmy Doyle that."

At the mention of Jimmy Doyle's name Gertie spoke up.

"Jimmy Doyle! Jimmy Doyle! I knew I had something to ask you, Jane. Are you two not going steady anymore?"

"They are as far as she's concerned," sneered Nuala, and Jane's face flushed.

Gertie continued. "The reason I ask is because he was in here a little while ago with Mary Lonnigan. At least I think it was Mary Lonnigan. I never knew her all that well."

"Isn't that the one who used to carry God's Cows around in a matchbox?" Nuala asked. "But I thought she was married and living up in Dublin!"

Jane said we thought so too, not mentioning what Billy Bood had told us about the home for wayward women.

"How do you know they were actually together?" Jane inquired, hoping, I supposed, that Gertie would say she didn't.

But Gertie was explicit. "Any fool could see that. He was all over her. Kissing her on the face and everything."

Mercifully Jane's cold came to her rescue. She began to sneeze and moved away abruptly.

Gertie gave her a weird look, then beckoned Nuala closer. Not caring to hear what she had to say I moved to another aisle.

A few minutes later Jane came and stood beside me. She was alone.

"Where's Nuala?" I asked.

"She's gone to get her wages. They're closing now," Jane explained, and we headed for the door.

It was dark when we got outside again, with a few stars peeping through the broken clouds. Traffic on the street had lessened, but a few last-minute shoppers were still abroad. A group of girls from the Monster House strode toward us along the path, the smell of soap and soft cologne preceding them. They passed in front of us laughing and talking excitedly. Jane spoke to one of them, who told her they were heading to the Club House Hotel. Jane sighed and said she wished we were going with them.

"I have never been to that hotel, and I'd love to go just for the sake of it."

"I doubt if they would welcome you."

"Oh! I don't know," said Jane. "My money is as good as theirs." She stepped out to the centre of the sidewalk and looked up at the sky. "The rain has stopped," she called across her shoulder, and whipped off her scarf, arranging it neatly about her neck. The wind, too, had dropped so I took off mine.

What's keeping Nuala? we wondered. We started to turn back when across the road near Walkin Street we spotted Jimmy Doyle coming out of Tynan's with a parcel in his hand.

He stood outside the shop looking up and down, and I felt Jane's excitement as she raised her arm to wave. He looked across and saw her, then turned his head away and scurried around the corner like a harried dog. Utterly disgusted I turned to Jane.

"I can't believe..." I started, but Jane swung her head abruptly and looked the other way. I could hear her breath going in and out with a sort of staggered motion. I wished the ground would open up and swallow me. Why did I have to be here when this happened? I wanted so much to say something, but I couldn't think of anything, so mad was I with Jimmy Doyle.

After a while Jane turned to me. "Well, if I don't know now, I'll never know," she said in a saddened voice.

"I can't believe what he just did," was all I managed.

"Nor can I. I never expected that of him. Some men are dogs, plain and simple." She hesitated, then continued. "But I'll get over it, don't worry. I see now that he isn't worth it. I just wish I hadn't found it out like this."

"Me too," I said, "but it's just as well it happened now, so you won't have to spend the Christmas wondering."

She started to speak again, then stopped, on the verge of tears. "It will be nice to see old Ladybug again, though, won't it?" she managed, and I agreed.

"If it really was Ladybug, and not just somebody who looks like her." For Jane's sake I hoped it was Ladybug. At least she was someone we both knew and liked and who would never willingly hurt Jane.

"Don't mention anything about me and Jimmy Doyle if we do run into her. And don't say anything to Nuala about what just happened."

We moved off along the sidewalk looking in the windows and waiting for Nuala to catch up. Finally she did and we turned the corner to the Grand Parade where a small band of choristers had gathered on a bunting-covered podium tossed together for the occasion. We stood in Elliot's doorway listening. A young girl with a tin mug in her hand held it out to passersby. She saw us and hurried over. We each put in a penny and stayed there listening for a little while. Then Jane blew her nose and said her feet were cold, so we carried on along Rose Inn Street.

The shops here were already closed, but their windows were unshuttered and bright with blinking lights and tinsel. Overhead, strings of coloured bulbs stretched clear across the road, reflecting their colours on the wet pavement below. Of all the streets in Ireland this one was the most enchanting, a veritable fairyland of lights. Or so I thought back then, having no other means by which to judge, born and bred as I was to small-town standards. Yet in spite of its attractiveness the street was bare.

"It looks like any other night, if it weren't for the lights," Nuala remarked, plaintive with disappointment at the absence of male company. "I don't understand it. Where have they all gone?"

"Pubbing, I suppose," I said, unwittingly giving her food for thought.

"Well, maybe that's where we should go." She looked at Jane, who shrugged and passed the suggestion, unacknowledged, back to me.

"Not on your life. You're not getting me inside a pub. The Imperial, maybe, or the Metropole, but not a pub."

"Oh, you're no fun. You never want to..." Nuala started and then stopped, her eyes wide with revelation as the implication of my statement passed through her mind. "Well, maybe that's not such a bad idea. The Metropole I mean. It might turn out to my advantage." She grinned roguishly at Jane who offered no response, and for the first time Nuala noticed her distinctly altered mood. She gave her a lengthy sideways glance, then looked at me as though I knew what was in Jane's mind. Which of course I did, and felt a certain sneaking pride at knowing something Nuala didn't.

"I know where Jane would like to go," I offered, taking her off guard.

"Where?"

"The Club House."

"Oh yeah. I'm sure they'd love us there. That place is only for the rich."

"Our money is as good as theirs," I said, repeating Jane's earlier words.

"Yeah. Well, when have you ever been in there?"

"That's just the point, Nuala."

She failed to understand. "I'm not going there only to be turned away at the door, and that's final."

Jane, whose tummy had been rumbling noticeably from lack of food all day, suggested we go to the chip shop first and then decide. To that Nuala was agreeable, provided she was allowed to treat. This was one of the more pleasant aspects of her nature, her readiness to share what few pennies she might have. She had, I must confess, some irritating ways, but meanness was never one of them.

"I have my wages, don't forget," she said, waving aside our protest. We agreed finally, on condition that she would not ask to pay for anything else in the coming year. We drifted across the concrete bridge spanning the River Nore, stopping in the centre to look down at the swollen river.

"If this rainy weather continues, we'll have another flood," Nuala remarked to Jane, who was standing with her back to us, gazing forlornly at the river and not bothering to answer.

Nuala, having managed up to now to keep the Christmas spirit, turned impatiently to me. "Can she not try to be more cheerful? She's making me depressed. If she keeps this up, I'm going home." As though it were in my power to change the situation!

"Leave her alone. She doesn't feel cheerful, Nuala. And she doesn't have to be, if she doesn't want to."

"Well, if she doesn't want to be, she doesn't have to be. But that doesn't mean she should make other people miserable."

"Shut up," Nuala, I said. "To hear you speak, anyone would think she was doing it deliberately. How would you feel in her shoes? Hearing news like that!"

Nuala shrugged. "Well let's face it. She must have known he was up to something, or at least suspected."

"Exactly. She may have suspected, but she did not know. And to hear it like that, from gossiping Gertie Gallivan."

"Gossiping Gertie!" Nuala broke into a raucous laugh. "She isn't that bad. Nor is Jimmy Doyle the last man on earth. There's plenty of fish in the ocean."

"Yes, we know that, Nuala, but we're not all as adept at catching them as you are. It isn't a matter of a man, Nuala. It's a matter of pride. Jane does have some you know." Jane flashed me a grateful smile, not because of what I had said but rather because of what I hadn't, though I was sorely tempted to reveal the hurt and humiliation she had suffered.

Nuala thought it over in silence for a while, then pulled Jane close. "Tess is right. I should be more considerate. I won't say another word. But that Jimmy Doyle wants thrashing. He'll pay for it, you'll see. God will strike him down."

I made the mistake of agreeing with her, and she continued in this vein until Jane snapped. "Nuala, if you don't shut up this minute, I'll strike you down myself."

It was then the smell of zesty salt and vinegar reached our twitching noses and we hurried to the shop. The chips were fresh and crispy when we got them, the bags filled to over-flowing. We stood inside the window eating, not wanting to be seen outside. Jane's gloomy mood was broken as she savoured the aroma and filled her stomach.

The only downside to our pleasure was the presence of two lads, either waiting for an order or for someone to arrive. One lad was busy looking at the ceiling enumerating flies, while the other was busy excavating rubble from his nose. He dug something out and held it up in front of him, examining it minutely as one might assess some microscopic specimen. We glanced disgusted at each other but said nothing. He continued doing it.

"Could you try not to be so disgusting? There are people eating here," Nuala finally blurted.

The lad looked at her surprised, said nothing, then with a flourish of his arm popped his finger into his mouth.

"Oh Christ!" groaned Nuala, throwing down her chips and walking out. We followed.

There was little else to look at, so we wandered back across the bridge and up Patrick Street to the Club House.

"Well," Jane asked, "are we going in or what?" I was all in favour, but Nuala hung back. "We can't just walk in there like we own the place."

"I don't see why not," I said, and in a moment of bravado I galloped up the steps. Looking back now I can scarcely believe I had the nerve to do this, for people of our status seldom frequented the Club House Hotel. I stood outside the door and peered through the glass at the sparkling chandelier. The others watched me from the street. The hall, as far as I could see, was empty, so I stepped inside, undecided as to what course of action to pursue should I be confronted. Ankle deep in crimson carpet I crept along the hall, aware of my reflection in the polished oak and brass.

Halfway along a door opened and two men stepped out. One of them looked up and saw me. The other, the bartender, I assumed from the empty glasses in his hand and the white towel draped around his shoulder, disappeared into another room. My first reaction was to flee as the second man approached. The manager, or proprietor, I thought, noting his attire, his aquiline nose and carefully tended white wavy hair.

"Hello there. Can I help you find someone?" he asked, in a voice so kind and friendly that I was taken by surprise. With some trepidation I explained my presence. He listened courteously, then nodded and looked out at the apprehensive faces of the others, who seemed ready to take flight at the first sign of trouble. The man chuckled and looked more closely at my face.

"Your name wouldn't be Lennon by any chance?" he asked, as he beckoned to the others, still wide-eyed on the path. Unbelieving, I asked him how he knew. "You look just like your mother did at your age. A grand little woman she was. I knew her well."

By this time Jane and Nuala had arrived at the door. Nuala, having removed her raincoat, looked radiant, she imagined, in her mutton-sleeve blouse and navy skirt, the blouse having been dyed a not-too-successful cherry-blossom pink. She looked glowingly around, drinking in her surroundings. The man spoke to Jane and in a dreamlike state we followed him along the hall and up a flight of stairs to a large room filled with gleaming furniture.

There was a bright fire in the marble fireplace, with a leather armchair on each side. For some strange reason I remember little else about that room, which should have remained a beacon in my memory. I do remember its quiet cosy atmosphere, the gleam of the mahogany and the flames dancing in the green marble around the chimney. The man asked what we would like to drink, and seeing the blank expression on our faces left us to consider.

Nuala settled her fat self in the nearest chair and looked around contentedly. "What are we going to have?" she asked excitedly, and Jane said she was going to have a sherry. I wanted a Baby Cham. "You can't ask for a Baby Cham in here," laughed Nuala, "a liqueur or something nice like that, you silly." Jane agreed that port or sherry might be more appropriate.

"Well, I don't like port wine or sherry."

Nuala shook her head. "It's easy knowing she's not used to anything."

"Just order it, why can't you, and Jane or I will drink it."

The man returned while we were still arguing and Jane told him we would each have a sherry. He hurried off to fetch it.

"I'm not drinking it," I said. "If I can't have a Baby Cham, I'm not having anything."

"Oh, for crying out loud! It won't kill you just this once." Nuala turned to Jane in exasperation.

"She's frightened she'll get drunk on it," Jane told her. "She can't handle spirits. Gets drunk on wine gums, she does." They both dissolved in laughter.

The man returned with a silver tray, three glasses filled with sherry and some ladyfingers on a plate. The biscuits were on the house he told us, sensing our concern as to whether we could afford them. Jane handed him the money as we had pre-arranged and he thanked her and left.

Hooking a finger around one glass Nuala pulled it gently toward her. "Go on, try a drop," she said, handing it to me.

"Oh, all right then! Just this once, but I know I won't like it." I sipped it with repulsion, hating the aroma and the taste.

"Try a biscuit with it and you won't notice it," said Jane, and we all reached for one.

Nuala leaned back in her chair and looked around the room. "This is grand. I can't believe we're here."

"Well, you can thank me for it. If I had left it up to you two, we would still be outside."

"I know. I don't know how you managed it. Is he the manager then?"

"Or proprietor," I replied, bursting to reveal his reference to Mother. Many times in the past I had dreamed of an occasion such as this. Some chance to elevate my mother, to vindicate her character, especially to Nuala, for I had not forgotten all those years before when she had so enraged me with her comments. Now that the opportunity was here I strove to make the most of it, though I knew by her expression that she didn't believe a word I said.

About fifteen minutes later the man returned. He put his head around the door and asked if all was going well. A short while later as we were leaving we looked for him but could see no sign of him. Somewhere from behind the white and gold painted panels came the sound of clinking glasses, and through an opening in one panel a man with his shirtsleeves rolled up looked out and smiled.

Nuala stuck her head in through the opening, then raced after us. "There's a bar back there," she said, squeezing between us through the door.

Jane shoved her out and whispered, "I'll bet she can't wait to tell Gertie Gallivan."

"I heard that," cried Nuala. "And you're right, I can't." She hurried down the steps in front of us, her unbuttoned raincoat flapping in the wind.

"I'm disappointed we didn't see that man again," I said. "I would have liked to thank him. He didn't have to do all that, put us in a private room and everything."

"Ah well! We may see him again. Who knows?" said Jane, and we continued down the steps.

About to step into the street, we saw him coming toward us on the path, but he was not alone and good manners prevented our approaching him. He nodded as we went by and we offered him our thanks. "Not at all," he said, bowing slightly to the side. "Merry Christmas to you now," and looking pointedly at me, "and best wishes to your mother."

I was jubilant with pride and didn't dare look at Nuala for fear she might say something to break the spell. But Nuala didn't say anything, speechless for the first time since I'd known her. I could feel Jane grinning to herself, sharing in my pride for our mother. We could hardly wait to get home and tell her. It was past eleven when we did get home, and she was in her chair beside the fire, her head resting on her chest and Timmy the terrier sleeping in her lap.

Probably drunk, was my first thought, for it was always my way to expect the worst. Mother opened her eyes when she heard us.

"So you've come home. Where have you been 'til this hour?"

She picked up a glass from beside her chair and took a sip from it. I could tell by her voice that she wasn't drunk, one or two drinks maybe but nothing more. Relief flushed over me.

We hurried to remove our coats and sit beside her at the fire. "I brought that for you," she said, before we got a chance, nodding at the bottle of Bailey's on the table. "Get yourselves some glasses now and have a drop of it."

Jane walked over to the table. "Have you been home long, then?" she asked across her shoulder, and Mother said she had, that she came home especially, thinking to find us in the house.

"Where's everybody else?"

Mother shrugged. "Your father went to bed some time ago, and so did Uncle. Peg and Tom just went this minute. I was going to go myself if you hadn't come." Jane poured herself a drink and brought her glass back to the fire. Mother raised hers. "Well, here's to you," she began, then noticed my empty hand. "Are you not having any?"

I shook my head.

"She only drinks Baby Cham," said Jane, and Mother nodded.

"Your father will never be dead while that one is alive." There was no judgment in her voice, merely in her choice of words.

"You'll never guess where we've been this evening," I finally got in, and began to relate the story.

Mother listened patiently, then shook her head. "And he knew me, he said?"

278

"Best wishes to your mother. I heard him myself," Jane teased.

Mother took another sip to enhance her concentration. "A little man you say, with white wavy hair and no glasses?" She thought some more, shaking her head in frustration.

"We thought he might be the manager or the proprietor," I offered hopefully. "He was so spic and span."

Something in my statement jogged her memory. "Wait a minute now. Did you happen to notice if he had a scar anywhere about his face?"

I looked at Jane. "Now that you mention it, I think he did."

Jane nodded her head. "That's right. I remember it now. Just above his eye. I thought it was just a deep wrinkle, it was so faint."

"Well it would be, wouldn't it? He was only a lad when he got it."

"So you do know him, then?"

"There is no one else it can be but Johnny Dunne. He was the doorman there for years. Though he might as well have been the manager for all the work he did. Even ran the bar at one time."

"He doesn't work there now?"

"Not a bit of it. He's been retired these many years and living down in Waterford."

"Then how come he was there tonight, I wonder?"

"Probably just helping out, or maybe visiting. That place was his home for years, you know."

"And how did you get to know him?" Jane asked, and Mother explained that she had worked as a maid in the big house opposite the hotel.

"It belonged to the Kennedys then, and every morning I would see Johnny washing down the steps of the hotel. Hail, rain or snow, he was out there. That was before they put that carpet down. 'Spic and span' put me in mind of it. It was how he got the scar, poor lad. Slipped on ice one morning and went right down to the bottom. Almost killed himself, he did. Was in hospital for weeks. I was the one who found him and ran all the way to his uncle's house to tell him."

"Where was his mother and father then?"

"He didn't have a mother or a father. He was an orphan, poor lad."

Jane poured herself another drink and filled Mother's glass. "What happened to his mother and father?" she asked.

Mother said either she never knew or couldn't remember. "I was just a girl myself back then."

"Did Johnny ever ask you out?" Jane asked.

Mother laughed. "We went to the pictures once or twice, but that was all. Johnny was never one for girls. He never had the time. He worked like a slave at that place."

"So he never married?"

"Not to my knowledge. And more's the pity, for a nicer lad you couldn't hope to meet. The last I heard of Johnny was when his uncle died. He left Kilkenny shortly after and went to Waterford."

"He is still a nice man," I told her, happy to have learned about him yet disappointed that he wasn't of more importance. We continued talking until the fire went down and the room began to chill. Without warning Jane grabbed the poker from the corner and began to clear the loose ash from the bottom of the grate, sending clouds of dust and particles all over us.

"Lord God Almighty!" Mother coughed and spluttered, "is it trying to smother me you are?" She pushed back her chair with such a force that it almost toppled over, and Timmy leaped in terror from her lap.

"Sorry! Sorry! I didn't mean to do that," Jane giggled, adding that she wanted to clear the grate before going to bed.

"Can you not leave it until morning?" Mother asked.

"No. I plan to go to early Mass, and I want to light the fire before I go."

Amused, Mother set her glass down on the table. "Well, I suppose it's time I went to bed. Don't stay up too late now," she advised, and left the kitchen.

I helped Jane put the glasses away and set the table for the morning meal. Then we rolled her hair again, this time in metal curlers.

"Is it really worth it, all this torture just to look attractive for some thankless man?" Jane moaned. She was still upset about Jimmy Doyle, she told me, yet happy to have brought it to an end. The experience had taught her a lesson, though. From now on she would be more ruthless and not believe everything a fellow said.

"More like you," she added, meaning it as a compliment. "All in all I had a pleasant evening," she remarked, reflecting on the hours passed, on Mother's unexpected gesture, and her obvious effort to stay sober. We continued talking, musing about people's disappointments, how they mould or change a person's character, and Jane told me things she had never told before and I, to my amazement, revealed some of mine.

"I see now that it's better to face up to things, to tell the truth and not try to fool yourself," she said.

"Does that mean you are going to tell Nuala that our friend was only a doorman then?"

Her face took on a righteous look as she thought on this awhile. Then, with an impish smile, "Naw. I don't think so. What she doesn't know won't trouble her."

We put out the light and went to bed.

Epilogue

Summer came again, but this time with great changes. Nuala got herself engaged and soon after left the town. Then, one evening, Madge met her intended and began to break away. We had long ago lost interest in the Meadows, and though Jane and I were seldom lost for male attention, neither of us forged a special bond. I, for one, still felt lost and miserable, drifting aimlessly, and searching for what I knew I was never going to find. There seemed no reprieve from the days' routine. The tedium I had endured today, I would endure again tomorrow. Each day seemed dull and endless.

Now more than ever I longed to get away, especially since Mother was still at her old game, drinking heavily, her behaviour rivalling that of any drunk around the city. Once or twice she was carried home. As usual Father retreated in despair, leaving us to cope and staying out all hours walking with little Timmy. Then one day the little dog died, poisoned by a heartless neighbour. It was more than Father could endure.

Shortly after he began to change, becoming more estranged from us and talking to himself. He never sang and seldom laughed. Without Timmy to fill the lonely hours of evening he began spending more time with his friends at the club. Now and then he arrived home with the smell of drink on him, and though he never shamed us by becoming drunk I found his careless attitude unbearable. Drinking was drinking no matter who was doing it, and the fact that it was tolerated more in men did not lessen its disgrace.

Before we knew it the home became an empty angry place again, with Mother rowing every chance she got and Father rising to her accusations. Many a night Jane and I stood outside at the garden gate too frightened to go in. Or we would hide behind the lilac bush waiting until we felt it safe to enter. Other times I would take my bike and ride far out into the country, wanting never to return.

"I'm not putting up with this," I said to Jane one evening, after one particular argument and a vicious cruel remark by Mother. No longer could I look upon my father's face and witness his humiliation or the perpetual sadness in his eyes.

"Tomorrow I'm going to see about my passport, and as soon as I am twenty-one I'm going to England."

"But you'll be twenty-one in August. That's only weeks away."

"I've made up my mind," I told her, and so I had. Nothing could ever change it.

"I'll have to go too," she said. "I can't stay here without you," and she began to cry.

And so it was decided. Mother did her best to talk us out of it and Father too, but my mind was set.

The morning of departure came.

We said goodbye to Father before he left for work. I watched as he walked in sorrow to the gate, his head bent, the tears in rivulets on his face. Every fibre in my body was crying out to him, wanting to run after him, to tell him I would stay, but I knew that I could not.

With a heart too heavy to contemplate I fastened up my case. Then we made our way around the neighbourhood for a last farewell. Everyone was sorry we were leaving, at least that was what they said. Mother came with us to the station, in one way sorry we were going, in another way relieved, for she was tired of our constant supervision and her own failed efforts to behave. Crying openly she clung to Jane, remarking on my rigidness and my heart of stone.

The final whistle blew and we climbed into the train.

Jane leaned out the window waving.

"I'll write as soon as we get there, Mam," I heard her call as the train pulled out. I don't know if Mother answered, because I could not look.

Jane sat down beside me. "I wish I could be hard like you," she said, with no unkind intent. "I'm such a baby when it comes to things like this." She blew her nose, then dabbed her eyes.

I kept mine on the passing fields and made no reply, for I knew that in a little while the pain would pass.

ONE EVENING ON MY WAY from work I had gone to visit the Old Man. Little mounds of bluebells had sprung up where I planted them around Meggie's bell, and I could almost hear him crowing at their presence. Of all the many flowers in his garden the bluebells most of all delighted him. I sat myself upon the grass and told him I was leaving.

Didn't I always say ye wud. Th'Lord knows I'll miss ye, came the answer, *but there's no comfort in yer stayin, if yer heart is somewhere else. F'r two pins I'd come along with ye.*

I looked up at the sky where a host of twinkling stars were charting courses to foreign lands around the Old Man's silver ship. For a little while I lingered, recalling this and that, and without the least embarrassment I heard myself declare, "I loved you Mr. Dempsey and longed to tell you so."

I rose and kissed the iron cross, long since erected and shining in the sun.

Theresa Lennon was born in Kilkenny, Ireland in 1931. At twenty-one she left for Brighton, England to work, where she met and married her husband, Keith Blunt. In 1957, she emigrated to Canada, where she currently resides. *Judas in Kilkenny* is her first book.